Thurkill's Revenge

PAUL BERNARDI

CONTENTS

THURKILL'S REVENGE

ONE

"No!" Harold's gloved fist slammed down on the oak table around which his leading nobles were gathered. Wooden platters and cups were sent flying in all directions, clattering noisily as they hit the straw-covered stone floor. "I have made my decision and that is an end to the matter." Harold, King of the English, glared about him, his face set like thunder, as if daring any of the assembled lords to challenge his word.

Thurkill, just seventeen summers old and a newcomer to the councils of great men, did not flinch. As an honour to his father, Scalpi, one of the King's most trusted and loyal huscarls, he had been allowed to stand as a door warden within the king's great hall at Wintanceastre. Normally such an honour would go to more experienced, battle-hardened warriors, and Thurkill was neither. True, he had shown great promise from an early age, displaying admirable prowess in weapons-craft under his father's tutelage, but he remained, nonetheless, untested and unbloodied in battle. He was here simply because he was the great Scalpi's son and the king wished to favour his thegn.

Their family had served the Godwines for several generations and their reputation was fearsome and well-deserved. Always to be found where the fighting was thickest, standing foursquare with the other huscarls; men who would surround their lord, ready to give their life in his defence if the occasion demanded. It was a life of honour and duty and Thurkill longed to add his name to those of his father, his grandfather and his father before him.

Their lord, Harold, head of the powerful Godwin family and – since the beginning of the year – king of all England – needed all the men he could find, young or old. The threat of invasion had hung over him since the very start of his short reign just eight months ago. Across the channel, Duke William of Normandy had made no secret of the fact that he intended to take the throne by force, to make good – he claimed – on a promise made to him by King Edward; a promise which Harold had supposedly endorsed not two years since.

All year, word had been reaching the English court that men were flocking to the Duke's banner; his own retinue being swelled by hundreds of landless adventurers eager for the chance of booty in one of the wealthiest lands in Christendom.

But, as the long summer months had dragged on, no ships had been sighted along the southern coast. Day after day, the army watched and waited, expecting – at any moment – to see the horizon awash with bright sails billowing in the wind. Hopes had begun to rise that the danger had passed – at least for this year. Everyone knew that the channel between Normandy and England was best avoided in the autumn months. Storms could blow up out of nothing, blowing ships miles off course, dashing them against rocks, sending men to a watery grave. Surely, it would soon be too late for William to risk a crossing?

But, just when thoughts had turned to winter preparations, Harold's spies had reported a great army and a huge fleet – said to be one of the greatest fleets ever seen, bigger even that the Danish invaders of old – had gathered in the harbour of St Valery, no more than a day's sail from England. All that stood between him and the southern shores of England was a favourable wind.

To make matters worse, the fyrd - the common men of England's towns and villages whose duty it was to provide military service to their king – was restless. It had been assembled for almost five months; more than double what was normally required. The men, thousands of them living cheek by jowl in huge camps, had been idle for weeks, with little to do other than eat, sleep and drill all day. Supplies were dwindling and men were going hungry, giving rise to the risk of thieving and murder. A few miscreants had been hanged, as an example to the rest, but discipline was wavering. And then there was the risk of disease. It was a miracle that no foul pestilence had so far swept through their ranks.

Above all, though, they yearned to be released. Those who came from the land needed to return home to help bring in the harvest. If the crops were not gathered in before they withered, it could mean death by starvation for many over the long winter months. Many more would die than from any battle. Almost daily now, groups of men would arrive at Harold's tent, petitioning the king to be allowed to leave, but – so far – he had refused every one of them.

But many thegns were now speaking of rumours of mass desertion, of mutiny even. They knew their people; there was only so far they could be pushed and that line was fast approaching. Never afraid to listen to those below him, Harold had called today's great council to debate the problem. It had begun calmly enough, but things were now getting out of hand with voices raised on all sides, until Harold had been forced to intervene to impose order.

The sudden outburst had shocked Thurkill, but he managed to keep his emotions in check. He had been trained to stand fast in the face of the enemy, no matter what, so the young Saxon remained stock still, as straight as the shaft of the finely crafted spear he held in his right hand. He was a tall man, standing over six feet in height and, with his helmet on, he towered over most others.

In his left hand, his fingers gripped the leather straps of his shield so hard that the whites of his knuckles showed. The shield, a circular piece of wood made from a number of planks glued together, was like a dead weight, dragging on his arm, but he dared not let it slip lest he draw attention to himself. The shame it would cause his father was unthinkable. It was covered with leather on which a design had been painted around the central iron boss: the golden wyvern of Wessex standing proud on a red background. It was pristine, having – like him – never seen battle.

He longed for that day. The day when he would stand by Scalpi's side in the shieldwall; his shield overlapping his father's, protecting his left side, just as that of the man to his left would protect his. He had been brought up on the stories of old; stories of great battles against the Vikings, of feats of great daring and courage. Sitting by the hearth fire in his father's hall in Haslow, he would sit, open-mouthed, as Scalpi related tale after tale until his aunt, Aga, had shooed him away to bed, his eyelids drooping as he sat. One day, he had promised himself as he lay in his bed thinking back over what he had heard, he would be a great warrior too. Like his father. One day, his name would strike fear into the hearts of his enemies on the field of battle, like Byrhtnoth at Maldon, or even Alfred himself.

Back in the present, he wished his sister, Edith, could see him. Two years younger than him, she had been left with Aga back in Haslow. She had pleaded with their father to let her go, but he had been steadfast in his resistance. Since their mother had died of the sweating sickness some years back, Scalpi had been fiercely protective of his daughter and he was not, he had yelled – his patience finally exhausted - about to let her be surrounded by so many uncouth, hairy-arsed ruffians. Edith had run sobbing from the hall and had not emerged from her room before they had left the next day. Thurkill felt the pain of separation particularly hard. He valued her above all other things and they had never been apart for so long before. Yes, they bickered and fought like any siblings, but underneath it all was a bond that was stronger than oak. For now, though, he comforted himself with the thought of how proud she would be if she were there to see him. He looked every inch the noble warrior even if he were still just a boy with only the first wisps of a moustache showing on his face.

Scolding himself for allowing his mind to wander, he tried, once again, to focus on what was being said. It was hard, though; the heat of the fire was oppressive, made worse by the smoke that clung to the walls like a winter's fog that hugged the land. Although summer was not long passed, the weather had already become unsettled. High winds had brought thick, dark clouds laden with rain in from the east, increasing the men's clamour to return to their farms before their crops were destroyed. Without the fire, they would have had to stand shivering in damp clothes.

As he watched, the air above the fire shimmied, making the people on the other side look, to his watery eyes, as if they were dancing. Smoke swirled around the flames, fighting to make its way up and out of the small hole in the roof above.

Under the weight of his clothes and armour, Thurkill was sweating heavily now. Most of the burden came from his byrnie.

Made from small rings of iron riveted together, the mailshirt reached all the way down to his elbows and knees. It was a costly piece of equipment that only the wealthiest warriors – huscarls like him, in the service of a great lord - could afford, but it was also a lifesaver. As heavy as it was, the protection it gave from sword cuts, spear thrusts and even arrow shots, was invaluable. After long hours of use, though, wearing it could become almost intolerable, like carrying a small child for hours on end. Under it, he wore a padded, long-sleeved tunic that shielded his body from bruising or abrasions caused by blows to the mailshirt. Although the tunic made the byrnie more comfortable, it also made him incredibly hot. He could feel small rivers of sweat trickling down his back, while yet more dripped down from the helmet's sweatband and into his eyes, stinging them until he could blink them away.

The king's outburst had silenced the hall. Even the thralls had stopped in their tracks, midway to refilling cups or clearing platters from the tables. The only sounds were the crackling and spitting of the logs in the fire and the whining of one of the king's dogs, woken from its dream-filled slumber in front of the hearth.

Now Harold stood with both fists pressed down on the table, his head bowed forward so that his features were obscured by his shoulder length blonde hair. It was plain to see that the pressure of the past few weeks was wearing him down. He must know that the decisions he made in the coming days could seal his fate one way or another, to say nothing of that of hundreds if not thousands of his countrymen whose lives it was his sworn duty to protect.

Eventually, Harold rubbed his hands over his face and flopped down heavily in the great oak chair that stood behind him, draped in furs. It was Gyrth Godwineson who first dared to break the silence. As the king's brother, he – more than most – could speak plainly and honestly to the king, without fear of rebuke.

"Lord, we understand the reasons for you decision, but is it wise to let the fyrd disband at this critical moment? We may soon have dire need of them. William's ships are gathered not far from us."

Harold looked up at his beloved kinsman. "Dear brother, we don't have a choice. They have been held here far longer than our laws allow. You've heard the mutterings as much as I have; they need to be away to their farms. Whatever else may happen, just think how much worse things will be for my people if they fail to bring in the harvest."

Leofwine, the youngest of the three siblings, now joined the debate in support of Gyrth. But where Gyrth was measured in his words, Leofwine had ever been headstrong and impulsive. "My noble brother is right, Lord. Whilst the weather is bad now, who's to say things won't improve to allow the Normans to sail in a few days? With no army to protect the coast, we would be destroyed. It is folly to let the men go now; at least wait until the end of Haligmonath."

Harold sighed impatiently as if he were having to explain things to a dim-witted child. "That would be too late, Leofwine. The harvest may well have ruined by then, especially if these storms continue. For as long as I remain king, my first duty is to care for my people and I would not have them dying of hunger this winter. I will not stand at gates of heaven with that on my conscience."

"Lord." Thurkill realised with a start that his father had spoken.

"Speak, Scalpi. I would have your opinion on this matter. My brothers' brains have become clouded by this damned smoke."

"Whether we keep the fyrd in the field or not, we cannot ignore that our supplies are dwindling. We have bled these lands dry over the last four months and we are having to forage further and further afield to find sufficient victuals. None of this comes cheap to your coffers; as the food becomes more scarce, so the price goes up. Either we must send the men home or else to move the army several days' march from here where we might find new stocks of grain and livestock to feed our seven thousand mouths."

Harold nodded, rubbing his stubbled chin as he considered Scalpi's counsel. "As ever you speak wisely, my loyal thegn."

Then rising to his feet, he continued. "My mind is made up.

I would bring this council to a close as we have talked enough. The fyrd will disband one week hence. We must place our faith in God that the year is far enough advanced to deter the threat of invasion. My people shall return to their farms to gather in their crops and prepare for the winter. But we will plan ahead for the spring when, I am certain, we will feel the wrath of our Norman cousins. Until then we rest, grow strong and make ready to receive them."

Gyrth nodded slowly in grudging acceptance of Harold's ruling. Like most men, he knew that a royal decree once issued, must be supported. It was a lesson that Leofwine, however, was yet to learn as his youth and impetuosity combined to give vent to his feelings.

"Madness! The Normans will come and we will be defenceless. Because of you, brother, none of us will live to see the feast of our Lord's nativity." With that he stormed from the hall into the night, kicking over a bench on his way out.

"Leofwine!" Gyrth shouted as his back.

Harold laid a restraining hand on his brother's arm. "Leave him be, brother. Let the night air cool his temper. He is loyal and stalwart but lacks the maturity to see the fuller picture, as I must."

"That may be, Lord, but you are too soft with him. He needs to learn respect for your position. Talking to you like that when you were Earl of Wessex would be bad, but now that you are king, he should not be seen to challenge your word in front of others."

"I will speak to him about it tomorrow, Gyrth, but for now my bed awaits. I am tired and would put an end to this day. I will pray to God that he is not right about the Normans. If he is, I may just have made the biggest mistake of my life."

But Leofwine was wrong. It was not the Normans who came.

TWO

10 September, Flamborough Head

The two men stood on the cliffs overlooking the sea, their thick woollen cloaks flapping behind them, buffeted by the strong easterly breeze. Both men were dressed as for war, each equipped with spear and shield, though there would be no fighting for them that day. Rather, their role was to maintain a lonely vigil on this bleak, desolate stretch of Northumbrian coastline, two days' hard ride to the east of the great city that was Eoforwic.

All around them, seabirds swirled and swooped, diving in and out of the angry waves, hunting for fish. Many more clung to the cliffs, seeking shelter from the stiffening wind. On a clear day, the height of the cliffs would allow the watchmen to see for miles, but with the dark, forbidding clouds on that day, they could see no further than a mile at most. No matter, though, as neither of them believed this day would be any different to the others. Yet again, their lot was to spend the day in mind-numbing tedium, staring out across the waves for signs of invaders. Both knew that, with the approach of autumn and with the weather as unruly as it was, the chances of anyone being foolhardy enough to brave the waters were small to say the least. But watch they must, lest they incur the wrath of Sheriff Osric.

Behind them came the gentle sound of chomping from over by the small clump of trees where they had tethered their horses. The rhythmic sound of them ripping the wispy grass out of the ground before stoically munching it had an almost soporific effect on the two watchers. They had been there since sunrise and it was now well into the afternoon. It was hard to tell exactly, though, as the sun had not once managed to break through the impenetrable layer of thick, dark cloud lay across the sky in every direction.

At least it's not raining, Eoppa thought to himself. He hated watch duty; there was nothing more boring than standing alone on top of this god-forsaken cliff with only Aelric for company. It was a necessary evil, though, that his village - and many others like it up and down the coast - had performed for well over two hundred years. Ever since the first long ships carrying the marauding Norsemen had arrived on their shores, ravaging and pillaging everywhere they went, they had taken to posting watchers on the cliffs to provide early warning of an attack. Many lives had been saved over the years as riders carried warnings from village to village allowing time for the inhabitants to seek shelter in the forests and hills and for the local lords to muster their men to defend their halls.

But it was slow work: long periods of inactivity with nothing but the birds for entertainment. If he were honest, though, they were marginally more interesting than his companion, Aelric. He was the dullest of all the men in their village and it was just Eoppa's luck to draw the same duty as him. To help pass the time, Eoppa had feigned a stomach upset brought on, he claimed, by some the fish he'd eaten last evening. At least that gave him the excuse to wander off every now and then, ostensibly to take a shit, but really just to avoid his companion's monotonous ramblings.

On the bright side, though, it would soon be evening. They could head home to the village and the warmth of the fireside and a good, hot meal. What's more, he had his eye on Siward the farmer's daughter and he was reasonably sure that she liked him too from the looks she had been giving him recently. An evening in the barn with Mildryth was definitely something to look forward to on a day as miserable as this. She had udders that rivalled many of her father's cows and he longed to get his hands on them.

"Hey, Eoppa, look yonder!"

Aelric's sudden shout broke rudely into his daydream. *This had better be worth dragging me away from Mildryth's teats,* he swore under his breath. *If this was just another one of those damned birds he likes, the ones with the colourful beaks ....* he left the thought unfinished, though, as, following the line of his companion's outstretched arm, he saw a sight that made his blood run cold. The entire horizon was slowly filling with ship after ship. The shape and form of the sails and the wooden hulls were unmistakeable: Norsemen, and thousands of them by the looks of it.

"How many ships?" Aelric shouted over the wind. He had rushed forward towards the very edge of the cliff to get a better view.

"Quiet, I'm trying to count." Eoppa was one of the few men in the village who'd had a bit of learning, including the ability to do numbers, after a fashion. As the third son of a poor miller's family, his father had hoped he would go into the church so as not to be an extra mouth to feed. He had started as a novice in the local abbey but found the rules too stringent for his liking and was kicked out after less than a year when he was caught with his hand under the skirts of one of the kitchen maids. Still, he smiled at the memory, at least he had managed to learn a thing or two in his time there.

"Way over two hundred, I'd say." In truth, he had managed to count to one hundred and given up. He was fairly sure that the ones he had managed to count were fewer than half of the overall total.

"Quick, we must light the beacon."

Aelric was right. They must give the warning. Earl Morcar, back in Eoforwic, needed to know of the danger as soon as possible. Dropping his spear and shield, he raced over to where the great pyre stood ready. He grabbed the nearby ceramic pot filled with pig fat and began to pour it over the kindling at the base, before working to create a spark with which to ignite the wood. With the fire thus started, he threw the remains of the pot into the centre of the pyre and watched with satisfaction as the flames shot up high into the sky.

Looking back out to sea, the ships were much closer now, driven on by the vicious wind. They were close enough for him to see the men on board. Each vessel was lined with dozens of shields slung over the edge of the bulwarks showing that these men were definitely not here to trade. To his horror, the fleet began to turn south to follow the coast. They were looking for the entrance to the Humber, the great river that would take them inland to Eoforwic.

Tearing his eyes away from the vast fleet, Eoppa scanned the western horizon, willing the next beacon to appear. What was taking them so long? They'd better not have fallen asleep or, worse still, deserted their post. Wait. Yes. There it was, a small red smudge on the next ridge of hills. He breathed a sigh of relief; their job was done. The message would reach Morcar before nightfall.

"Come on, Aelric. There's nothing more we can do here. Let's ride south to track them."

All thoughts of Mildryth's charms now forgotten, he untied his horse from the branch and pulled himself up into the saddle. The Norsemen had returned to Northumbria once again.

***

Thurkill crested the ridge and smiled. The sight of their hall nestling in the valley below never failed to fill him with joy. The imposing, oak-framed building sat centre stage, surrounded by assorted dwellings, craft shops and out-houses all grouped together on either side of the stream that wound its way through the middle of it all. In truth, it had not long been in his family's possession but, so happy was he here that it felt like it had been home all his life. Harold had gifted it to his father some six or so years ago, back when he was the Earl of Wessex, as reward for his years of loyal service. The previous lord had died of wounds received in battle with the Welsh. And with no heir to succeed him, it suited Harold to have a trusted thegn take his place as quickly as possible. The tenants needed protection from bandits, the giving of justice, but – above all – to pay their taxes.

It was a moderate sized village that went by the name of Haslow. Home to just twenty or so families and set deep within the ancient kingdom of Kent, it was surrounded by fertile farmland that yielded a strong and plentiful crop each year. They also had some pigs, a handful of sheep and two dozen head of cattle that were set to graze on the surrounding slopes of the downs each summer before being brought back to the barns in winter to keep them safe from the wolves whose desperate search for food in the snows had seen them become more and more daring. In the worst of winters a generation or so back, the older villagers had told of a time when beasts had been seen prowling the tracks between the dwellings, scratching at the walls behind which the livestock sheltered. So one of Scalpi's first acts had been to set the villagers to building a wooden palisade. Built from trees felled in the nearby woods, it stood higher than the tallest of men and had the added bonus of keeping out bandits as well as wolves. Set in the south facing section, a single gate remained open during the hours of daylight, after which it was closed and secured with a heavy, cross-beam that rested snugly within a pair of stout, iron brackets.

The lord's hall which stood next to the small wooden church in the centre of the settlement was nothing like on the scale of the king's great hall in Wintanceastre, of course, but it was a decent size nonetheless; more than enough for their modest needs. It was large enough for all the families of Haslow to assemble on feast days but it was also cosy enough for just Scalpi and his kin. The walls were sturdy, with well-shaped beams packed with plaster in between so that there was little or no room for the cold winter winds to penetrate. The fire pit set in the centre of the floor was large enough to ensure that the heat reached every corner. Behind the lord's chair a thin screen separated the main room from the chamber where Scalpi and his family would retire to sleep, allowing them some privacy from the rest of the hall's occupants.

The four Haslow men who had gone to join the fyrd – Wulfrid, Ubba, Halfdan and Aelfwine – had returned home with them, following Harold's decision to disband the army. Reunited with their families, they were now hard at work in the fields beyond the wall, gathering the harvest before the autumn rains came. Thurkill could see them as he sat atop the ridge, no bigger than ants, labouring away in the late summer sunshine, cutting the stalks with sharp scythes and loading the crops into the nearby carts.

Thurkill turned in his saddle, shielding his eyes as he did so against the glare of the sun. He could hear his father labouring up the final stretch of the incline, followed closely by the two huntsmen who had accompanied them and who now carried between them a freshly killed stag slung by its bound legs from a thin willow branch. He grinned as he saw his father's face red with exertion, sweat dripping from the end of his nose.

"Come on, father! I swear by almighty God that you get slower every day."

Pausing to catch his breath, Scalpi blew out his cheeks but chuckled good-naturedly, all the same. "Less of your cheek, young lad. I could still give you a good thrashing if I had a mind to and don't you forget it."

At thirty-seven, Scalpi was well into his middle age, but he was still a strong man and one of the most renowned warriors in the king's warband. A reputation that he had earned fighting for Harold in numerous battles over the last ten years or so against Gruffydd ap Llewellyn, king of the Waelesc. The fighting had been fierce and brutal and Scalpi had shown great skill, both as a warrior and as a leader of men. It was after the most recent rebellion, in which Gruffydd had been killed, that Harold had seen fit to reward Scalpi with the gift of this land.

Thurkill laughed. "That I would like to see, father. I would put you on your arse and you know it. The only reason I don't is that it would not be right to embarrass the Lord of Haslow in front of his people."

He loved spending time with his father. It was still something of a novelty for him as Scalpi had often been away on his lord's business. And with no mother to care for him, he had been sent away for several years to learn the skills of the warrior in the household of one of Harold's thegns. Now, several years later, he had few memories of his mother. No more than a vague pciture of a mass of blonde curls, a bright, round face that was always ready with a smile and a voice that was often singing. Scalpi would never speak of her and he did not have the courage to ask. Many times, he had seen his father alone, late at night and having drunk deeply from the mead barrel. He would sit, head in hands, weeping quietly while his shoulders heaved with emotion. He had never remarried, nor even shown interest in any other woman. It was as if he felt there could never be another to replace what he had lost.

By all accounts, his sister, Edith, was the very image of her mother. The same blonde curls, quick to laugh and always singing much like, he imagined, their mother would have done. She was tireless around the village, gladly helping everyone with all manner of tasks. Though her station should have precluded her from menial work, that was not her way. Whether it be bringing a lamb into the world in the middle of a cold spring night or gathering in the harvest as she was now, nothing was beneath her or too much trouble.

If he were honest with himself, Thurkill was in awe of his sister. The night before he had left to join the thegn's household, he had sworn an oath to protect her from all danger for the rest of his life. He remembered it clearly as if it were yesterday, down by the river on a moonlit night. He had taken a knife to his palm and then gripped his sister's hand as tight as he could, until she squealed with pain, while blood seeped through his fingers. He had sworn to the old gods and the new one that he would kill any who hurt her. Though he had been a foolish boy of no more than seven or eight summers, it was an oath to which he knew he would always hold true. He glanced down at this left hand; the angry red scar was still visible, a fitting reminder for all time of his solemnly sworn promise.

In the absence of a wife, management of the lord's hall had become the responsibility of Scalpi's younger sister, Aga. She had come to live with them when her husband had been killed in battle three winters ago. It seemed that she, too, was content to be on her own, throwing herself instead into the business of running the estate, not to mention keeping Scalpi and Thurkill in order. She was a plump, red-faced, joyful woman and Thurkill loved her as much as if she had been his own mother. True, she was strict with him, never slow to give him a clip him round the ear if he should forget his chores or be late to the dinner table, even nowadays when he towered over her. But she was also fair and generous and could never stay angry with him for long.

As they ambled down the slope towards the village, Thurkill could see Aga waiting for them. Word of their arrival must have preceded them for she had come out of the hall to greet them. Her sleeves were rolled up and her hands and forearms bloodied, where she had been preparing a slaughtered pig for the evening meal. The thought of it made his stomach rumble; he'd had nothing to eat all day save a few mouthfuls of bread and cheese several hours past. She'd have more work to do now, he grinned, skinning and gutting the stag before hanging it in the storeroom to bleed dry.

Edith had also noticed their arrival, for she was now running back from the fields towards the hall. She seemed to look older, more womanly, every time he saw her. At times, and now was no different, he felt a deep sadness within his soul as he knew that, sooner or later, he would lose her to a husband. A few of Harold's thegns had already approached Scalpi to press a claim to her hand in marriage, but he had turned them all down, citing her youthfulness. The truth was, however, that even though Edith was old enough to be wed, she reminded her father so much of his wife that he could not yet bear the thought of her leaving him as well. Doubtless, he hoped to put the moment off as long as possible, while knowing all along that he could not resist the inevitable forever.

As they drew closer, Thurkill could see that Aga was waving her arms at them, urging them to hurry.

"What does the old hag want now?" Scalpi shouted, not unkindly, but loudly enough to ensure his sister would hear him. All the same, he did as he was bid and dug his heels into his mount's flank to force it into a trot. Thurkill said nothing but fell into line behind his father, a sense of anxiety and dread spreading through his body.

As they pulled up by the hall, Aga bustled forward to grab the reins of Scalpi's horse as he vaulted out of the saddle. "Thanks be to God you're back, brother. Where have you been for so long? I've sent men out to look for you but to no avail."

"Out hunting in the south woods as I said I would be. But never mind that now, woman, what is it? Speak." The slightly irritated tone of his voice showed that Scalpi had become infected with the same sense of apprehension as his son.

"A messenger has come from the king."

"Well, show me to him. Where is he?"

"He had no time to wait for you to return, you oaf. He had many more people to reach before sundown. But he left a message."

Scalpi could not contain himself any longer. "Well tell me

then, woman," he yelled. "For the sake of our Lord, Jesus Christ, piss or get off the pot."

Red-faced, Aga bit back on the insult that had formed in her lips. "The Norsemen have come. You and the fyrdsmen are to assemble in Lundenburh before dawn."

"What? They've actually come? So late in the season too?" Scalpi was incredulous. "But wait. Why do we assemble in Lundenburh if the Normans have come? Surely, we should be heading to the coast, south of here?"

Thurkill interjected, excitedly hopping from foot to foot. "Age dulls your hearing, father. Aunt Aga said Norsemen. The Danes have landed, somewhere to the north, no doubt. All summer we have looked to Normandy for the coming of the Bastard only for the hammer to fall elsewhere while our back was turned."

"My God!" Scalpi turned back to his sister. "Did the messenger say where or how many?"

"Only that they have landed not far from Eoforwic, and even now the brother earls, Morcar and Eadwine, are riding out to confront them."

Thurkill gave a shout. "Yes! They are good men with many thousands of brave warriors to call on. I'll wager we'll have no need to fight for those lads will see them off long before we arrive."

"I wouldn't be too sure too soon, son. Many's the chicken that fails to hatch from the egg. The Norse are a dread foe not easily dealt with and we underestimate them at our peril. It may be that Harold has more news of the size of their army; perhaps the brothers are outnumbered. Either way, it is prudent that Harold takes an army north to deal with them. Come, let's gather our gear; we must be away within the hour."

Thurkill realised with a thrill, but also a pang of disappointment, that he would be going with his father. Having spent much of the summer away from Haslow, he had been looking forward to time at home with Aga and Edith. He had missed them both, especially Aga's cooking. As variable as it could be, her portions were legendary and, doubtless, a significant factor in his great stature. She was forever fussing over him, urging him to eat, lest he waste away. Swallowing his emotion, he went forward to embrace his sister.

"I am sorry, little chicken. I would have liked to stay a little longer to tell you all about Harold's court and the great lords and ladies I saw there."

Edith buried her head in his shoulder as she returned his hug. Her face was wet when she pulled away. "Hurry back, Killi, I would hear those stories before you forget them."

Aga then grabbed him and pulled him tight to her ample bosom, all the while shouting after Scalpi who was already away to see to the horses and gather the men. "You keep him safe, brother, do you hear? Or you'll have me to answer to. And make sure he eats properly. You know what he's like when he gets hungry."

Scalpi threw up his arms in mock outrage. "Leave off him, woman. He's big enough and ugly enough to look after himself. Come on, boy, we need to be going. As long as you can drag yourself away from your aunt's skirts, that is."

THREE

16 September, Lundenburh

The city was in uproar. Every street was a heaving mass of men, women, horses, oxen, carts and all manner of other contraptions, all moving in every direction. It was a seething maelstrom all with a single, common purpose: to be ready to march north. Having travelled through the night, Scalpi, Thurkill and their four fyrdsmen had reached the city shortly before dawn. The gates would normally have been closed at that time of day, but they stood gaping, as the steady stream of men and materiel flowed into the city.

Lundenburh lay just to the north of the great river Thames, within the walls of the old Roman city, built many hundreds of years earlier. Scalpi and Thurkill reached the river at the point where the more recent settlement called Suthweca stood on what had once been a patch of marshy ground. Nowadays, it acted like a funnel, being the one place where you could cross the river, by means of a wooden bridge just wide enough for two carts to pass side by side. Suthweca formed the southernmost defence for the city, having been established to guard the southern end of the bridge into Lundenburh and was – as always – garrisoned strongly.

Their little party was quickly ushered through the gates and on to the bridge, at which point they dismounted to lead their horses across, lest the beasts turn skittish at the unfamiliar surroundings. It was the widest stretch of water Thurkill had ever seen, other than the sea of course. He marvelled at the width of the crossing, counting the paces it took to walk its length as he wondered at the skill required to build it. It was slow going, though; the walkway was rammed with people and carts, mostly heading north to the assembly point. It was a time for patience, though, as there was nowhere for them to go other than to follow the backs of the men in front.

Once on the far side, they followed the road north until they came to Cheapside, one of Lundenburh's greatest markets where all manner of goods were traded by merchants from all four corners of the known world. There, they turned west, heading towards the church of St Paul's, which was said to be built on the site of one of the earliest Christian churches in all England, dating back to the time of St Augustine who had been sent from Rome to teach Christ to the English.

The crowds showed no sign of easing; if anything, the press was becoming worse. It seemed as though the whole city had turned out to fill the narrow streets. Ever quick to spot an opportunity, Tradesmen were – despite the hour – already loudly proclaiming their wares from their tightly packed shop fronts on either side. Sellers of bread, cheese and salted meat were doing a particularly brisk business as the more well-off warriors sought to bolster their provisions for the long march north.

"There's nothing worse than being hungry before a battle, boy," Scalpi grinned as he handed over a couple of silver pennies for two loaves of bread and a roundel of strong-smelling, hard cheese. The grin turned to a laugh as Thurkill took a sniff of the cheese and wrinkled his nose at the heady aroma. "That'll help put hair on your chin as well as your chest, you'll see if it doesn't."

After what seemed an age, tramping along the busy thoroughfare, they rounded a corner into a more open space, at the centre of which stood the largest church Thurkill had ever seen. In front of it were gathered several hundred warriors, many on horseback and all in armour with shields slung over their backs.

"I thought the fyrd had been disbanded, father. Surely they cannot have been called back so quickly?"

"Indeed not, for that would be a miracle worthy of our Lord Jesus. This is just the king's huscarls together with those of his brothers and whatever other great lords are here. I'll wager there are no more than five hundred men here, but good men and true, every one of them." Scalpi's voice caught in his throat, betraying the pride he felt at the sight of the country's best warriors all gathered in the once place.

"Will that be enough to defeat the Norsemen?"

Scalpi chuckled. "I wouldn't think so for a moment; even

though I don't doubt that each one of us is worth two or maybe even three of the Viking scum. Remember, though, we have a long march ahead; Harold will have sent messengers north already to muster the men from the counties between here and Eoforwic." At that moment, Scalpi held up his hand for quiet and then pointed towards the door of the church. "Look, there is Harold now. He is going to speak to us."

Harold had indeed emerged from the church where he had been praying for victory over the pagan invader. In one easy movement, he swung himself up on to the back of a wagon where he could be seen clearly by all those assembled. The gold band around his head shone in the flickering light of the torches held aloft by those around him; an effect which made it look as if it were a burning halo. Before speaking, he threw back the sides of his thick cloak so they could see his mail-coat and the great sword that was buckled to his waist. He looked every inch the great warrior king and Thurkill felt a sharp thrill of excitement at the thought of following him into battle to defend his kingdom.

Then Harold held up both arms to call for quiet. He had a strong, confident voice that carried easily across the square, so that no man struggled to hear his words. "Countrymen! I had hoped not to have to stand before you on a day like today. I had hoped that our lands would be free from threat at least until the spring; but it was not to be. Once again, the Norsemen have come to our shores as they have done many times before in the time of our forefathers. As I speak, our great city of Eoforwic is under attack from a fleet of more than two hundred ships led by Harald Sigurdsson, King of Norway; he who is also known as Hardrada. What's more, my brother, Tostig, recently banished from his earldom of Northumbria, is said to be with him. Their intentions remain unclear, but mine is not. I will not have my people threatened or killed by foreign invaders. I will not have my women beaten or raped. I will not have their children left as orphans or taken into slavery."

A great roar of anger greeted his words, so loud and prolonged that Harold eventually had to appeal for calm. "I share your pain, my friends. We will not allow this insult to go unpunished. Our noble Lords Eadwine and Morcar hold Eoforwic for me and I have sent messengers north to tell them to defend it at all costs, while we march to join them. Today we are few, but we will gather the fyrd from Berkshire, Mercia and Lindsay as we go. By the time we reach Eoforwic, I promise you we will have a mighty army with which to destroy the enemy."

The shout this time was even louder as men thrust their swords and spears in the air and yelled their support. "Gather your strength now, brave huscarls. You will need it for the fight to come. We ride now and will not stop until sundown. I do not know how long Eoforwic can hold out so we must reach them with all haste."

With that, the king stepped down and made his way through the crowd towards his lodgings. As he went, men thronged around him to swear loyalty or to call for his blessing. Many knelt before him and held out their sword hilts for the king to touch. As he walked, Harold called out names of those he recognised, greeting them with warmth and humility. It was not hard to see why he, above all others, had been acclaimed king on Edward's death, Thurkill thought.

Suddenly, Harold was no more than ten paces from where they stood. "Hail, Scalpi, my loyal friend!" Thurkill swelled with pride to see his father so honoured in front of this great gathering. Only then did he realise that his father had knelt before the king. Shamed, he quickly followed suit almost stumbling forward in his eagerness. Harold grabbed Scalpi's forearm, pulling him to his feet before embracing him warmly. Still smiling, he turned to Thurkill and beckoned him to stand also. As he did so, he saw the surprise in Harold's eyes as he reached his full height.

"By God's bones, Scalpi, what manner of beast is this with you? He's huge."

Scalpi smiled broadly, pride emanating from every pore. "Lord King, this is my son, Thurkill. He is not yet eighteen summers but is already as strong as an ox."

"And he looks like he's eaten a fair few in his time. Are you sure he's yours?"

Men all around them laughed at the king's joke but Scalpi showed no sign of embarrassment. "Either that, Lord, or my late wife was squired by a bear, when I wasn't looking."

Harold joined in the laughter. "When we march, I want you two up near me at the front. With your cunning and his strength, I should be safe from all danger."

Scalpi bowed low in acknowledgement. "Gladly, Lord. You do us great honour."

FOUR

24 September, Tadcaster

Thurkill was almost asleep in the saddle when they reached the small town of Tadcaster just before sunset. It had been a long hard ride: six days solid, stopping only to rest and water the horses every few hours. Food and sleep had been grabbed wherever possible and everyone, without exception, was tired and hungry. For the most part, the men just plodded on, faces sullen or glum, keeping their thoughts to themselves. Every now and then, an altercation or scuffle would break out somewhere and would be over almost as quickly as it had begun, even before the captains had the chance to wade in and break a few heads to restore order. It was ever thus when large numbers of men gathered together; a wrong glance, an ill-chosen jest or simply knocking into the wrong person could result in a flurry of blows.

The bread and cheese they had purchased had seen him and his father as far as Lincoln but, since then, they had hardly eaten because the supply wagons had fallen a long way behind. Pulled by huge oxen, the heavy carts lumbered along at a much slower pace. On good days, they would arrive at dawn, just as the army was about to set off, causing a mad scramble to fill their provision sacks. But more often than not, they had to make do with what they could buy from the few farms or towns they passed. If they were in luck, they'd find wild bushes alongside the road every now and then, affording them access to handfuls of ripe berries that helped take the edge off their hunger.

Morale had been high when they set out, with much singing among the ranks of horsemen. Some were songs retelling heroic tales of past battles or other great deeds from ancient times; while others were bawdy romps more commonly heard after a night's drinking in the tavern. Songs that would make the face of many a young maiden blush were they but to be within earshot. Things had taken a turn for the worse at Lincoln though. Not only was food in short supply, but also news arrived that the army of the north under the brother earls, Eadwine and

Morcar, had been defeated by the Norwegian king. By the time the exhausted rider had finished relaying the tale of woe, Harold could no longer contain his rage.

"What in God's holy name did they think they were doing?" He shouted. "My orders were clear: hold Eoforwic until my arrival. But now you tell me they wilfully disobeyed my command and chose to leave the safety of the city walls to go out to meet the enemy?" Throwing his arms wide in exasperation, he continued. "Have I not always said they could not be trusted? Those two bastards never wanted a Godwine on the throne and this just goes to prove I was right!"

"Yes, Lord King." The rider had kept his head low, unsure how else to respond. "When Earl Eadwine arrived from Chester with the men of Mercia, Earl Morcar felt that together they were strong enough to defeat Hardrada. They had more than five thousand warriors, all well armoured, rested and prepared for battle."

"And all now dead or dispersed, and Eoforwic lost as well I daresay." Harold had spat the words while, at the same time, aiming a vicious kick at a nearby pail which splintered under his assault.

The rider had not dared to speak further for fear of being the next target for the king's ire. Instead, he had been ordered back with all haste with a message to the two earls to meet their king at Tadcaster in two days on pain of death. Harold wanted to hear what had befallen his army and his city directly from the mouths of those responsible.

Now, as they approached the town, Thurkill could see that a small contingent of warriors awaited them on the other side of river. Two of them, both tall with long dark hair and remarkably similar looking, stepped forward as the advanced guard began to wade through the fast flowing, but shallow waters.

"Well met, Harold." called the taller of the two, bowing to show his respect.

"Hmmph", Harold snorted, unable to speak for fear of giving vent to his anger. Leaving his captains to oversee the crossing, the king strode over towards where a huge fire had been set, indicating that the two earls should follow.

24

"You." Harold pointed to Morcar without ceremony as soon as they arrived. "Tell me all that happened. I want to know what strength you have left to you. I pray God for your sake that it's more than the few men you brought here to the ford? I want to know how many Norsemen were killed before they routed you. What numbers do they have left to them? Where they are now and what do you know of their plans?"

Morcar began confidently. "Lord, word reached us of the arrival of the Norse fleet several days back. Our scouts brought news that their ships had set course up the Humber and were advancing upon Eoforwic. In council with the other lords here, we determined that our best form of defence would be to confront them as soon as we could."

"Why in God's name did you not wait? Did my messenger not make my wishes clear? You were to stay within the safety of the city walls until I arrived." Harold shouted, unable to contain himself any longer.

"Lord, the walls are weak in several places, following years of neglect under your brother, Tostig. We feared that the enemy would exploit those weaknesses and break through our defences. Besides, have our people not always trusted in the strength of our shieldwall? We fight face to face with the enemy rather than cowering behind walls like frightened children behind our mothers' skirts."

"What's more," Eadwine interjected, "we had no idea where you were or if you were even coming. And even if we had known, we could never have expected you to cover the distance from Lundenburh so quickly."

Without warning, Harold sprang to his feet and slammed his fist into Eadwine's face. To his credit, the earl stood his ground despite the force of the sudden blow which would have floored many lesser men. Nevertheless, blood flowed from his split lip. "Silence!" Harold roared. "I do not recall giving you leave to speak, you young pup."

Eadwine stood transfixed, his arms hanging limply by his side. But then, as suddenly as it had come, the fire left Harold's eyes and he slumped back down on the tree stump on which he had been sitting. "Continue." he barked.

Morcar swallowed nervously, before taking up the tale once more. "We marched out to meet them four days since, on ground of our choosing. The Norse were advancing from the east up the old road that runs parallel to the great river on which the city stands. We chose a good position to block their path just beyond the village of Fulford, a mile or so outside of the city walls. Our front was drawn up behind a small stream with our flank secured against the river."

Harold snorted. "Well that, at least, sounds sensible. I am glad that your wits had not completely deserted you. Nonetheless, you must have been either brainless or boneless to lose the field from there. How many men did you have?"

Morcar bristled at the criticism but chose not rise to the bait. "We numbered just over five thousand souls, Lord. My brother held the right flank with his huscarls opposite Harald of Norway. I was on the left with mine."

"And who, pray tell, did you face?"

Morcar hesitated.

"Spit it out, man. Or do you want to feel my fist too?"

"It was your brother, Lord."

"I feared as much. Ever since we heard that he had gone north to Scotland, I felt certain he would return to haunt me soon enough." Harold leapt to his feet once more, punching a sack of grain that sat on the back of a nearby supply wagon. "So the traitorous, ungrateful bastard is here after all, is he? And you're sure of this?"

"Yes, Lord, there can be no doubt. We all recognised him, standing beneath his own banner on the battlefield."

"Did he survive the battle?" To Thurkill's ear it was not clear what answer Harold wanted to hear, and from the look on Morcar's face, he was similarly troubled by the question.

"I cannot say for certain, Lord, but I believe so. No one told me they saw him fall, at least. When we first saw his banner raised opposite us, there was much anger among the men of the fyrd as they do not remember his rule over them here in Northumbria with much fondness. My captains did their best to restrain them but they surged forward all the same. I believe it was this that was our undoing. But for this our shieldwall would have stood all day long, but once the flank had moved forward, opening a gap between us, our fate was sealed."

Harold paced around the fire, rubbing his chin as he listened. "Hmmm, it is clear to me now why you lost. When one half of your force abandoned its strong defensive position behind the river, you left your flanks exposed to counter attack. Am I right, Morcar?"

"Initially we made good progress. We pushed Tostig back and many of his best warriors fell beneath our spears. But when we were on the point of destroying Tostig's warband, Harald of Norway launched his attack. Though we fought bravely, we could not withstand the ferocity and fury of the Norsemen, led by this heathen devil. This Harald is a man like no other, Lord. He towers over all other men."

Harold scoffed and pointed at Thurkill, who felt his cheeks redden as all eyes turned in his direction. "What? Even taller than Scalpi's boy, there?"

Morcar looked Thurkill up and down. "Easily, Lord. I would swear on the bones of our Lord Jesus that Harald stands at least a head taller."

Harold grunted sceptically but nodded all the same, before Morcar continued. "He fought like a man possessed and his warriors followed his example. They drove my brother's men back before turning to take us in the flank. By now our doom was inevitable; we had no choice but to flee back to the safety of Eoforwic's walls. Many were lost attempting to cross the river, weighed down, as they were, by their armour. Another group, perhaps some five hundred men, were cut off and surrounded. To their eternal honour, they refused to surrender and fought to the last man. Not one survived."

"Yet you two lived." Harold sneered.

"Our duty was to you, Lord. We had to try to save as many men as we could so that we might yet defend the city."

"And just how many of my brave Englishmen did you save?"

"We led just over a thousand back to Eoforwic. By the end of the day a few hundred more had also come in singly or in small groups. Many were wounded and all were exhausted, but I would say that those that are able to fight again number just over eight hundred."

Harold was visibly shaken. "So many lost?" He slumped down with his head in his hands, contemplating the path he must now take. "I came north without my full army as I had to move fast but also because I had to leave numbers in the south in case of need. I had hoped that together we would be strong enough to force the Norse back to their boats."

Eadwine, perhaps keen to regain some lost ground, dared to speak up once again. "Lord King, from what we saw at the ford earlier, you still have a mighty host. Surely it will be enough to put the heathen to flight?"

Harold seemed to have forgotten he was angry with the younger earl.

"Yes, but it is not enough, I fear, to force them to surrender. We will have to fight and place our trust in Almighty God to deliver us victory."

Silence descended once more as Harold paced up and down, deep in thought. Other than the low murmur of the army settling in for the night, there was little to be heard. A few of the assembled lords glanced at each other, their faces etched with worry. With the loss of the northern fyrd, their chances of victory had diminished considerably. Eventually, Harold stopped mid-stride and turned back to the group assembled round the fire.

"Where are the Norsemen now, exactly?"

"Back with their ships, drawn up on the banks of the river at a place called Riccall; about a day's march from here." Morcar then bowed his head in shame. "After the battle, they said they would return in three days to take hostages; one hundred and fifty sons of the best families within the city, else they will sack Eoforwic and slaughter everyone within. With so few men fit enough to fight, we could not hope to defy them. We are to bring them to a place called Stamford Bridge, mid-way between the city and Riccall."

Harold considered this information for a while. "Stamford Bridge, you say? If I am right, those three days expire tomorrow?"

"Indeed so, Lord," Morcar confirmed. "The chosen ones are

ready to leave Eoforwic at dawn."

Harold turned his back to the fire, a look of excitement and anticipation spreading across his face. "Well, I say we go meet them, but we give them more than they bargained for."

"What's on your mind, brother?" Leofwine rose to his feet, his face breaking into a grin as his mind leaped ahead.

"In their minds, the Norse feel secure. They have won a great battle, taken Eoforwic and demanded tribute. But, they do not know that we are here, eh? So rather than sending them hostages, I will send them my army instead. With luck we will catch them unawares and make them regret ever coming here."

"Is that wise, Lord?" Gyrth was ever the more cautious of the siblings. "Should we not negotiate a settlement? You said yourself that our numbers are not sufficient to guarantee success."

"Wise be damned! We have no choice, Gyrth. We do not have the strength to force them to surrender; our noble brothers here have seen to that. And I will not spend hard-earned English coin on bribing these Norse scum to go away. I need all the money I have to face the Norman bastard next year, should he come. No, let us be bold and make use of this chance the Lord has given us to achieve a great victory. Let us not forget we have an even greater enemy to the south, Would William not shake with fear when he hears of our great victory here. With luck he may even decide to put aside any thoughts of invasion."

Gyrth nodded in acceptance. "What are your plans then, brother? We should act now as there will be much to do this night if we are to be ready."

Harold laughed, his tone more good-natured now that his path was clear. "You're right as ever, Gyrth. Send word that we march to Eoforwic at dawn."

"Why so, Lord?" Leofwine asked. "The enemy is to the east of the city."

"For two reasons, Leofwine. First, we link up with the remaining men from Morcar and Eadwine's fyrd; we will have need of them, I think. Second, we can then take the road east from the city which will be quicker."

"Also, that way, we will approach the Norse from the

direction from which they expect the hostages to come?"

"Exactly, Scalpi. You are not just a big dumb brute after all; you also have a brain hiding up there under that shaggy thatch of yours. If we arrive along the road from Eoforwic, it may help to buy us time to get close to them before they realise who we are. With luck we will fall on them before they work it out. Right," he clapped his hands together. "Enough talk. Be about your business."

***

"What's it like, father?"

Scalpi yawned. "Eh? What's what like?"

"Battle."

The older man rolled over on to his right side so he could face his son, fidgeting with his cloak as he did so, to make sure the thick woollen folds covered him as far as possible. Despite the day's warmth, there was a definite autumnal chill in the air; the clear night sky doing nothing to prevent the heat from escaping.

"Can't you sleep, son? It's been a long day and you need to rest before tomorrow."

"I can't. There's too much going on in my head."

Scalpi grunted and raised himself up on to one elbow, his grizzled features illuminated in the last flickering flames of the camp fire. "I remember I was the same before my first battle. It's natural to feel scared."

Thurkill sniffed. "I'm not scared." He was grateful for the shadows, though, so his father could not see his cheeks redden. "I just want to know what it's like to be in a battle, that's all."

"I meant no insult in my words, son. Mark me, though; a little fear is a good thing. It keeps you sharp and you will need all your senses about you if you want to come through the battle unscathed. The man who tells me he has no fear of battle is either a liar or stupid."

"What was your first time like?"

"I don't recall a lot about it, if I am honest. I could not have been much older than you are now. All I remember was that I had no idea what was going on. I seemed to be stuck in the middle of a heaving press of bodies, mostly standing, but many underfoot also, either dead or dying. It was all I could do to stay upright. First lesson I was taught was to stay on your feet at all costs; for once you were down, there's no way you're getting back up. You'll either be trampled to death or someone will stick you like a pig you as you lay there defenceless. In all the time I was there, I'm not sure I landed a single meaningful blow. And I'm certain," he chuckled at the memory, "I didn't manage to kill anyone that day.

"But, don't worry, son. You're well trained – unlike I was, I should mention - and me and the rest of our lads will be there to look out for you too. God knows your aunt will have my guts if I let anything happen to you." As he finished speaking, Scalpi reached over to give Thurkill a playful cuff round the head. "Now get some sleep, or at least shut up and let me get some."

Thurkill lay on his back staring up at the sky, mulling over his father's words as he watched the stars. With only the wispiest of clouds scudding across an otherwise clear night sky, he could see hundreds of them spread across the vast expanse of blackness above him. It took him back to his childhood when he and Edith had loved nothing more than to lie on their backs counting stars in the meadow behind Haslow on a warm summer's night. He wondered what life would bring him, should it not end tomorrow of course. If God saw fit to spare him, what would be his destiny? He knew there were other, far off lands out there; he had seen many a merchant at the king's court and he often found himself wondering whence they had come and what it was like in their homeland. Some of them had dark skin, brown like an otter or bear. Others were almost as dark as the night sky itself. Having spoken to a few of them, they'd told him it was so hot where they came from that the sun had changed their colour. At first he had found this hard to believe and had long assumed they were making fun of him. They even claimed that it rarely if ever rained. How could that be true? Surely it rained there almost every other day just like in England?

Whatever the truth of it, he hoped one day to see such far-off places to find out for himself. No sooner had that thought entered his mind than he felt a pang of guilt. He could not abandon Edith. He'd sworn an oath to protect her for all time,

31

even should she marry and have a family of her own. He would have to put thoughts of travelling to foreign lands out of his mind. Duty came first.

He glanced over to where his father lay and saw that he had long since fallen asleep. His breathing, now slow and regular, was comforting, reassuring even. It made him feel like he was back at home in their hall where they often slept close together by the hearth. Despite his father's advice, though, he doubted he would sleep at all tonight. Tomorrow would be his first taste of battle. Tomorrow he would, for the first time, face a man who would be trying to kill him.

FIVE

25 September, Tadcaster

"Come on, you lazy-arsed pig. It's time to kill some Vikings."

Thurkill groaned, rolled over and opened one eye. His father was up and already shrugging his byrnie over his shoulders, shaking it down into place along his arms and legs. The metal gleamed in the early morning sun, the result of Aga's hours of scouring and polishing in readiness for just such a day.

Despite everything, he must have dropped off for at least a short while. The fug in his head, however, suggested it can't have been much more than an hour or two, but anything was better than no sleep at all, he supposed. Grunting with the effort, he pulled himself to his feet and wandered over to where an open barrel stood next to one of the supply carts. The grass under foot was sodden with early morning dew and he could feel the damp seeping through the leather of his boots as he walked. Shedding his heavy cloak, he dunked his whole head beneath the freezing cold water before standing up to shake his shaggy mane, cascading water in all directions to the loud complaints of those nearby. The sharp, stinging sensation helped to clear his head but he still felt groggy. He balled his fists into his eyes to try to clear the sleep from them; they felt as if they were buried in sand.

Yawning heavily, he trudged back to where they'd been sleeping, using his cloak to dry off his hair as much as possible. His father was already strapping on his sword and looking round to collect his spear and shield. "Hurry up, son. If you're quick there'll be time to get some food. I hear they have eggs and porridge on the go."

"Gmmmph", the sudden thought of food caused Thurkill to retch. He'd felt queasy since waking but had put it down to a lack of sleep, but this was something else. Clapping his hand over his mouth, he rushed away from the camp to a nearby clump of bushes. As he ran he realised with horror that his bowels were also demanding immediate attention. *Dear God,* he prayed, *let me get behind those bushes before it's too late.*

A while later, he stumbled back into the camp, still clutching his guts. Scalpi stood waiting for him, hands on hips, shaking with laughter. "I guess you'll not be wanting breakfast then? Still, that little clear out should help. Nothing like a good shit and a puke to make you lighter on your feet in battle, eh?"

"Father!" Thurkill hissed. He was already embarrassed and did not want everyone around to know what he'd just been through.

"Ha ha, don't you worry, boy. Everyone goes through it one time or another. It's natural. In fact, you're one of the lucky ones; you've managed to get it out of the way before we fight. It's much worse when you need a shit in the middle of the battle, I can tell you that for nothing."

Thurkill doubled over in pain again, holding his stomach, "I'm not sure that's the end of it yet. It feels like the world is trying to escape from my arse."

Two more trips to the bushes later, Thurkill was finally dressed and ready. Together with the rest of Harold's huscarls, they were now formed up ready for the march to Eoforwic. His guts were still doing occasional somersaults but at least he felt he had it under control now. Being active helped; it took his mind off his anxiety. His father had been right, he realised, once things were up and running you felt much better.

It promised to be a warm day. The sun was climbing steadily, warming the land as it went, burning off the early morning dew. There was no breeze and the shockingly blue sky was devoid of all cloud. When the sun finally did reach its peak, he thought, they really would be sweating like oxen pulling at the yoke. Ever the leader, his father had warned all those in earshot several times now: "Drink plenty, lads. If you get too thirsty you'll be too tired to fight and then you will die. Don't worry about needing a piss; you'll be losing so much through sweat there'll be nothing there."

Before long, they were on their way, following Harold's standard – the fighting man of Wessex – that was held aloft for all to see. The king rode at the front with his brothers. Behind them came their huscarls, Thurkill and his father in a place of honour in the second rank. Though mounted, they travelled at walking pace as they were now accompanied by the bulk of the northern fyrd who marched on foot.

Though the day was getting steadily warmer, the men were still fresh and well supplied with water. Spirits were high as the prospect of battle grew ever closer. The thought of catching the Norsemen unaware gave the men an extra spring in their step. Here and there, snatches of song were belted out lustily, interspersed with jests and insults thrown about good-naturedly. Many had not been in these parts before and men looked around them with the excitement of children at the new sights and sounds around them.

They reached the city just after midday. If any had been concerned about the reception that awaited them, they need not have worried. Though they might have taken against Harold's rapacious brother, Tostig, that enmity did not seem to extend to the king. Many hundreds of Eoforwic's inhabitants lined the walls of the city, waving and cheering as the army approached. The fyrd came to a halt fifty or so paces outside the southern gate, where Harold, his brothers and a number of their senior lords dismounted and went forward on foot. They were met at the gate by Eadwine and Morcar who had returned earlier to make arrangements for their arrival. Behind the two earls stood a group of young boys; in their teens mostly by the looks of them, Thurkill thought, many of them the same age or even younger than his beloved Edith.

Harold strode straight over to the group, embracing each of the earls in a show of warmth and respect for the benefit of the townsfolk. "Who are these fine looking children?" he smiled, tousling the hair of the nearest boy.

Eadwine stepped forward. "Lord King, these are the hostages that were demanded by Harald Sigurdsson. They were due to be sent to the Norsemen today as a guarantee for the safety of the people of Eoforwic."

"Yes, but what are they doing here like this, as if ready to leave? There is no need to send hostages now that I am here."

"Yes, Lord, but they wanted to greet you all the same, to give you thanks for their deliverance."

Harold smiled broadly and held out his arms to encompass

the assembled crowds. "My loyal people, what sort of king would I be if I could not protect your children? We have hastened here from Lundenburh to deliver you from the ravages visited upon you by the Danes and - with God's help - we will bring the invader to heel and make them rue the day they invaded my kingdom."

A great cheer greeted his words. Amid the tumult, Scalpi cupped his hand round his son's ear and spoke as loudly as he dared. "This is a welcome omen, son. Harold has never travelled this far north; it was thought that he and his family were not well liked here. To see him welcomed like this is wondrous indeed. It is a sign we may yet carry this day."

Thurkill was less convinced, "I guess when you have a horde of marauding Norsemen on your doorstep it's easier to put aside any other feelings."

His father grinned before punching him playfully on the arm. "Who taught you to be so cynical? It surely cannot have been me. Come on, enjoy the moment. The people are cheering us and great deeds will be done this day. Let us fight together, you and me, side by side and pray that we bring honour and glory to our name."

Scalpi then turned to face the rest of the huscarls, drew his sword and thrust it into the air. "For God and for Harold. Let us drive these pagan bastards back into the sea. Let us burn their boats and make them swim back home!"

***

They stayed in Eoforwic no longer than the time it took to take on more water, eat a quick meal and for the remains of Eadwine and Morcar's army to join the king's host. They were about to leave when a scout came galloping up to Harold, jumping from the horse's back almost before it had stopped and running the last few yards to where the king stood. Panting heavily, he knelt to make his report. "Lord, I come from the bridge at Stamford."

"Well met, friend. What can you tell me of the Norse strength and disposition?"

The scout could barely contain his enthusiasm. "The fools. It is God's will that they be destroyed this day."

Growing impatient, Harold barked. "Explain yourself properly, man. Unless you now claim to be a great war leader, just give me facts."

"Forgive me, Lord. Excitement clouded my judgement. The Norse are drawn up west of the bridge. It looks like they are getting ready to move closer to Eoforwic."

"Hmmm, this side of the river, you say. And about to move further in this direction?" The scout nodded, still breathless from exertion.

"And why do you believe them to be fools? It is not a description of our enemy that I readily recognise."

"Two reasons, Lord. Firstly, they appear to have left a good portion of their army back with their boats at Riccall. I reckon they have fewer than five thousand men."

For the first time, Harold smiled. "So we outnumber them by about half as much again. And your other reason?"

"They appear to be unprepared for battle."

"What do you mean, man? How can you be sure?"

"I was not close to them, but it was clear to me that many have no mail shirts. Several were lying on the ground with no tunics at all, their skin bare to the sky. There appeared to be much merriment as if it were a holy day."

Harold turned to his brother. "Gyrth, what do you make of this? What sort of madness has taken hold of them?"

Gyrth grinned. "I can only assume, brother, that they are enjoying a nice walk on a summer's day in this fair land of Northumbria."

"What? Speak plainly."

"Remember, they have no knowledge of our presence. They believe the people in these parts beaten; cowed and fearful since their defeat at Gate Fulford. They're coming to receive one hundred and fifty of our young folk as hostages. It would seem to me that our foe has grown complacent and has not bothered either to send their whole force, or to make sure they are properly equipped for battle."

Harold threw back his head and laughed. "It would seem that God may yet be with us this day. Let us go quickly now and show them the full extent of their misjudgement."

SIX

25 September, Stamford Bridge

They left Eoforwic on the old Roman road heading east; the king's banners, fluttering noisily in the breeze as they were borne aloft at the head of the column. The men were ready for battle; they carried their shields slung across their backs, but in such a way that they could be quickly pulled into position if required. Each man also carried a long ash-shafted spear, the gleaming points of which looked, from afar, like a forest of ice as they danced in the sunlight.

Thurkill marched along beside his father and their four fyrdsmen; their mounts having been left in the city to rest after the long ride north. Though his anxiety increased with every step, he took comfort from the companionship of those around him. Men told jokes and swapped stories as if they were simply marching from one camp to another, rather than to their possible deaths. He didn't think he was afraid of dying; after all, he said his prayers and believed what the priest in Haslow said about a life after death. He was more worried about his courage failing him on the field of battle; of embarrassing his father in front of the others. If he were to die, please God let him die bravely. Let him be worthy of his family name and be remembered well by his kin. He closed his eyes briefly to offer up his silent prayer.

His mind was wrenched back to the present by the sound of a shout at the head of the column. Harold had reined in his horse, halting on the crest of a ridge which lay a few short miles from the city. Leaning on his father's shoulder, Thurkill strained his neck to see what had caused them to stop.

"What can you see, son?"

"By God's holy bones," Thurkill hissed in excitement. "It's them! It's the Norse army!"

Immediately a great clamour broke out all around them. One of their fyrdsmen shoved Thurkill in the back. "What do you see? Come on, lad, tell us everything."

"There's thousands of them – about half a mile away - and they're heading this way. But they're not really marching as such."

Scalpi frowned. "What do you mean, not marching?"

"They're more like...walking. As if they've got no destination in mind, no real purpose. No, wait. They've stopped. They've seen us and they've stopped."

"This is it, lads. It's time to dip your blades in Norse blood." Scalpi's voice had taken on a hardness that Thurkill had not heard before.

In response to new orders from the king, the Saxon host resumed its march but with a noticeably quicker pace. How that the enemy had sighted them, it was critical that they brought them to battle as soon as possible, lest they try to escape. As they descended the ridge, they had a good view of the enemy. It seemed that confusion now reigned amongst their ranks; men milled about in small groups pointing and gesticulating towards the approaching Saxons.

And the truth of the scout's words was now revealed; only one man in every three or four was wearing a mailshirt, while many of the others were, indeed, bare-chested under the hot sun. But, as they watched, they could see their captains starting to restore order with liberal use of wooden staves. Rather than withdraw, though, they formed up into a loosely circular shieldwall, apparently waiting for the Saxons to come on and give battle. At the same time, Thurkill noted that three men jumped on to horses before racing off to the east.

"Why don't they retreat, father? They are outnumbered and many have no byrnie, it makes no sense to stand. Are they mad?"

"One thing you will come to learn about the Norse before this day is done, son, is that they are proud men. They won't ever take a step backwards if they don't have to. They will stand and fight us here, you mark my words. Besides, did you see those three riders heading off?"

Thurkill nodded.

"I'll swear on our Lord's mother that they'll be galloping hard back to the boats to gather the rest of their men, as if the very Devil were after them. If those reinforcements reach us in time, we'll soon know we're in a fight."

"In which case," Thurkill shouted, his frustration getting the better of him, "we should attack them now, before it's too late."

"Well said, that man!" Gyrth swivelled in his saddle to look back at Thurkill. "There's someone with a good head on his shoulders. You see it stays firmly attached there today, won't you? We need men with your guts, if not also your size!" He then raised his voice to address those around him.

"There they are, lads. It's like the scout said, they are fewer than us by far and most have left their armour behind. They are ours for the taking."

Harold heard his brother's words and laughed. "You are never normally this keen to join battle, Gyrth. You sound more like Leofwine. Before we put spear and sword to work, however, I would speak with them. My brother, Tostig, may be with them and I would entreat him to give up this fight before it's too late."

"You are too generous, brother. Tostig has made his choice and he must live or die with the consequences."

"No, Gyrth," Harold said gently. "Whatever he has done in the past, he remains our blood. We owe him a chance to atone for his sins."

Gyrth scowled but offered no further challenge. When they were no more than one hundred paces from the Norse shieldwall, Harold held up his hand to halt the men. "Gyrth, Morcar, bring twenty of the best men and come forward with me. Let us see what they have to say for themselves. We may yet avoid bloodshed and still achieve our victory."

Moments later, the small group walked slowly forward, making great show that they posed no threat. With Harold, Gyrth and Morcar, were Eadwine, Scalpi, Thurkill and another fifteen of the biggest, most imposing huscarls in Harold's household. As they drew close, a similar number of the Norse army broke free from the shieldwall to meet them.

As he walked, the king shielded his eyes from the glaring sun. "Ah, I see Tostig among them but who is that with him? Is that Harald? He's huge. He truly is more than a match for your lad, Scalpi."

Before Scalpi could reply, however, Harold held up a hand

in greeting. "Hail, brother. By God, it is good to see you but I cannot pretend I am not saddened to meet in such circumstances."

"That is as much your doing as it is mine." Tostig's reply was nothing other than surly, like a young boy after having been scolded by his mother.

Harold continued unperturbed. "That may be, but the past is the past and there is no sense in dwelling there longer than we have to. Rather, we should look forward to happier times when we can, perhaps, live in peace once more."

"The time for peace is over, brother. Now is the time for war. Eoforwic has already fallen to us and we are of a mind to take the rest of your kingdom too. The force you see before you is but a fraction of our strength; you will not be able to withstand our fury. You should think of your people; surrender to us now and spare them from further bloodshed. Rest assured, if you do so, we will guarantee your safety and let you leave in peace. But you must disband the fyrd and leave this island for good."

Harold paused, as if to consider the offer. Thurkill looked sideways to his father, concern etched on his face. Surely the king could not seriously entertain such a suggestion? But if Scalpi knew his son was staring at him, he did not show it. He kept his steely gaze directed at the Norseman opposite him.

Thurkill knew that Harold was no coward, but he could not imagine the burden of responsibility that must weigh on his shoulders. Win or lose, many of his followers would die if he chose battle over surrender. It was a decision he was glad he did not have to take.

Finally, Harold responded. "I would make you a different offer, Tostig, if you would but hear it."

The Saxon raised an eyebrow in response, looking wary of what was to come. "What trickery would you have me fall for now, brother?"

"No trick. I simply desire to put an end to the enmity between us. For the sake of the land and the people, we should be together as a family once more. You, me, Gyrth and Leofwine. We four brothers should be united in friendship. Our kinship should not be cast aside so readily."

Tostig had lost patience, though, as he threw his arms in the air and snorted his reply. "And how would you propose we do that, Harold? Too much bad blood has flowed under the bridge for me to forget the past that easily. Where was our kinship when you kicked me out of my earldom rather than support me? I've had enough of your empty words."

Despite the venom with which Tostig spat out his tirade, Harold continued in the same calm, assured manner. "Well, if you would reconcile with me now, I would offer you this earldom of Northumbria that was yours once before. Take it back but rule it more wisely and in my name."

Before Tostig could reply, however, an angry shout came from behind the king. "No! This land is mine!"

Red-faced with indignation, Harold rounded on Morcar. "Be silent, fool! You have no voice here. As king of this land, it is mine to do with as I please. Besides, you forfeited your rights by your defeat not five days since."

Tostig couldn't resist a chuckle, only adding to Morcar's embarrassment. In disgust, the earl spat at Tostig's feet, turned his back and strutted back to the Saxon host.

Harold turned back to face his brother. "Well? Do we have an agreement?"

Tostig rubbed his beardless chin, as if mulling over the offer. When he spoke, he pointed at Harald who stood by his side, unable to follow the conversation. "What of my noble lord, the King of Norway? If I accept your offer, what would you give him? He has come a long distance in support of my claim. I would not have him return home with no reward."

Harold looked the giant Norseman up and down. He stood a good head taller than Tostig, who was no small man himself. His feet were firmly planted a shoulder's width apart; his hands placed, one on top of the other, on the end of the shaft of his huge, two-handed battle-axe, the blade of which rested on the ground. His piercing blue eyes peered out from amidst the huge mass of unkempt blond hair which sprouted fearsomely in all directions from under his iron helm. He seemed to realise that the conversation had turned to him as he squared his shoulders, emitting a low growl, which only added to his menacing aura.

Harold smiled at him before turning back to reply to Tostig, still smiling as if he were offering the Norse king a compliment. "As he is so keen on this noble land of England, I would offer him seven feet of it, all to himself." He paused to steal another glance at the Norseman as if measuring him, "or as much more as would be needed to hold his body, as I see he is taller than most normal men."

It took a moment for the full meaning of Harold's words to sink in, but when they did, Tostig's face was like thunder. "You would insult my Lord Harald so? Where is your honour?"

"It was no insult, Tostig, merely a promise of what will become of him should he not leave my kingdom, reward or no reward."

"Enough talk. There can be no accord. We fight!"

The Norse king evidently understood that matters were concluded for he uttered what sounded like a curse at Harold before spitting at his feet. Then he turned and stomped back towards his lines, battle-axe slung over his shoulder with Tostig following like an obedient hound.

Harold sighed and turned towards Gyrth and Eadwine. "Ready the men. We do battle this day."

***

Thurkill followed his father back to the massed ranks of Harold's army; back towards the centre of the shieldwall where the rest of the huscarls were formed up; grim-faced warriors standing ready for a fight. As they took their place in the front rank, several called out for news even though it was clear to most what the outcome had been.

"We fight," Scalpi growled.

As they waited, Scalpi offered some final advice. "Keep your shield up at all times, son, even when you get tired and it feels like it weighs as much as a horse. The shieldwall is only as strong as its weakest link. Let your guard down for a moment and you'll find a Norse spear in your guts or an axe in your neck. Not only will you be dead, but then the bastards will come pouring through the gap you leave and the rest of us will die as a result. Stay close to me, especially if it all turns to shit. A man running on his own is a dead man. Stick together, come what may, and we stand a chance of getting through this alive. Understood?"

Thurkill swallowed hard and nodded, his mouth suddenly dry, despite all the water he had been drinking that morning. Conversely, his palms felt slick with sweat; so much so that he had to continually wipe them on his trews to stop his grip from slipping. The true horror of his situation had become all too real, now. All the anticipation with which he had awaited his first battle; all those long hour spent wondering what it would be like. It all came down to this moment.

He prayed he was not going to disgrace himself. Live or die, he wanted his father to be proud of him. He was no coward but he was petrified right now; his father had been right, he thought ruefully. He could feel his guts clenching once again; he could only hope he had nothing left to void. He whispered a quick prayer that victory would be theirs, before wiping his hands once more. Then, he spat on the ground for luck, feeling a slight pang of guilt as he did so and checking around nervously to see who had seen him do it. It was an ancient practice dating back to the days before the Christians had come from Rome and he knew some would be quick to take offence.

He was not the only one praying; a few paces to his right – close by to where the king stood - the Bishop of Eoforwic implored God in strident tones to protect Harold and his host and to cast down the pagan Norsemen into the very pits of hell. He could see the king kneeling in front of the churchman, his head bared and his gloved hands resting on the pommel of his great sword, its point dug into the ground. When the prayer ended, the bishop pushed through the ranks to the rear; the shieldwall was no place for a man of God. Harold rose to his feet, donned his helmet once more, and pointed to where the Norse waited in their circular shieldwall on a low ridge, a hundred or so paces to the east. Without waiting a moment longer, he ordered the advance.

The Saxons moved surged forward, keeping an even pace so that their ranks remained unbroken. Thurkill, his heart pounding in his chest, could see the enemy waiting for them. Many of them were brandishing their weapons while yelling curses and challenges in their direction.

They didn't look much different to themselves, Thurkill reflected. They were just men, with the same hopes and fears as the Saxons. And yet, ever since he'd been a young boy, these men had been spoken of in hushed tones, almost as if they were invincible giants of men. Stories were told in every hall, how the Vikings had terrorised the land for generations. Mothers still used their menace to scare their children into obedience. He had lost count of the number of times his aunt had told him as a boy: *Don't wander off too far into the woods or a hairy Viking might chop your head off.* The threat had worked at the time, but now here was a whole host of them, hairy and otherwise, waiting to remove his head from his shoulders.

The Saxons began to chant their own battle cry, drowning out the noise of the enemy. There were no words to it as such, just a single guttural shout that approximated to the word "KILL!" It alternated with the sound of sword pommel and spear haft being rammed against the rear of their shields, in time with each step they took. Kill! Thump! Kill! Thump! To Thurkill's inexperienced ears, it was nothing short of terrifying.

The two armies were just a few short paces apart now. Several of the enemy looked as if they were straining at the leash to be let loose, like dogs eager to chase down a rabbit. Here and there one or two rushed forward, launching themselves at the Saxons. Whether they were intoxicated on ale or simply overcome with the blood-lust, Thurkill did not know, but he admired them nonetheless. It was suicidal, though: there was no way they could break through their ranks on their own, but it was brave nonetheless, boosting the courage of their companions who howled and spat at their foes.

Then the moment was upon him. He gripped his shield straps even tighter, holding it up like his father had said, so that he could only peer over the rim at the hellish sight ahead of him. Already, the stench of fear had begun to assail his nostrils. Someone nearby had shat his breeches, though he knew not whether Saxon or Viking. Behind him came the sound of a man vomiting, some of the effluent splashing the back of his legs.

But rather than freeze in fear, Thurkill was astonished to find that his mind grew calm. Fear gave way to lucidity as the two shieldwalls closed together. Looking ahead, he set his sights on the bare-chested warrior in front of him. He was a beast of a man, not much shorter than him, his beard twisted to a point and held in place with some sort of thin metal band. In his hands, he held a huge two-handed axe, which he was swinging about his head, ready to cleave Thurkill's skull. All the while he was hurling abuse in his direction, daring him to come on and meet his doom under his murderous looking blade.

Thurkill gripped his spear tightly and raised it above his shoulder. He would need to be quick to make sure the Norseman did not have time to hack the shaft in two. Three paces, two paces, lunge! He put all the strength of his right shoulder and upper body into the thrust. At the same time, he ducked and raised his shield; just in time as he felt the rush of air as the axe swung harmlessly above his helmeted head. But then he felt the point of his spear connect. There was a momentary resistance before the it broke through the skin to plunge deeply into his neck. Exhilarated by the thought of his first kill, Thurkill kept pushing until the spear protruded a good foot's length from the other side, blood spurting in all directions from both entry and exit wounds. Death was instantaneous; the axe dropped harmlessly from the man's lifeless hands and the body crumpled in a heap. The sudden realisation of what he had done shocked Thurkill so much that he forgot to hold on to the spear shaft. Before he could react, the weapon was wrenched from his hand as the man fell.

"Sword, boy, draw your sword. Quickly!"

His father's warning came not a moment too soon. Looking up from the prostrate body of his first kill, Thurkill saw that another Norseman, just as large as the first, had stepped into the gap and was already raising his axe ready to crush his skull. Still, he did not panic. Instinctively, he knew there was neither time or space to drag his sword from its scabbard; he would be dead long before he released it from the fur-lined sheath. Instead, he chose the only option left to him. In one movement, he dropped to his knee, lifting his shield over his head at the same time. Almost immediately, he felt a paralysing blow as the axe landed with a dull thud, its sharpened iron edge biting deep into the layered wooden board.

The shock reverberated all the way along Thurkill's arm, up to his shoulder. There was a short burst of intense pain which made him fear that his arm might be broken. Panic flashed into his mind; without his shield, he would not last more than a few heartbeats. But, as quickly as it had come, so the pain receded, leaving nothing more than a dull ache in its place. Meanwhile, his snarling, sweating enemy had dropped his own shield so he could grasp the shaft of his axe in both hands, desperately trying to free it from the shield. With a surge of adrenaline, Thurkill saw the man was now defenceless. Using all the strength in his tree-like thighs, he pushed himself up and forwards into the Norseman. The metal boss of the shield caught him squarely in his unprotected face, sending him down with blood and snot gushing from his crushed nose. Without thought or mercy, Thurkill moved to end his life. Lifting his boot, he stamped down as hard as he could on the exposed throat. If the Norseman had been wearing his armour, he might have survived, but with nothing but a woollen shirt to protect him, his fate was sealed. Thurkill felt the crunch of bone and cartilage breaking under his heel as he killed his second man in as many moments.

"Bravo, lad!" He turned his head to see his father standing next to him. Though Scalpi was grinning at him, a strange look had – nevertheless – come over him. It was as if he was shocked to see the man his son had become. The day had now dawned when childhood had been put aside for good; his son was now a warrior. But more than that, his son was a killer with neither pause or scruple.

Meanwhile, the battle raged on around them; men on both sides falling, limbs and torsos cruelly hacked, crushed or otherwise broken. The noise was horrific, something he had not expected; men screaming in pain, others calling for their mothers, still more begging for an end to their agony. Part of him wanted to give in to the terror that surrounded him; wanting to curl into a ball like a startled hedgehog. The longer it went on, the more he wanted to shut his eyes tight and stuff his fists into his ears to block out the sights and sounds that threatened to engulf him. Everywhere he looked, men were slashing and stabbing at each other, their faces twisted in hate and fear. By now, the ground was slippery with blood and entrails, making it hard to keep a sure footing. On more than one occasion, Thurkill felt his leading foot slide away from him as he stepped forward. He gave thanks to God each time he managed to avoid falling, for that would have been the end of him for sure.

In the thick of the melee as he was, it was impossible to know which side was winning. All he could do was stand firm and keep fighting along with the rest. The men on either side relied on him, just as he relied on them. Though, his shield arm was growing tired he dared not let it slip. His father's warning still rang in his ears. *Keep your shield up or we are lost.*

The sun beat down mercilessly as the afternoon wore on. Pressed up against the enemy, surrounded by warriors in front and behind, there was no relief from its glare. And little in the way of breeze to cool their bodies, either. Sweat poured down from his head, dripping into his eyes, making it ever more difficult to see what was going on around him. His lips were dry and cracked, his tongue stuck to the roof of his mouth; he could feel the energy slowly sapping from his limbs as the battle wore on. He had no idea how long they had been fighting, but it seemed like for ever.

After the initial clash, the two shieldwalls had stabilised. Now, as men tired, fewer blows were exchanged as the two sides resorted to pushing and shoving against each other instead. Every now and then, someone would spot a gap between, above or below a shield – an exposed arm perhaps, or a neck or leg – and a blade or spear would flick out to take advantage. Often, the target reacted in time, closing the gap or parrying the blow, but many times, the weapon would find its target. A scream, a gout of blood and the man was out of the fight. If he were lucky, and the wound not too bad, his friends would drag him back from the front line to rest and have the wound bound up with cloth strips. More often than not, however, the man fell where he was, beyond help. If he were not dead already, he would soon be trampled underfoot or gutted by some wicked blade darting downwards to finish him off.

Suddenly, through the fog of his fatigue, Thurkill realised he had taken two steps forward without having been pushed back. To his front, a man collapsed, a gaping wound where his neck had once been, but his place was not filled. By his side, his father – veteran of many battles – realised what was happening. "They're breaking, lads. They're breaking. Push on. Push on!"

Shouts of encouragement went up all along the Saxon line. Exhaustion was forgotten, thirst ignored. Now was the moment to seal victory. If they could but break the Norse shieldwall, they could be slaughtered as they ran. Despite their lack of numbers and armour, the Vikings had put up a staunch fight, but now the weight of the greater Saxon force was beginning to tell. If they could rout them now there would be no escape, penned in as they were against the fast flowing river that ran several yards to their rear.

Thurkill joined in with the shouting, stepping forward in unison with those around him. Everywhere, the enemy had begun to pull back in confusion. It was the tipping point his father had spoken about; the moment when one side gained the upper hand and the fate of their opponents hung in the balance. One more effort and they would surely break and run. No sooner had the thought entered his mind, however, than his hopes were cruelly dashed. Just as it seemed the Saxons were about to triumph, they were hit by a new and sudden onslaught. Had the reinforcements arrived from Riccall already? Surely, there could not have been time?

The new attack struck the Saxons right in the centre of their line, a few paces to Thurkill's right. And there, right in the middle of it, was Harald Sigurdsson, towering over all those around him, laying waste on all sides with his huge, two-handed war-axe which he swung in wide, looping arcs so fast and so ferociously that few dared come within its range to attack him. Those that had now lay dead or dying at his feet. Even shields offered little protection as his strength was such that the wood simply splintered on impact.

Having been so close to victory, the Saxons now found themselves on the back foot. Almost all the ground they had gained had already been ceded. Here and there one or two warriors were even showing signs of wavering in the face of the new onslaught. The king had timed his intervention to perfection. Even though fewer than fifty men were with Hardrada, they had stopped the Saxon advance in its tracks, giving the rest of the Viking host valuable time to reform their shieldwall.

Once again, Thurkill found himself fighting for his life, side by side with his father and the rest of Harold's huscarls. Blows were raining down on his shield relentlessly – like the heaviest winter hail storm; it was all he could do to ward them off. His shield was pitted heavily around the edges as strike after strike tore splinters of wood from it. His sword arm was numb from the effort of stopping strike after strike, while his left still ached from the earlier blow. Only the thought of not letting his comrades down kept him going. It was now, though, that the long hours of incessant training paid off. The huscarls stood firm, their shields overlapping with that of the man to the right, soaking up the pressure as best they could. Men fell; it was inevitable under the ferocity of the Norse counter-attack; but the gaps were quickly plugged. But still, the fate of the battle hung in the balance, though their shieldwall had bent, it had buckled, but it had not been broken.

But then the Norse king overreached himself. With a furious roar, he smashed his way through the shieldwall, hacking the head clean off the huscarl in front of him as he did so. But before his men could follow him through, the gap was sealed off, cutting Harald off from the rest of his men. Yet he refused to yield, roaring his defiance, daring all to fight him. None would accept his offer, though, and soon a small clearing had grown around him, as if he were a boar cornered on the hunt, a forest of spears pointed towards him Then, without warning, Harald's huge axe suddenly dropped to the ground, landing with a mighty thud. The king's hands shot up to his neck in shock, gripping the shaft of an arrow that had pierced his throat; its white goose feathers now streaked red. He was choking, the blood from the mortal wound flooding into his lungs. He dropped to his knees, still clutching the arrow, trying to pull it free. The surrounding huscarls stood in awe, each looking at the other wondering what to do until, finally, one of their number seized the courage to step forward to thrust his sword into the his heart. Harald watched his fate approaching and met it with dignity. Lowering his arms, he stared defiantly at the Saxon. His mouth moved as if he were trying to curse his executioner, but no sound came but for that of his lifeblood gurgling in his throat.

The king's death ended the attack as abruptly as it had begun. Without their talismanic leader, the Norse warriors fell back in confusion. Like a rudderless ship in the midst of a great storm, they floundered until, finally, they streamed away.

The Saxons, too tired to follow, were content to let them go for now. The scene they left behind was one of unspeakable carnage; corpses lay everywhere, piled on top of each other with blood-spattered limbs twisted grotesquely or severed from their bodies. Scores more lay wounded, close to death. For the time being, however, the Saxons had not the strength to go to their aid. There was little that could be done in any event; those that could not walk were likely to die sooner rather than later. For now, it was all that they could do to slump to the ground, or lean heavily on shields or spears, blowing hard trying to recover their breath as best they could.

Thurkill turned to his father with a look of triumph despite his fatigue, animated by a sense of relief at having survived his first battle. "The field is ours. The Norse are defeated!"

SEVEN

25 September, Stamford Bridge

Grimacing, Scalpi pointed down the slope towards the river. "I fear not, son. There's no victory yet. We have but won the first encounter. Look," he panted. "They retreat in good order; there is no panic. Tostig has raised his banner; he has rallied them. My guess is they will cross the river to reform on the other side."

Standing nearby, Gyrth overheard them. His face was covered in blood, the result of a wicked-looking gash just under the rim of his helmet. "Your father is right, boy. They cannot bear the taste of defeat. I'd say they will hold out until their reinforcements arrive."

"So we must destroy them before that happens." Harold strode up to them, sweating profusely but otherwise looking as fresh as he had at the start of the day. "Gyrth, rouse the men. We must press home our advantage. There is much slaughter still to be done before we can call the day ours."

Gyrth spread his arms wide, taking in the expanse of warriors on both sides. "Look around you, brother. The men are exhausted. They need rest from this furnace-like heat."

"I know, Gyrth but there is no time. If we tarry too long, the Riccall men will come and then their two forces combined may be too strong for us. We must attack them now."

Scalpi intervened. "Their king is dead, Lord. Perhaps the fight has gone out of them? Maybe they will seek terms?"

"They will only come back again next year with a new leader and more ships. Besides, Tostig is still with them. I will not have him free to roam where he will, causing trouble. Not while Duke William threatens us in the south. He is a warrior of renown and too proud to ask for a truce. I should know; it's a trait that runs in the family."

Gyrth continued to press the case. "Nevertheless, Lord, the men need time to recover. To attack now would be folly."

"To wait for them to be reinforced, or allow them to escape, would be a greater folly. Get the churls to bring up water skins and ale. Pass out whatever bread and other food we have. They can eat and drink as they march."

Slowly, the Saxons began to follow the retreating enemy down the slope. Already, a good proportion of their host had been herded across the bridge as fast as its narrow span would allow. But with only two or three men able to walk abreast, it had become a vast bottleneck. Many Vikings still swarmed around its entrance, waiting for their turn to cross, all the while looking anxiously over their shoulders at the advancing Saxons. Some, in their desperation to escape the coming slaughter, had chosen to swim, but the river was wide and fast-flowing, so only the strongest swimmers could make it. Several men had been swept away by the current, arms thrashing ever more weakly as they struggled in vain to stay afloat.

By the time Harold's advance guard reached the river, most of them had reached the other side or had drowned trying. Those few that were left were swiftly put to the sword after little more than token resistance. With those few souls dispatched, Harold immediately began to harangue his captains and thegns to cross the bridge.

Thurkill and his father were near the front, a few ranks back from the riverbank, but it soon became clear that the way forward was blocked. No one was moving, though there was much shouting, cursing and shoving from those in front and behind.

"Boy, can you see what's happening? Why is no one moving?"

Thurkill spied a fallen tree trunk nearby. Clambering up, he looked ahead to the bridge. "There's a Norseman on the bridge, father."

"What? Just one?"

"Yes."

"I don't understand. Why in the name of God does someone not kill him?"

"I don't think it's as simple as that. You should see him. He's as tall and as wide as their king and twice as angry by the looks of it. He has one of those massive war axes and knows how to use it from what I can see. What's more, he's one of the few that's wearing a mailshirt."

"Surely it can't be that hard to kill him?"

"Several have tried and failed already, father. There's bodies everywhere on the bridge, and still more in the water. Oh!"

"What?"

"There goes another one." As Thurkill spoke, they heard a short scream followed by a heavy splash as another huscarl fell from the bridge, his right forearm left behind on the bridge, still gripping his sword.

Moments later, Harold arrived shouting up to Thurkill for news. "Send for the archers. Shoot him down," he ordered as soon as Thurkill had explained the situation.

"That is not possible, brother."

Harold's face flushed bright red with indignation. "Don't presume to tell me what can or can't be done, Gyrth. Fetch the archers up here now!"

"It is not possible, Lord, because they are not here. They have loosed all their arrows, so we left them back on the field to forage for spent shafts. It will take them a good while to arrive."

Harold roared in anger and stormed off towards the bridge. "Swarm him then. Kill him, now! We cannot delay any further."

Another wave surged forward on to the bridge in response to the king's demands. The result was the same, however, as the width of the wooden span played into the hands of the defender. Though it was wider enough for two, maybe three, men to walk side by side, there was only really space for one to properly wield a weapon. The bodies on the bridge only made matters worse by impeding the next man's attempts to close in on the Viking axeman.

Two more huscarls went forward, working as a pair. The first man moved in close with his sword held in front of him, while the second stood back, seeking the opportunity to thrust his spear point into any exposed part of the body. Such was the Norseman's skill, however, that even this failed to dent his defiance. Thurkill had to admire the man's ability. He had settled into an easy rhythm – parry and strike, parry and strike – and showed no sign of tiring. And all the while the Saxons were held up here, the remainder of the enemy host had ample time to form a new defensive line a few hundred paces beyond.

As Thurkill watched, growing more and more impatient, something caught his eye, giving him the germ of an idea.

Grabbing Scalpi's arm, he led him fifty paces up stream before making their way down the pitted slope to the edge of the water. It was an area thick with undergrowth, shielding them from sight.

Nestling amongst the overhanging trees, however, was a boat, probably belonging to a fisherman from the nearby village. It was this that Thurkill had seen from his vantage point atop the log. Working in tandem, they pushed the small craft down the bank and into the water. Thurkill threw a spear into the boat before wading in alongside it, the water soon coming up to his knees. Then he climbed in and lay down at the bottom to ensure that he was hidden as much as possible. Meanwhile, Scalpi was gently pushing the boat out into the middle of the water. Slowly, he slipped deeper under the surface, crouching down until only his face was visible. Holding on to the stern, and keeping his head out of sight as much as possible, he began to direct the little fishing boat downstream towards the bridge.

As they drew closer, the sounds of fighting grew louder. Silently, they floated slowly along with the current, keeping as close to the bank and the undergrowth as they could. At any moment, Thurkill feared they might be spotted, bringing their enterprise to a premature end; but their luck held. Eventually, they arrived beneath the wooden structure, Thurkill holding up his hand to signal his father to hold the boat in position. The bridge had been constructed from half a dozen roughly hewn logs lashed together as tightly as possible. The uneven nature of the trunks meant that, here and there, there were gaps through which Thurkill could see the cloudless blue sky. A pause in hostilities appeared to have occurred for the warrior was standing with his axe head resting on the bridge, breathing heavily. It seemed he had some mastery of the Saxon tongue, and he was using it to hurl insults at the Saxons who now stood back from him, deriding them as cowards, no better than womenfolk, daring them to come forward to meet their deaths.

"Are none of you man enough to take me on? I have killed

twenty of you at least and not one of them was worthy of my blade. Come on, what are you waiting for? My axe is thirsty for more of your Saxon blood."

Meanwhile, Thurkill waved his hand gently to the right, letting his father know he needed to move the boat further towards the middle of the river. While he waited, he offered up silent thanks that the current was slower here, helping to keep the boat steady in the water. He raised himself on to his knees, careful to avoid tipping the boat too far. His father, holding on to the sides, did his best to help keep the swaying movement to a minimum.

Just as he was about to grab hold of the spear, a huge splash not two feet away from them soaked him as another Saxon met his end at the hands of the axeman. The waves caused the boat to rock wildly, making him forget the spear and grab on to the sides to stop himself from being thrown into the water.

As soon as the motion had died down, Thurkill braced his knees against the edges of the boat and grasped the spear in both hands. Peering upwards, he positioned it carefully between two of the logs, gathering himself for what was to come. As he waited, another huscarl chose that moment to attack. The Norseman took a step forward to meet his assailant, opening his stance as he did so. Thurkill knew he had to seize the chance he had been given. Gripping the shaft of his spear as tightly as he could, he launched himself upwards, thrusting the tip through the gap in the logs as hard as he could. Almost immediately, he felt the point hit home. The scream that came from the Norseman's lungs was the most terrifying thing Thurkill had ever heard. The blade had penetrated his unprotected groin and had proceeded to lay waste to his bowels as it continued its death-bringing journey. Blood and entrails splashed down the shaft, onto the bridge, even splattering on to Thurkill's upturned face. The defender's axe fell with a clatter onto the bridge as he grasped his riven gut with both hands. With a triumphant yell, the next Saxon in line hacked his sword down on to his neck, ending his heroic defence for good.

Released, the Saxon host lost no time running forward across the bridge, the first of them shoving the fallen warrior unceremoniously over the edge so that he plummeted into the water just to Thurkill's side. Despite his elation, he felt a pang of guilt as well. The man had fought bravely and with honour; he did not deserve to die by such foul means.

Vaulting out of the boat, he waded over to grab the body, dragging it to the far bank where, with the help of his father, he hauled the lifeless form out of the water and up on to the grass. He straightened the legs, hiding the cruel wound as best he could. Taking a discarded sword, he arranged the warrior's arms across his chest, folded over the blade. He would at least meet his forefathers in the afterlife, weapon in hand. Then, bowing his head briefly, Thurkill uttered a quick prayer to speed the warrior's soul to its final resting place.

EIGHT

25 September, Stamford Bridge

Looking back across the river, Thurkill could hear Harold, Gyrth and the other leaders urging the men of the fyrd to hurry across the bridge. Much time had been lost to the lone defender; time enough for what was left of the enemy host to regroup on the far side. And yet, crossing the narrow structure remained a slow business, merely adding to the king's frustration. Even now, he was gesticulating furiously, shouting at anyone who caught his eye and - every now and then - slapping the flat of his blade across the rump of any warrior he deemed to be moving too slowly.

Scalpi stood alongside him on the muddy riverbank, looking up at the bridge. "The longer this takes, the more likely it is that their men will arrive from Riccall. Come on, son. Let's get back to the rest of the lads. Your deeds here will have won you great renown; there'll be many a song sung about you around the fireside for years to come, you mark my words. But only if we win."

Climbing up the steep bank, they joined with the rest of the huscarls as they made their way towards the ridge on which the new Norse shieldwall now stood. Though it was smaller than before, it looked no less formidable for that. It would not be an easy nut to crack.

They halted at the base of the ridge. The slope was not steep by any means, but an uphill attack would still sap what remained of their strength. Looking up, Thurkill could see the massed ranks of the enemy, gathered around Tostig. The king's brother stood in the centre of the line, under King Harald's raven banner, which hung limply from its staff, next to his own, in the breezeless afternoon.

Once again, Harold strode forward, alone this time. When he was within earshot, he halted.

"You have fought well today. But your king is dead and there is no need for further bloodshed. Honour has been satisfied. Lay down your arms so that you may retrieve his body and leave this place in peace. All that I ask is that you return to your ships and sail from these lands, never to return."

A growl greeted his offer. A huge bear of a man stepped forward, challenging Harold to fight him, but the king dismissed him with an imperious waft of his hand; it was beneath his rank to engage with an ordinary warrior in such circumstances.

"Think of your families. Think of your homes. You don't have to die here, far away from your wives; you can leave now; you can go home with no impediment. I swear it in the name of Almighty God. But be aware, if you refuse my offer, I shall show no mercy. Your bodies will lie here, unburied; to serve as a permanent reminder to all those that would invade my lands and lay waste to my people. They will be food for the crows, picked clean until there is just the white of your bones left. Your souls will be left to wander the earth in perpetual torment, excluded from the heavenly realm for eternity."

When Harold finished speaking, Tostig shouted back. "We fight on, brother. We will not turn our backs on the enemy. You may retreat if you wish to avoid further death and destruction, but we will not leave this ridge while there is one among us who yet lives."

Harold paused briefly, a look of profound sadness flitting across his face, before sighing. "So be it." He turned abruptly to walk back down the slope to the shieldwall, which parted to allow him passage.

Moments later, the Saxon host began its advance. The sun had at last begun its slow descent towards the horizon, but there was still plenty of heat in it. Many of those around Thurkill were already panting with the effort of climbing the slope. Although many had slaked their thirst from the river as they crossed, they were still tired, nonetheless. Long hours of fighting under the blazing sun had taken its toll on both sides. But now that the enemy had refused Harold's offer of quarter, it would be a brutal fight to the death.

The two armies clashed for a second time with a cacophony of noise; screams intermingled with the sound of metal striking metal or wood. Straightaway, the Norse were pushed back. They had been outnumbered from the start, and the losses they had suffered on the western side of the river had only served to exacerbate the situation. They fought bravely and sold their lives dearly but their shieldwall was visibly shrinking as more and more men fell, either through wounds or exhaustion. For the Saxons, however, their fatigue seemed to lessen as every step took then closer to victory. They spurred each other on to greater efforts, ignoring the pain from which they suffered.

A great shout went up to Thurkill's right. "What's happening?" He yelled as he thrust his shield forward to block another blow.

A voice came back. "It's Tostig. He's down. Dead, I think."

"Surely they will surrender now?"

"Don't count on it, son", Scalpi replied, his face a mask of sweat and concentration. These fellows don't know the meaning of the word, surrender. We won't see the last of this fight for a while yet."

Sure enough, there was no let-up in the ranks of the Norse army. Though they were being pushed back all the time, they were still steadfast in their defence. But their losses were taking their toll. They no longer had the numbers to match the Saxon shieldwall, allowing the latter to start to envelope their flanks. Much more of this and they would be encircled before the sun went down.

Thurkill, his father and their four fyrdsmen were now gathered on the far left wing of the Saxon line. It was a miracle they all still lived. Two of the fyrdsmen had been wounded, though not seriously. Ubba had a gash to his cheek from which blood still dripped, while Halfdan had a piece of cloth, ripped from his tunic, wound tightly around his right forearm. It had stained red where the blood had seeped through, but it appeared to be doing the job. "A lucky spear thrust while I was off balance," Halfdan scowled ruefully, more in embarrassment than pain. Neither wound appeared to be affecting their agility, though, as they both hacked and stomped their way forward against the opposing line.

But just when they thought that the enemy must be on the point of collapse, they were suddenly thrown back on to the defensive by a huge surge. Immediately, they began to yield ground, step after step, slipping and sliding in the guts and blood of the fallen. All around them, men looked at each other in horror; they had been on the point of victory after all.

"What in God's name is happening?" Scalpi yelled above the tumult.

Thurkill pointed with his sword. "Look, father. The rest of the Norse army has arrived at last."

King Harold must have also realised the threat, for he arrived at that moment with a party of huscarls taken from the centre where the battle was less intense. Immediately, they threw themselves into the thick of the fighting, with the king shouting encouragement to all those around. "Hold them! Hold them! Do not let them steal your victory."

Thurkill had no concept of how long this last phase of the battle went on, but it was – without doubt – the fiercest it had been all day. The fresh warriors, in full armour, fought with the desperation of men who knew that they stood but one pace from annihilation. Their leaders were dead, they had suffered grievous losses in their ranks but there was no other option for them but to stand and fight. There could be no retreat. They fought for honour, glory and, above all now, revenge. They fought so that those who came after them would sing songs of their deeds around the hearth in every great hall across their homeland. The knowledge lent them an extra ferocity that was terrible to behold and which gave them the strength to cut huge new swathes through the Saxon host.

Everywhere he looked, Thurkill was confronted with cruelly twisted and misshapen bodies from both sides littering the field. He had long since passed the point of exhaustion; his body moved through some will of its own now, independent of his fatigued mind. His thirst was almost overpowering now; he was no longer even sweating. He felt as if every last drop of moisture had been leeched from his body. He had so little strength left, he knew it was only a matter of time until he fell; either at the hand of an enemy or from sheer physical breakdown. His father still fought alongside him, shouting encouragement every now and then, but clearly also at the limits of his endurance. Three of their fyrdsmen were still by their side. All save Halfdan; his wounded arm limiting his ability to fight, to such an extent that he was finally cut down by two Norsemen working in tandem, despite the best efforts of those around him.

When he thought he could stand no more, Thurkill suddenly found that where there was once a snarling, cursing Norseman in front of him, there was now a gap. Dumbstruck, he turned to the left and right, wincing at the pain in his aching neck muscles. It was the same story on both sides. Here and there the odd duel continued, but there was now an unmistakably huge sensation of space where, only moments before, there had been an intense sprawling press of men, hacking and hurling abuse at each other. Did he dare hope? Was it true? Had they finally had enough?

It was true, he realised, relief flooding his soul. Already the few remaining Vikings were streaming down the slope away from the slaughter, heading east towards their boats.

A handful of Saxons pursued them but, for the most part, the victors slumped to the ground where they stood. Like many around him, Thurkill dropped to his knees. A wave of nausea swept over him, causing him to turn his head to puke his guts on to the churned up soil around him. He wiped his mouth on his sleeve before collapsing on to his back, still sufficiently sentient to avoid the mess he had made. Scalpi squatted next to him and tousled his hair, perhaps finding it hard to let go of the child and accept the man his son had become that day.

"I'm proud of you, boy. You've fought well and brought honour to our family."

Thurkill smiled thinly, but his father's words warmed his heart nevertheless. He could not have hoped for more from the day.

"Why did they give up like that? I thought they had us beaten at the end there." His voice was weak, croaking for lack of saliva.

Scalpi wiped his sleeve across his forehead and sighed wearily. "I don't rightly know. I can only imagine they were even more spent than us. Losing both Harald and Tostig must have taken its toll as well. There's only so much you can do without strong leadership."

"But they had all those fresh warriors. They were pushing us back."

"They were, that's true. But remember, too, that they had come all the way from Riccall; a good few miles away from here. They must have run most, if not all, of the way. On a hot day like this, in full armour, that's going to take a lot out of a man."

Scalpi stood and reached out his hand to pull Thurkill to his feet. "Come on. Let's go find Harold and see what's happening."

***

Every step they took brought ever more gruesome sights. Bodies lay everywhere, in many cases hacked and stabbed to the point of unrecognisability. In those places where the fighting had been fiercest, they lay so thick on the ground that they had to chart a course around the bodies lest they tread on them. Thurkill glanced at his father; his face was ashen with shock.

"I've been in a fair few fights in my time, as you know, but this is the worst I've ever seen".

Thurkill said nothing, not wishing to disturb his father's thoughts. He too was shocked to the core by what he had seen and done that day. It was as if someone had reached into him and wrenched his childhood out in one brutal, gut-wrenching movement. There could be no turning back, now; he had joined the ranks of men, like it or not. Though he was sickened by what he had seen and done, at the same time his heart was bursting with a mix of excitement and pride. He had fought his first battle and survived. Not only survived, but played his part well by his own reckoning, if not also by his father's.

But alongside those feelings, somewhere deep inside, a part of him was scared of what he had become. He had found an enjoyment in the act of killing his enemy; seeing them fall before him, faces contorted in a rictus of pain. Did that make him evil? Would he go to hell? Surely, he had been doing nothing more than the king's bidding? Following orders he had been given?. Did that not also make it God's work? Besides, any one of those he had killed would have done the same as him were they but quicker or more skilful.

He resolved to go to see the village priest when he got home. Would it help him to talk about it, seek some assurance that he was not damned for eternity? The thought of home also made him wonder what Edith would think of him if she could see him now, covered in blood, standing over the broken forms of those he had killed. Would she be proud, or would she recoil in horror at what he had become?

"Hail Scalpi, well met! It brings me joy to see you still alive, you ugly troll." Harold strode forward to embrace him warmly. He looked to have come through the battle without a scratch, despite being covered almost head to foot in blood; a testament to his having been in the thick of the action throughout.

"Aye, Lord. It will take more than a few hairy-arsed Norsemen to finish me off."

"Ha! I'm glad to hear it, old friend. Though there are many who have paid dearly for today's victory all the same. We must honour them in time, raise a cup of ale in their memory."

Harold then turned to face his son. Though he was much taller, Thurkill still felt small in the presence of the warrior king. Harold stood silently for a moment, looking the boy up and down as if measuring his worth.

"Now then. What do we do with you, lad?"

Thurkill blushed and looked down awkwardly at his feet. Words did not come; he had no idea what Harold meant. The king chuckled at his discomfort, while Scalpi grinned stupidly, his face beaming with paternal pride.

The king continued. "My brother tells me that without you, the battle might have gone very differently."

Thurkill bowed his head, his cheeks burning red in consternation. "I did but play my part, Lord, as well as any other man here today."

"You are too modest, Thurkill. Without your intervention at the bridge, we may have been stuck there for a good while longer; long enough for their reinforcements to arrive well before we could defeat them. We owe you a great debt of gratitude."

Thurkill lifted his eyes to meet Harold's. He could feel a

warm glow spreading through his gut, swelling up to his chest. Then, he dropped to one knee, overwhelmed in the presence of this great war-leader. "It is my honour and privilege to serve you, Lord. My sword is yours for all time."

Harold nodded approvingly, raising him back to his feet. "Well, you should have more than just a sword with which to fight for me." He beckoned Gyrth to come forward. "Thurkill, son of Scalpi, I gift you this war-axe, the very same that was carried by the brave Norseman who held my army at bay for so long on the bridge. May you bear it henceforth as skilfully and as courageously as did our foe."

Harold then removed a gold band from his arm and handed that to Thurkill also. "This token I also give you as a mark of my thanks; as reward for a brave warrior who fought well in my service; in recognition of a boy who today became a man. Wear it with pride and give thanks to God each time you look at it and remember this day. In years to come when you are old and sitting by the fire, with grandchildren playing around your knees, you may look at it and recall the day you first went into battle and how you won it in my service."

Turning to Scalpi, the king continued. "He is a fine boy, my friend. You have raised him well and should be justly proud of him."

Thurkill was dumbfounded. He stood there, mouth agape, hands grasping the two gifts, surrounded by a great gaggle of warriors all staring at him. He knew he had to say something, but the struggle to find the right words was as hard as anything else he had experienced that day. He searched for the inspiration that would save him from appearing an arse in such vaunted company.

"Lord," he began nervously. "You honour me greatly with these gifts, more than I could have ever hoped. I give thanks to God that I have survived this day so that I may have the chance once more to prove myself worthy of them in your service."

Harold clapped a hand on Thurkill's shoulder and laughed. "The boy speaks almost as well as he fights. Are you sure he is yours, Scalpi? I don't ever recall you being so eloquent."

Harold then turned to the assembled lords and captains.

"Tend to the wounded as best you can and then let us go from this place to Eoforwic where we will celebrate this victory."

NINE

25 September, Eoforwic

Thurkill stood on the parapet of the wall that surrounded the city of Eoforwic, looking out to the south. The evening was cool after the heat of the day, but a sharp breeze was beginning to blow in from the south west, causing him to draw his cloak more tightly around his shoulders. The sun had long since fallen below the horizon but the sky still clung on to the last vestiges of light as if trying to hold back the all-encompassing darkness that threatened to take over. He was alone with his thoughts, brooding over the events of the day. The guards who patrolled the wall stepped round him, rather than disturb his reverie, aware, perhaps, that this was a man with a troubled soul.

The reality of the day's events had finally sunk in. He had killed for the first time and not only that, he had found he was good at it and – in the darkest recesses of his soul – he knew he had enjoyed the feelings of power and invincibility that came with it. But something else in his soul fought against it, was repulsed by what he had become. It was a turmoil of emotions, each fighting for supremacy, and he knew not which would win.

His stomach cramped once again, his body shuddering as he retched, leaning far out over the wall. It was this, more than anything, that had caused him to step away from the feasting hall. Like a fool, he had gorged himself on choice cuts of pork and beef, washed down with copious amounts of ale from a cup that was refilled after almost every sip – however small – by the legion of waiting churls. Eventually he had stumbled outside claiming the need to take a piss, only to throw up instead, behind a stinking byre. His head swam as he leaned over the parapet, allowing the breeze to cool his forehead. To make matters worse, every muscle ached and throbbed. The exhilaration of the battle had long since worn off as they trudged back to the city and – with each step – he had begun to feel every bruise from all the blows he had received. On top of which, his back, shoulders and all four limbs protested continually at the amount of effort demanded of them. He longed to find a bed to rest but he knew that the feasting would go on for some while yet, not to mention the songs and tales to come after that. Come to think of it, he was surprised he had not already been missed.

"Hey. What are you doing skulking out here? You're missing all the fun."

Thurkill groaned. He had spoken too soon. Turning towards the sound of the voice, he forced a smile on to his lips to disguise his feelings.

"Alright, Ubba, can't a man take a piss in peace?"

***

Inside the hall, the atmosphere was even more oppressive than it had been before. The stench of unwashed bodies combined with the aroma of the rich meat made for a distinctly pungent smell. Furthermore, the heat and smoke from the hearth fire was making it difficult to breathe. Someone had thrown the doors open to allow some fresh air into the place, but it helped only those sat nearby. Thurkill took his seat between Wulfrid and Ubba, the latter still with bloodstained bandage wrapped tightly around his head. Together with Scalpi, they sat at a bench close to Harold's own table, in recognition of the king's favour.

Eventually, the churls began to clear away what remained of the food after which a hush fell over the assembly. Looking up, Thurkill smiled as he saw Eadric the scop take to the floor. Eadric's reputation as the best storyteller of them all was known in almost every corner of the kingdom. Thurkill had had no idea that he was even here in Eoforwic, but he supposed it made sense as Harold would want news of the great victory to be recorded for just such an occasion as this, and for many years to come.

Now he stepped into the space before Harold's table and introduced his latest composition: The Saga of Stamford Bridge. In his hand he held a small lyre with which he introduced each new verse ...

They stood together, shield overlapping shield,
The host of Harold, Lord of England and giver of rings.
No man shrank back from
The blizzard of spear points.

No man lost heart in the face of
the foemen as they drew their swords.
Thegn did not shrink from thegn
Nor warrior from warrior.
As it always was with our fathers
And their fathers before them.

The host of England, sons of those Angles and Saxons
Who came to these shores many centuries ago,
Stood shoulder to shoulder to defend this land once more.
With their might, they broke the shieldwall,
split many a shield asunder.
With their might, they sent many a Viking to Valhalla,
to meet with their ancestors.
And the field flowed with the blood of the enemy,
As they fell beneath our swords.

All morning the host of Harold stood and fought,
Under the glare of the burning sun.
Then the great king, Harald, known as Hardrada, fell
His throat pierced by a Saxon arrow.
But his people did not crumble, nor did they flee, but instead
they crossed the Stamford Bridge to fight again.

But our warriors could not follow, could not reach the enemy
with their swords,
For their way was blocked by an axe-wielding Norseman,
charging a toll of blood to cross.
Around him lay many a brave warrior fallen,
hewn down by the giant Norseman.
Now came to the fight, Thurkill, son of Scalpi.

As his name was mentioned, a huge cheer went up from the
assembled warriors, led by Harold, his brother, Gyrth, and all
those sat at the king's table. Those nearest to the young warrior
slapped him on his back and yelled in his ear. All around the
hall, men banged their cups and platters against table tops.
Thurkill grinned sheepishly, his cheeks burning hotter than the

fire. It was some while before the uproar had dimmed to a level that allowed Eadric to continue.

Now came to the fight, Thurkill, son of Scalpi.

Carved from oak, with strength and height to match.

With cunning and guile he speared the axeman,

His bowels laid waste, no more was he to rise.

The tale went on for what seemed like an age. Like all good scops, he had the knack of mentioning key moments from the battle and the names of those involved and every time he did, a new round of back-slapping, yelling and banging of tables ensued.

As the saga went on and on, Thurkill's could feel his head swimming. He could barely focus on what was going on any more apart, that was, from the dark-haired serving girl who kept refilling his cup. Earlier in the evening he had wondered, idly, whether she was looking at him but he had put it out of his mind; why would she be interested in him? Now, however, he wasn't so sure. Every time she passed by, she fixed her eyes on his and smiled, her curly dark hair cascading around her shoulders as she looked from side to side. Was it his imagination or was she pressing herself against him more than she needed to when she leaned in to pour the ale? He blamed the drink. In truth, he could not remember ever being this drunk before, and it gave him a courage that otherwise would be lacking. *I suppose it's not every day you fight your first battle and get rewarded personally by the king,* he grinned foolishly to himself. *Why wouldn't she be interested in me?*

He shook his head, trying to clear the image from his mind, but he found his eyes following the girl around the hall as she swayed through the crowd carrying a brimming jug full of ale in each hand. As he watched he felt a sharp dig in his ribs. Turning, he saw Ubba grinning stupidly at him, blood still dripping, unnoticed, down his face from beneath his bandage. He looked as if he were even more drunk than Thurkill, if that were possible.

"You'd like to have her keep you warm on a cold, dark night, eh?" he leered.

Thurkill felt himself flush as he slurred. "Shut up, Ubba. You don't know what you're talking about!"

Ubba said nothing but chuckled knowingly as he returned to his ale. Thurkill looked down at his own cup, acutely aware that the other men around him were all nudging each other and pointing at him and the girl. Even his father was smiling at him, seemingly fully aware of the cause of his embarrassment. He wished the ground would open up and swallow him whole.

He had never been with a woman, not properly, despite his age; he was practically a man after all. Well, that was if you didn't count a quick fumble in the woods with Agnes, a farmer's daughter, a year or so ago. She had been a few years older than him and definitely much more experienced. He remembered burying his face between her ample breasts as she fiddled with his breeches. To his eternal shame he had spilled his seed almost as soon as she had got her hands around him, her touch alone being enough to make him erupt. To her credit she had not laughed too much, but had instead tried to reassure him as he mumbled a red-faced apology. Even so, he was sure that, for the next few days, he heard the odd snigger from a number of the women folk as he went about his business. He supposed that, despite her promises to the contrary, Agnes had not been able to resist confiding in her friends about the time she tried to bed the lord's son.

Remembering the shame of the memory, he didn't spot that the girl had appeared alongside him once more. Without a word she held out her hand to him, her eyes smiling and encouraging all at once. Almost in a trance, Thurkill took her hand in his, noting how his huge paw enveloped her slender fingers as if they were but tiny twigs. He allowed himself to be pulled to his feet, oblivious to the whistles and shouts all around him. Without a word, she guided him deftly between the benches and the prostrate, snoring forms of those who had already succumbed to the ale.

Outside in the cool air, she led him to a nearby barn. Inside it was warm and cosy with piles of clean straw freshly strewn around the floor. He stood dumbly, his arms hanging uselessly by his side, while – in one smooth movement – she stepped out of her dress to stand naked before him. He stood transfixed, in awe of her beauty, his eyes as round as the moon which gently shone through the gaps in the oak beams. The light playing across the curves of her body, casting shade in placed that served only to accentuate her allure.

He had faced a horde of Vikings without fear earlier that same day, but the sight of this one beautiful woman had defeated him where they could not. He could neither move nor could he could run away. He must have looked ridiculous; swaying slightly with the effects of the beer, his mouth agape, unable to speak. Sensing his awkwardness, the girl lay down in the straw before reaching up with one arm to draw him down to her. He rolled sideways on to his back as she drew his cloak over them. As he lay there, he felt the weariness flow through his body. Closing his eyes, he gave himself over to her to do with as she willed.

TEN

27 September, St Valery, Normandy

Duke William of Normandy stood on the high bluffs overlooking the town of St Valery, surveying the bustling scene below him. From his vantage point he had a clear view of the weather vane sitting proudly atop the small stone church, the focal point of the town. For the past few weeks that God-damned piece of iron had been stubbornly pointing in the wrong direction. Day after day, the winds had persistently blown in from the north west, keeping his fleet firmly anchored in the harbour. With every day that passed, his frustration had grown and his temper worsened. He knew the autumn storms could hit any day now, making the journey across the channel to England perilous to the point of being foolhardy. It was already late enough in the season to be a significant risk as it was. The distance might only be short but to be caught in the eye of a storm in the middle of the crossing could destroy his plans in one fell swoop. If they did not set sail soon, however, he would have to send the army home until the spring. His coffers were already severely depleted, on top of which he had also had to borrow vast amounts at exorbitant prices to make good the shortfall. God alone knew where he would find the money to do it all again the following year.

Finally, however, his prayers – and those of the priests in the town – had been answered. He should think so too, as he had paid them enough gold for their efforts, after all. He had emerged from his lodgings that morning to feel a definite change in the breeze. From up here on the bluffs, he was able to confirm his suspicion; the weather vane had changed direction. Now it pointed squarely north, the direction of his prize. Finally, he had his longed-for southerly wind and now, at last, he could put his plans into action.

The day was bright with just a few fluffy white clouds scudding across an otherwise clear blue sky. It was still quite warm for the time of year, the heat helping to keep the wild autumn weather at bay. He turned his face to the north and raised his right hand to shield his eyes from the glare of the sun in the east. Though he could not see any distinct detail of England's coast, there was, undeniably, a dark smudge on the horizon. That must be land, he thought to himself. She awaits me, a few short miles away. The culmination of years of expectation and nine months of solid planning was but a day or two away.

Smiling grimly, he turned back to the assembled group of knights. "It is time, my friends. Let us make good use of this divine intervention. The Pope himself has blessed our enterprise and now our prayers have been answered." He pointed at the pale blue banner with the gold cross fluttering in the strengthening breeze, "and now God has smiled on us and sent us this fair wind. To the boats. And thence to England where I shall take my throne from the usurper, that traitor, Harold."

"To England!" The men roared their approval.

As they turned to go, William grabbed the arm of the man holding the staff from which the papal banner fluttered. Richard FitzGilbert was the third son of the ageing Count Gilbert of Clare. With two older brothers before him, he'd had no chance of succeeding his father to the lands and title, Rather, he had been expected to follow his uncle into the church. He would have done so too, but for the fact that he was eminently unsuited to a life of prayer and meditation. After a year or two of apprenticeship in which he spent more time fighting with the other novices than he did praying or learning, he had been kicked out of the abbey of Fecamp. Further ignominy had then been heaped on his young shoulders when his father had cast him out of the household for failing to follow his wishes. He had been left to make his own way in the world as best he could.

So, he had become a sell-sword, making use of the skills he had learnt as a boy before being packed off to the church. He pledged allegiance to any lord who would pay him well and who gave him opportunity for plunder. Much of the past ten years had been spent fighting for the Norman Hauteville lords in southern Italy, where he had established a fearsome reputation for brutality. He had quickly worked out that the most effective way to win a fight was to make the enemy fear you more than you feared them. For the price of a few well-chosen massacres of villagers who had foolishly resisted his men, the dividends had borne fruit. More often than not, a town would, from that point on, throw open their gates at the mere sight of his banner: a black raven on a yellow background.

But with the arrival of peace in that region, he had found his services less in demand. He had become restless, eager for new adventure, unwilling to live the sedentary life of a lord of the manor that his paymasters had offered him. He was young; he still needed to fight, to pillage, to win glory and renown. Reluctantly, he had decided to head back north to his homeland where he hoped the pickings might be greater. It was while he had been making a short stay in Rome that Norman envoys had arrived to secure the pope's backing for what they referred to as a crusade to England. Listening to them as they fervently made their case in front of Pope Alexander, he'd decided there and then to latch on to their coat tails. The promise of conquest and all that came with it was just what he was looking for. It was too great an adventure to resist.

Duke William had heard of his reputation and was only too pleased to welcome men of his calibre to his cause. "I want you in my flag-ship, FitzGilbert, with the papal flag streaming from the stern alongside mine. I want all to see that we sail under God's own banner, that God himself supports our claim. I also want you near my person when the fighting starts. A man of your capabilities will come in useful when the time comes to cross swords with our Saxon cousins."

"My sword is yours, Lord." FitzGilbert's reply was short and to the point. It mirrored his fighting style: economic in effort but with maximum effectiveness. He was not a tall man, nor was he particularly broad-shouldered, but his menacing demeanour more than made up for his lack of stature. He carried a sense of foreboding that made most others want to avoid him at all costs.

As was the Norman fashion, he was clean shaven and wore his dark hair short, gathered in a wavy mop on the top of his head. His jaw was firm and jutted forward as if constantly spoiling for a fight. His black eyebrows were thickly thatched, almost to the point that there was no gap between them, and sat on a forehead that overhung his face. Set beneath it and deep within its shadow, his eyes were piercingly blue and fixed in a permanent glare. Even when he was pleased, which was rare, the smile never reached as far as his eyes.

He was not what might be called classically handsome, and what looks he did possess had been ruined by an ugly red scar that ran from the corner of his mouth, across his cheek and up to his ear, the result of a dagger slashed across his face during a vicious brawl over a game of dice in southern Italy some years ago. Although he had been wounded, the other fellow had not lived to regret his accusation of cheating, even though it had been true. The gash had healed well enough, and he had done well to avoid any infection, but he would never be rid of the reminder. He had long become accustomed to it, even coming to enjoy the effect it had on people. If fear and revulsion were their first impressions, then that was no bad thing in his eyes.

William understood the unspoken meaning and chuckled. He had seen many of this type in his time. "As long as the pay is good, eh? Don't worry, FitzGilbert, play your part as well as your reputation suggests you might and I will see you well rewarded. A man like you will be looking to settle down with a nice bit of land eventually, I'm sure. I hear that this realm of England is carpeted with fertile fields, ideal for raising crops and livestock alike. There is much coin to be made there, I'm told. Something in the south, close enough to get back to Normandy at any time would suit you, would it not?"

"My fighting days are not yet done, Lord, but I confess I have always yearned to have estates to call my own one day; estates that have been denied me by accident of birth and no more."

"To England then and let's see what fortune and God's will brings."

ELEVEN

02 October, Eoforwic

The door of the barn crashed open, kicked so hard that it splintered away from its hinges. In a heartbeat, Thurkill was on his feet, reaching for his sword which he had left propped against the wall by his head. The serving girl screamed beside him, frantically pulling her dress around her to protect her modesty.

"What is the meaning of this?" he yelled, more in fright than anger. Visions of Norsemen rampaging through the city, murdering and raping as they went, filled his mind.

"Put your blade away, son, you'll do yourself an injury standing there naked like that!"

Suddenly embarrassed, Thurkill dropped his sword and reached for his trews. As he struggled to pull them on, he asked. "What's happening, father?"

"Well first of all, it's past midday and you've been in here with this young lady," he smiled politely at her, "for far too long. And secondly, and perhaps more importantly, a rider has just arrived to report that William the Bastard of Normandy has landed on our south coast four days ago, with a fleet numbering over five hundred ships."

"By God, what devilry is this? Surely it's too late in the season to launch such an attack?"

"There's many a wiser man than you or I who has made that very point to Harold this morning. But the fact is they are in Pevensey and, what's worse, we are not. The whole of the south of England, Wintanceastre, Lundenburh, all of it, is unprotected. The timing could not be worse."

Thurkill stopped for a moment, mid-way through lacing his trews tight around his waist. "So, we must go. We must march south as quickly as possible."

Scalpi slapped his hand against his forehead in mock surprise. "You're right! Wait here while I inform the king. For God's sake, Thurkill, do you not think we have thought of that? The men are ready to leave and we're just wasting time rounding up stragglers like you. Say your goodbyes and get out here now."

Before Thurkill could say another word, Scalpi had stomped off, leaving him red-faced and wondering what he should say to the woman whose name he could not even remember. As he stood there, his head bowed in shame, the woman resolved the issue for him. Still as bare as the day she was born, she walked over to where he stood and wrapped her arms around his neck, squeezing her body against his, so tightly that he felt the first stirrings of arousal once again. She kissed him full and hard on the lips before pulling back and looking him straight in the eyes.

"Go now, Thurkill. May God keep you safe from harm."

"My thanks, lady. I will not forget you or the time we spent together."

She said nothing, but smiled enigmatically, as if suggesting she thought he would forget her as soon as he lay with another woman. Instead, she turned to gather up her dress from the ground. As he stood looking at her back, Thurkill was seized by the desire to grab her and pull her back down into the hay. With a rueful smile and a shrug, though, he forced himself to turn away from the heavenly sight before him, striding out the door to find his father.

***

Back on the road south, Thurkill's mood had turned sour; matching the taste in his mouth, a legacy of having drunk too much ale these last several days. He had already emptied his water skin but to little or no effect; his thirst was still raging. With him and Scalpi were barely five hundred men, though all mounted; a far smaller number than had marched north to Eoforwic a few short days ago.

"Father, do we know how many men Duke William has brought to our shores?"

Scalpi jerked his head in his son's direction, having been lost in his own thoughts. "Eh? Um, I'm not sure. The messenger mentioned a fleet of well over five hundred ships carrying men, horses and supplies, but I doubt we know how many of each were in every ship. But we should expect a host of several thousand men; to bring any fewer would be foolhardy to say the least."

"Look around us, though. We do not have the numbers to match that. Why have so few come south with us?"

"Don't worry, son. The Duke may have forced our hand, but we will not go into battle with so few. We had to leave a good number in the north to replenish the garrison, while many others were too weak to travel after the battle. Then there were those who would have had to walk; we simply don't have time to wait for them. We must reach Lundenburh fast so we can stop William before he has the chance to do too much damage."

"But where will we find the numbers we need to make a stand? Huscarls may be worth at least two of any fyrdsman but even so there are too few of us to be anything other than an annoying bee that William will merely swat out of his way."

"True, but Harold has already sent riders ahead with orders to go with all haste to the counties to the south. They will call upon every lord to muster their men and bring them to the city. There, Harold will assemble the fyrd and march out to meet the Norman bastard. Those men will be fresh and ready for a fight, having not been involved up here in the north."

"But will it be enough?"

"If we wait long enough for the host to gather in full it will, but I fear that Harold will want to attack as soon as possible. Either way, whatever he decides, it will have to be enough, son. It will have to be."

All around them, as the horses trudged south, mile after long mile, the mood was sombre. Gone was the elation of defeating the Norsemen; the songs of glory and honour had died in their throats. The battle at the bridge had almost been forgotten now that a new threat had arisen; one that was felt more keenly by these huscarls whose lands and families were in the south. It was the same for Thurkill. Though he knew that Pevensey was some way from where their village lay, who was to say where the Normans had gone since? It was not much more than a day or two's ride from the coast to the Weald which spread across the ancient kingdom of Kent. Furthermore, their hall was on a direct line from Pevensey to the city of Canterbury, a site that could easily be a target for the Normans as the centre of the

English church.

***

They arrived in Lundenburh on the sixth day of October. They had ridden for long hours each day, setting off before the sun was up and stopping only when it had dropped below the horizon. Horses and men alike were exhausted but the prospect of a few days' rest in the city's taverns helped to restore morale a little. They had been joined by a number of lords and their followers in the last day or two – lifting their spirits still further – and many more were expected to arrive in the coming days. But from the reports coming back from the messengers, it would be at least a week before they had an army big enough to take on the Normans without fear.

Thurkill hoped to visit Haslow while the rest of the army rested. They were fewer than two days' ride from the family home and he longed to go and see his sister and aunt. Perhaps he could even persuade them to move to the city, away from the danger? But Scalpi would not hear of it. They could not risk being absent when the order to march was given. Instead, his father had agreed to send a rider to Aga, urging her to go north of the Thames to where their cousin lived.

"Fat lot of use it will do anyway," Scalpi had snorted as the rider clattered over the bridge to Suthweca to begin his journey south.

Thurkill had looked at him quizzically.

"Well, have you ever known your aunt to be anything other than a stubborn old mule? I promise you now, she will ignore my instructions and stay to protect my lands in some misguided sense of duty. Does she not realise that walls can be rebuilt, livestock replaced, crops replanted? Whereas, her and Edith cannot." With that, he had walked away, shaking his head sorrowfully.

Meanwhile, Harold was desperate to confront the Normans. Every day his forces grew in size but were still too few to risk a pitched battle. How much longer could they wait? How long could they allow William and his army to ravage the southlands – Harold's own lands – unchecked?

Scouts came and went by the hour, with news of the

movements of the enemy host. The Normans had stayed in Pevensey long enough only to pillage the town and surrounding area for supplies, but - soon after – they had moved east, a few miles up the coast towards the larger port town of Hastings.

Now, according to the latest reports, the Normans appeared to have settled, spending their time constructing a solid base from which to plan their next move. But with every day that passed, Harold became more and more agitated. Hastings and the surrounding area were Godwine lands and many of the nearby villages and manors had already been ransacked by Norman soldiers looking for supplies. Many houses had been burned down already, women and children thrown out to fend for themselves in the woods and several of the men slaughtered.

As the former Earl of Wessex, Harold fretted for his people. Kicking his heels in Lundenburh waiting for the fyrd to assemble, he was powerless to prevent the deprivations being visited upon them. He was failing in his first duty to protect his people from attack or injustice. It must have cut him to the quick to have to stand idle while they suffered. With every day that passed, his patience wore a little thinner until it was as threadbare as the most ancient of rugs.

TWELVE

10 October, Lundenburh

The atmosphere within the great hall at Harold's palace at Westminster was subdued. The great lords and ladies were gathered with the king to celebrate the saint's day of Bishop Paulinus but few, if any, were in the mood for celebration. At any other time, such a day would have seen great merriment, gluttony and drunkenness, but there was little in the way of good cheer in the hall. Lords, ladies and warriors sat side by side in almost total silence, picking at their food or taking small sips from their cups. No one seemed in the mood for levity or boisterousness, afraid that they might somehow offend the king. Serving girls went about their business carrying food and drink, keeping their heads bowed as if sensing the mood and being afraid to attract attention.

Earlier that day, after Stigand – the dour and joyless Archbishop of Canterbury – had performed a lengthy service to celebrate the saint's life in the nearby abbey, prayers for victory over the Normans had been offered. Afterwards they had processed the short journey from the abbey to the king's hall, following Stigand and his retinue of monks. Walking just behind the bishop, Harold's face was like thunder. All attempts to engage him in conversation had been met with monosyllabic grunts so that no one now dared to try to break into his mood for fear of rebuke. Even Gyrth and Leofwine left him to his own thoughts, conversing quietly between themselves instead, a few paces behind their brother.

The reason for Harold's foul mood was apparent to all; the mustering of the fyrd was taking far longer than he had hoped. Although their numbers had swelled to almost seven thousand now, by most reckonings this was still too few to risk battle with William. Scouts had numbered the enemy host at around a similar size, perhaps closer to eight thousand, but the difference was they were fresh and rested. But every day they waited was a day wasted as far as Harold was concerned. The enemy was despoiling his lands, abusing his people and yet all he could do sit impotent within the city walls, feasting the memory of some long-dead saint about whom few outside the church cared or could even remember.

Now, up at the top table, Harold was drinking heavily but eating little of the food on his platter. In turn, those around him did little more than pick at their food, unwilling to be seen to gorge themselves while the king did not. Even Harold's wife, sat to his right, could not rouse him from his torpor. Instead, she sat sullenly by his side, as if waiting for the whole sorry affair to be over.

Thurkill, however, had long since decided to ignore everyone else; the food was of a quality and variety that was unlike anything he had ever experienced. Even though his father commanded reasonable wealth, enabling them to eat as well as any lord, this was on a different level altogether. There were swans from the great river, whole pigs stuffed with all manner of forest fruits and great hunks of hot, fresh bread with which to mop up the juices from the meat. To wash everything down there were wines from Burgundy, brought over by the many merchants who plied their wares in the markets of Lundenburh. He remembered having had wine only once before – a rich red liquid with which they had celebrated the day of Christ's birth the previous year – but it was expensive and not readily available outside of the city. Not knowing better, he had gulped it down as if it were ale, and had been sick not long after. Looking around him now, however, he saw that most people took small sips rather than huge draughts, and he sought to emulate them as if he had been drinking wine every day for years. *Something else I can tell Edith,* he smiled to himself, *she will be so jealous!*

The sound of a commotion behind him – somewhere towards the rear of the hall – dragged his thoughts back to the present. Twisting round on the bench, he saw that a group of five newcomers had entered, surrounded by several huscarls who had been standing guard outside. The leader of the group appeared to be an older man, dressed in the simple, brown habit of a monk pulled in at his generous waist by a wound piece of cord. His head was shaved in the familiar tonsure, leaving wisps of silvery grey hair sprouting around his ears and the back of his head. The fact he was a portly man, Thurkill noted, suggested he was not a devotee of any strict fasting regime.

Alongside him stood a knight; a great lord by the looks of his cloak and the way he conducted himself. In his right hand he carried a long pole from the end of which hung a pale blue banner emblazoned with a golden cross, either side of which the symbols X and R had been stitched. The knight stood still, unblinking, apparently unfazed by his surroundings. He was not tall but he carried an indescribable air of menace. From where Thurkill sat near the head table, he could see a wicked-looking scar running across his cheek, giving him an even greater sense of dread. This was not a man to be taken lightly, Thurkill thought to himself. As he stared, the knight became aware of his gaze and half turned his head to face the young Saxon warrior. Taking no more than a moment to appraise the boy, he smirked disdainfully, as if unimpressed by what he saw, before turning back to face the king.

Thurkill felt shame and anger in equal measure. He started to rise to his feet, but felt his father's hand on his shoulder, holding him down. Turning towards him in frustration, he saw Scalpi silently shake his head, mouthing the words "Let it go, son."

Having witnessed the exchange, the knight's smirk turned into a mocking grin, causing his scar to stretch, the damaged red flesh look even more angry than before. Thurkill reddened still further, his burning cheeks merely adding to his shame. He swore to himself that the Norman would one day pay for his humiliation. Ignorant of his thoughts, the Norman dismissed the young Saxon, advancing alongside the monk towards the dais. As they walked, so a low growl arose from the assembled lords and thegns; they were in no doubt as to who these men were.

Once the party had come to within a few feet of the king's bench, Harold lurched unsteadily to his feet, holding his hand out before him. "Hold! Who comes uninvited to my hall, disturbing my people on this holy day. Whence come you? Speak." Harold's tone was curt and cold, in keeping with his mood.

The scar-faced knight showed no visible reaction to the

challenge, but the monk bowed low as a mark of respect. "Noble Lord Harold of Wessex, my name is Hugh Maigrot, a monk from the abbey near Caen in Normandy. I am sent here by my lord, Duke William of that province, with a message for your Lordship."

All around the hall, men's jaws dropped as the realisation dawned that the monk had deliberately not addressed Harold as king. Here and there a few of the more drunken warriors shouted threats at the emissary. Harold calmly called for quiet, before addressing the delegation. "Out with it then, monk. Do not dress your words in finery as I would have you gone from my hall as quickly as you may, so we might return to our feast."

Maigrot nodded. "Very well, Lord. My master, Duke William, would have you abandon the crown you stole from him, keeping the promise you made to him not two years since when you swore on relics sacred to us to support his claim to the throne bestowed upon him by the blessed King Edward."

"A promise made under duress is no promise at all. As a holy man, you more than any should know that."

"Be that as it may, Lord, it was a sacred oath, sworn over relics most holy and you stand perjured before God. This banner," he gestured loosely towards the knight by his side, "has been presented to the Duke by the Pope himself, God's anointed representative. It was given willingly and in good faith, in recognition of the righteousness of the Duke's claim. God is on our side and you would do well to heed that. Should you decide not to stand aside, you risk eternal damnation for yourself and all those that follow you."

A shocked hush fell over the hall; even Harold seemed taken aback. To be cast out of God's grace, destined to an eternity of damnation and hellfire was a punishment worse than death itself. The thought of falling in battle and being denied entry at the gates of heaven was enough to shake the resolve of any man.

Before Harold could reply, however, Maigrot continued. "All is not lost though, Lord. The Duke is not a vengeful man; he does not seek battle if battle might be avoided. He would rather not see thousands of brave warriors on both sides slaughtered unnecessarily.

"Therefore, the Duke would have me tell you that if you willingly set aside the crown of England he would gladly cede to you all the land north of the Humber to be held under his licence. In addition, your brother, Gyrth, may hold the estates of Wessex as its earl. All this may be yours if you but step down in Duke William's favour. Rule Northumbria in peace or suffer papal excommunication; that is your choice." As he finished speaking, the monk held up the wooden cross that hung round his neck to ensure the solemnity of his words was not lost on anyone present.

No one spoke. No one even moved. Even the dogs stretched out by the fire waiting for scraps of meat and bones to be thrown were silent. While Harold considered his response, Gyrth, sitting to his left, rose to his feet.

"Brother, fellow countrymen. Do not lose heart. Do not allow the honeyed words of this so-called man of God disturb your minds or interrupt your feasting. All is not as he would have us believe. This monk seeks only to frighten us with this baseless threat of God's wrath, but I say instead that if this bastard of Normandy had any honour he would not send this cur before us to do his bidding. If this Duke had faith in the strength of his host and the righteousness of his claim, he would not resort to ignoble threats. He would not waste time with this pointless parley.

"Everyone here knows that Harold is our rightful king. He was chosen by Edward himself as his successor before he died. I saw it with my own eyes. Later that same day, my brother was acclaimed king by the witan, most of whom are in this hall today, eating my brother's meats and supping his wines. You were all there that day. You know I speak the truth. His claim to this throne is sound"

Several lords around the hall nodded in agreement, banging their wooden platters against the tables to emphasise their point.

"This duke has overreached himself by coming here. He trembles at the thought of our swords. He fears our spear-forest. He knows his warriors will crash against our shieldwall as uselessly as waves against our cliffs. Doubtless, he has heard of our great victory over the Hardrada at Stamford Bridge and now he fears both for his life and for those of his men. Why else would he waste our time with these weasel words? Why else would he make this ridiculous offer? Why does he not attack? He won't because he cowers like a lamb before the wolf, deep in our noble king's shire of Sussex."

Gyrth's words were having the desired effect. Appealing to the thegns' sense of honour was overcoming the fear caused by the monk's earlier threat of excommunication.

Then Gyrth held up his hand to call for peace before continuing, eager to press home the advantage he had gained. "What's more, do not believe this false promise of Northumbria. Do not think for one moment that William would leave us to live out our days unmolested. At the first opportunity he would bring sword and fire to kill us all in our beds. I'm sure he has already promised our lands to his followers; every inch of your fields, every plank of your halls, every strand of wool on the fleece of your sheep. How else would he have secured so many hired swords to fight for him? Do you think they come here for the love of William? How else has he swollen his ranks enough to be able to challenge us? Us, the strongest kingdom in Christendom. By offering our estates, our homes and our livestock to the godless, landless men that follow this banner, that's how! Men like this wretched knight here. This man who despoils himself by carrying that holy banner."

As Gyrth pointed at the scarred knight, the hall erupted. Platters were hurled against walls, drinking vessels smashed against the floor as men snarled and yelled, whipped into a frenzy by Gyrth's well-chosen words.

But Thurkill did not join in. His gaze was fixed on the knight, already consumed by hate for one he had met so recently. But in spite of that, he had to admire the man's courage and his poise; his face had betrayed not even the merest hint of anxiety at the change of mood, retaining its disdainful smirk throughout. The monk on the other hand had become highly agitated. This encounter had not turned out as he had planned.

Gyrth was not yet done, though; he was still warming to the task. "Will you give up your lands and your rights so meekly? Will you allow yourselves to be bullied by this feeble duke and his pet snake that stands here before us? Or will you defend them with your sword, your spear, your bare hands if necessary? I for one will gladly give my life for this island if I could do so in the knowledge that we had prevailed and sent this Norman upstart back whence he came."

Maigrot was by now literally hopping from foot to foot, desperate to escape the howling mob, but he knew he could not leave without having an answer from Harold that he could take back to William. When the noise eventually subsided to a level where he could be confident of making himself heard, he attempted to bring matters to a conclusion. In doing so, Thurkill noted, with some satisfaction, that he was now more respectful than when he had first started.

"Lord King, I have listened to the words of this noble prince of your realm, but I would know your own mind that I may convey your response back to my master."

Harold shrugged, gesturing around the hall, spreading his arms wide to take in every bench that was filled with angry warriors. When he spoke, though, his words betrayed no malice or anger towards the monk. "I think my answer is plain to see, Maigrot. You may rest assured that my brother speaks for me in this matter; we are of one mind. We will make neither peace nor treaty with our Norman cousin. Rather we will expel him from this land, by force of arms if necessary. We will succeed or we will die trying."

"Very well, Lord King. If conflict cannot be avoided, then consider this final offer that Duke William authorised me to make to you in the event that you reused to stand down. To avoid the senseless slaughter of thousands of your people, William would challenge you, the mighty warrior King Harold, to settle this dispute by the time-honoured tradition of single combat. Why must thousands die in agony when just two men need fight? Would you step on to the field of battle and take up my lord's offer? To the victor the spoils."

It was a canny move, Thurkill saw; the idea of it would surely appeal to Harold's sense of honour. It also meant ensuring that no men need die in his name. The Duke was known to be a great warrior, but so was Harold. During his recent sojourn in

Normandy, he had fought alongside the Duke and acquitted himself well by all accounts; even earning praise from William himself, it was said. It would be an even fight, he was sure. Who could say who would win?

As Harold considered this latest offer, Gyrth leaned in close to whisper advice. "I know your mind, brother. You are tempted to accept if it means saving the lives of hundreds, if not thousands, of our people. But I do not trust William. This offer merely hides a lack of confidence. He must think the odds of beating you man to man are greater than if his host were to be matched against ours. That tells me that the better option would be to refuse."

Harold nodded sagely, recognising the strength of Gyrth's argument. He slumped back into his seat, apparently wearied by the whole affair, before turning his head to the monk. "You already have my answer, we will match our swords and spears against yours and see who triumphs, whom God favours. Now be gone from my hall before I have you thrown out."

THIRTEEN

11 October, Lundenburh

"We march today. I will not wait a moment longer."

It was not yet dawn but Harold had called for all the lords to assemble at the abbey. He looked as if he had not even been to bed as his tunic and cloak were crumpled and still stained with wine and food from the previous day's feast. Several others looked the worse for wear; the result of a hard night's drinking. Thurkill was tired but otherwise unaffected. His encounter with the sneering knight had had a sobering effect, leaving him with no stomach for further carousing. Instead he had excused himself soon after the Normans left and retired to his cot. Now he stood at the back of the assembled captains, in full armour and clutching his war-axe.

"But several lords and their retinues are yet to arrive, Lord. To leave before they do would be foolhardy. At least wait for one more day?"

Harold sighed before putting his arm round Gyrth's shoulders. "We have delayed here too long already, brother. This Norman bastard has been ravaging our lands with impunity these past two weeks; I must act now before the people start to question my right to rule."

"That would not happen. The people would never desert you in favour of the bastard from Normandy."

Harold smiled, pausing to allow a slow procession of monks to pass on their way to the altar at the far end of the abbey. Their sandalled feet scraping across the rough earthen floor as they shuffled past, punctuating the psalms they sang.

"Thank you, Scalpi, your words are a comfort to me. But you saw the arrogance of that monk last night. They believe they have God and the Pope on their side and you saw what impact the threat of excommunication had on my thegns in the hall. If it were not for Gyrth's fine words, who knows what may have happened? If Maigrot can have that effect on the most senior lords of the land, think how the common people will feel when the Normans spread the same lies to them. How long before they rise up against me for fear of eternal damnation?

"No." He shook his head wearily. "My mind is made up. I believe our army to be large enough now to deal with whatever they might throw at us. It will have to be. If we go now we may yet catch them by surprise. I don't doubt their spies are telling them that we wait here for reinforcements. If we favour the unexpected, then perhaps we will repeat our success at Stamford Bridge, eh?" The tone of his voice betrayed the fact that he did not fully believe his own words.

"Why not just wait them out, Lord? The longer we avoid battle, the more chance they run out of supplies or succumb to some foul pestilence."

Harold turned towards the new speaker. "My Lord, Beorhtric, would you have me cower and skulk here forever behind the walls of Lundenburh? There is no honour in that. I would not have people point and call me coward for refusing to defend my kingdom."

Leofwine was next to offer his advice. "I agree we must fight, brother, but why risk everything in one battle? Send me or Gyrth to lead the host against the invader. That way we defend the honour of the kingdom and may also succeed in driving the Normans into the sea. Should we be defeated, however, then all would not be lost. You would survive to raise a new army either now or in the spring. You would have time to bring the northern levies to bear and bring bloody battle to a foe already weakened by us."

Thurkill could see the sense in Leofwine's words. Harold was also considering them as he stared at his brother, rubbing his bearded chin as if deep in thought.

"There is merit in your words, Leofwine, I'll not deny it. To risk everything on a single throw of the dice does worry me. But what sort of king would that make me? How would the chroniclers remember me if I sent others to do my work? My place is in the front rank of the shieldwall, standing shoulder to shoulder with those who would give their lives fighting for me. They expect to see their king plant his banner where the fighting is fiercest. They want... No! They need their king to lead them to victory. I would not deny them their right."

Harold continued, but raised his voice so that all might hear and be in no doubt. "My mind is clear on this. We leave here today to bring destruction down on the heads of the Norman invader. I will not allow them to stay unmolested in my kingdom any longer. My scouts tell me they have not ventured forth from the area around Hastings so we will meet them there. It's as good a place as any. Let us assemble at the old muster point known to our forebears as the hoar apple tree on Caldbec Hill two days from now. Send riders now to all those who have yet to arrive here. Tell them to muster there. With God's will and good English oak we will teach Duke William a lesson."

***

As he gathered up his war gear, Thurkill felt anticipation mounting within his heart once again. The memory of his first battle was still fresh in his mind. The exhilaration, the feeling of power as he dealt death to foes on all sides was as intoxicating as the finest wine; he yearned to taste it once again. He had overcome his fear and wanted nothing more now than to kill as many of the enemy as he could.

"How are you feeling, son?" Scalpi's voice cut into his thoughts, bringing him sharply back to the present. No doubt his father recalled how sick he had been on the morning of his first battle. Despite himself, his cheeks reddened at the thought of how he had lost control of his guts so dramatically.

"I'm fine, father. Eager to put the Norman whoresons to the sword."

Scalpi smiled, playfully cuffing his son round the head as he did so. "Do not imagine for a moment that this will be as easy as that little scuffle against the Norsemen. This will be a proper fight, if I'm not mistaken."

"How so? Why would we not send these foreign bastards packing just as easily?"

"You forget that the Norse had not much more than half their host on the field at the start and most of those were not ready for a fight. These Normans are trained killers; they will be prepared. From what I hear, William has gathered the best fighters from his own and many neighbouring lands with the promise of wealth and glory. His warriors will be wearing the best mail shirts and carrying the finest weapons that money can buy. What's more, I've heard some of them fight on horseback."

"They what?"

"I know. A good number of them ride into battle on these huge horses, as big as the ones we use to pull our ploughs. They use them to try and ride down their enemies using the sheer weight of these beasts."

Thurkill stopped to think for a moment, suddenly feeling a little less sure of himself than he had been before. What was it like to face a horse, or even hundreds of horses, thundering towards you at full pelt? The thought of it alone would be enough to turn your bowels to water.

Seeing the look on his face, Scalpi laughed. "Don't piss your breeches, son. Well, not just yet anyway. On horse or on foot, they have not faced a Saxon shieldwall before. Horse and man alike will not be able to break us if we stand firm. Both will fall just as easily beneath our spears, axes and swords."

Thurkill smiled at his father's encouraging words, but deep inside he felt a growing anxiety. Would they be able to stand against these Norman horsemen? They had no choice though; they had no mounted warriors of their own. They would have to stand – the alternative did not bear thinking about.

FOURTEEN

13 October, Caldbec Hill

The sun had not long slipped below the horizon when the first men of the Saxon host arrived at the hoar apple tree. No one knew how long it had stood there; no one remembered a time when it had not been. It certainly looked ancient, half covered as it was in dry, grey lichen that was so brittle it flaked away to the touch. For generations it had been used as a marker between three neighbouring regions and was thus frequently referred to in land charters going back, some said, even to the days of Alfred, or even his grandfather, Egbert, the first truly great king of the West Saxons.

Harold jumped down from his horse, stretching as he did so. He pressed his hands into the small of his back, arching his spine to try and ease some of the tension built up over two long days in the saddle. Meanwhile, all around the hill and on its surrounding slopes, men flopped to the ground in weariness. Those who still had the energy started small fires with which to cook up food from their forage sacks, augmented with rabbits and the odd squirrel or two that had been caught on the way. For the most part though, men gathered quietly in small groups and munched sourly on bread, apples or cheese before wrapping their cloaks around themselves and curling up on the soft turf, as close to their comrades as possible for protection from the chill autumn air. Few were in any doubt there would be a battle the next day so sleep was essential to give their bodies a chance to recover from the long march from Lundenburh.

Harold, meanwhile, gathered his captains together at the base of the tree to confer on their plans for the morrow. Wiping the worst of the dirt of the road from his face with the help of some water and the sleeve of his tunic, Harold sighed wearily before opening the debate.

"In truth, I had hoped to find more men here awaiting our arrival; the fyrdsmen of this county at the very least."

Gyrth nodded. "Indeed, brother. Though I dare say they have been sorely stretched these last days defending against Norman raiding parties. Unless any more arrive during the night, I fear we will have to make do with what we have and trust in God to grant us victory."

Harold snorted, but not without grim humour. "I would prefer to trust in another thousand or two stout Saxon spearmen. To say nothing of the bowmen who are no doubt still toiling their way down the great north road from Eoforwic. I wish to God that we had more of them in our ranks; without them we have little defence against the Norman archers."

"We have those who have come from Essex, Berkshire and Kent. They may not be many but they are good men with a good eye. They will not fail you, Lord."

Harold smiled. "Hush now, Scalpi, I meant no insult to the men here with us. I have faith in each and every one of them. I simply would rather there were more of them to put the outcome of the coming struggle beyond doubt. I know no man here will shirk their duty to defend this land."

The sound of hooves pounding their way up the slope interrupted the king. In the gathering gloom, it was hard to make out with any certainty who was approaching. Instinctively, Thurkill stepped in front of the king, his hand dropping to his hilt in readiness. Harold, however, rose up and laid a steadying hand on his shoulder. "Fear not, lad, it's just two of our scouts returning with news of our enemy. Hail! Egric, Thoppa! What can you tell us of the Norman wastrels?"

The two horsemen didn't bother dismounting, knowing they would be sent back out in a few moments. Instead, they offered their obeisance by bowing from the saddle. "Lord, the Norman camp lies a few miles south of us as expected, just to the north of Hastings. Our arrival has not gone unnoticed, however, as they have had their own scouts out watching the roads. We saw several riders galloping back with news of our movements."

Harold nodded in understanding but refused to show any disappointment in case it disheartened the men in earshot. "'Tis of no great import either way. I need to force their hand, to make them attack us, so the sooner they find out the better."

He then turned to those around him. "We camp here for the night. This ridge is easily defended were the Normans to attack in the night. In the meantime, Egric," he turned back to the scout, "I pray you keep sharp eyes on our enemy and report as soon as they start to move."

"Yes, Lord." With that Egric and Thoppa yanked hard on the reins, wheeled their mounts round and galloped off south, their hooves tearing up great clods of turf and soil as they went.

When they had gone, Gyrth, Leofwine and the other lords gathered round Harold. "Your orders, brother?"

"We rest, Gyrth. Now that our presence is known, I think William will want to attack as soon as possible. He knows that the longer he waits, the stronger we become while his host may begin to suffer from disease and starvation. We will cross swords tomorrow, I'm sure of it. Have every tenth man stay awake, and order the rest to sleep. We will rise at dawn and take a position on this ridge. It bars the route north for William and so he must break us here if he wishes to take my kingdom."

***

Thurkill awoke while it was still dark. The sound of horses thundering across the grassy slope had him scrambling for his sword. But this was no sudden assault; rather it was the return of the scouts. Egric was exhausted, rolling in his saddle, doing his best to cling on with what strength remained to him. With great effort, he pulled up just shy of the king's tent, from which Harold was now emerging, already dressed for battle.

"Are the Normans come so soon?"

Breathlessly, the scout fumbled for words. "Lord, the Norman host is moving north towards us. I believe they will be here in a little under two hours."

"My thanks to you, Egric. It is as I expected. William would have the matter settled sooner rather than later as well. So be it." Harold then turned to the thegns who had begun to assemble, just as the sky began to lighten in the east. "Lords, rouse your men. Have them take up position on the ridge: huscarls to the front, men of the fyrd behind. Plant my wyvern banner in the centre so that all men may see it and know that there I stand and will do so 'til I am victorious or dead.

"Let us stand firm atop this ridge and hold our line. We will be a rock, standing for eternity, impervious to the winds and rains that assail it. We will force the Normans to attack us, as they must if they wish to push on from Hastings. But here they will find their path blocked. Here, they will break themselves against our shieldwall, until they are worn out by their endeavours. Then and only then will we rise up and crush them once and for all. Let every lord and captain carry this message to their men. Let no one leave the shieldwall without my express command. If we stand as one, we shall win; if we break apart, then we shall be destroyed."

***

As Thurkill took his place in the front rank, next to his father and in front of the men from their village, he found his thoughts turning once more to his sister. He had seen her only once since the disbandment of the fyrd the previous month and even then it had only been a short while before they had been forced to leave to fight the Norsemen. It might only have been a few weeks but it felt like an eternity. So much had happened in those days, so much he wanted to tell her about. The fact that he had not been able to go to Haslow while they waited in Lundenburh still weighed heavily on his mind. What if he were to fall today? What if he were never to see her again? What would become of her should neither he or his father make it home? His father saw the look on his face and mistook it for fear of the coming battle.

"Be strong, lad. These Normans do not scare me; I have faced worse than them before and no doubt will again in the future."

"I was not thinking of them, father. My thoughts instead were for Edith and Aga. I pray to God that we may live to see them again."

Scalpi nodded empathetically, making the sign of the cross as he did so. "Amen. We will, son, we will. You have not had the last of your aunt's cooking yet, I'm afraid."

Despite himself, Thurkill giggled childishly. He had lost count of the number of times he'd 'accidentally' dropped some of the most burnt offerings to the floor for the hounds to eat. Sometimes, if the food was too bad, even they would venture no further than sniffing it before wandering back to the fireplace, affronted to be presented with such poor fare.

"Ware! Ware!"

Thoughts of Aga's culinary shortcomings forgotten, Thurkill looked to where the huscarl a few paces to his left was pointing down the slope. There, in the valley below, where there had been empty fields was now starting to fill with enemy warriors beginning to appear from the tree-line on the opposite side. It seemed to take forever for the whole army to emerge. Every time he thought that there could be no more, another unit issued forth from the woods. Eventually, they stood there, rank upon rank of grey-blue immutable shapes, each clad in full length mail shirts that seemed to shimmer in the early morning sunlight. To Thurkill's eye, they looked far more numerous and no less menacing than the Norsemen he had faced just two short weeks ago.

They formed up in three distinct ranks. In front were hundreds of lightly armoured archers. After them, came the bulk of the army: the foot soldiers, each wearing a conical helmet with nose-guard and carrying a long-hafted spear and kite-shaped shield that covered their body from shoulder to knee. At the rear, towering above the others on their huge beasts, were the dreaded horsemen.

Finally, the movement ceased. The Normans stood at the base of the slope, silent, as still as statues, as if hoping their appearance alone would be enough to unsettle their opponents. But the huscarls massed in the front rank of the shieldwall would not quake in fear; they would not shrink from the fight, nor would they lose heart in the face of the enemy, no matter how numerous or how threatening they seemed. Their courage would give heart to the rest of the Saxon host.

Suddenly, a great shout went up from the Saxon ranks. Harold had appeared atop his own horse. Cantering along the ridge in front of the shieldwall, he was resplendent in burnished armour and crested helmet, its dyed red horse-hair plume flowing behind him in the breeze. He gripped the reins in his left hand while in his right he held a spear from which the red wyvern banner of Wessex fluttered proudly. He rode several hundred paces along the ridge to the far end of their lines before wheeling skilfully and coming back, making sure that everyone could see him. All along the fyrd, men raised their spears and roared defiance in acknowledgement of their king. Finally, he brought his mount to a halt in the centre of the line. Slipping gracefully out of the saddle, he handed the reins to a ceorl who had come forward to lead the beast away. With a final two-handed flourish of the banner, he then planted its shaft's tapered base deep into the soft earth. Spreading his arms wide, he then bellowed a challenge to the awaiting Normans.

"Here is my banner and here it will stand until every last one of us is dead. If you want it, come and take it!" Then turning to face his huscarls and fyrdsmen, he continued. "Do not fear them, lads, we will triumph here today. Their mounted warriors should not scare you. Our fight is with men, not horses. As our forefathers did before us, we will trust in our own strength. We will stand together and face the enemy. If God wills it that I should die today, I would count no higher honour than to die in battle with you, defending our land so that it may not pass under the yoke of another less worthy."

With that the shieldwall howled its support before taking three paces forward so that king and banner were protected behind a formidable barrier of grim-faced, axe and spear-wielding warriors determined to defend them to the death.

From his position in the front rank, Thurkill saw he was facing the centre division of the Norman host. Narrowing his eyes against the glare of the sun, he espied – almost directly opposite him – the pale blue banner with a golden cross. He has seen that sigil before, in the hands of the scar-faced Norman knight who had accompanied the monk emissary to the king's palace at Westminster. Yes, he would swear that the man holding the banner had the same shock of unruly black hair and the same dark skin, tanned by the hot sun of southern climes whence he had hailed. He knew that once battle was joined it would be a confused and brutal melee with men hacking at each other on all sides, but he could not help but wonder, if not hope, that he would find himself face to face with the banner-man at some point. If God saw fit to grant him his wish, he would teach that Norman whoreson what it meant to be a Saxon huscarl.

FIFTEEN

14 October, Senlac Ridge

A grim silence had fallen over the massed ranks of Saxon warriors. Other than the sound of the king's banner fluttering in the stiff easterly breeze and the occasional cough or sneeze, there was little or nothing to be heard. All along the ridge-line men waited, patient and still, save for those that shuffled from foot to foot to ease the strain on tensed-up muscles. The sun, pale and watery as it was, had risen much further now, casting its weak light across the whole battlefield. After a brief overnight squall, the day was now dry but cold, a cold that would slowly seep into their bones the longer they stood idle; a cold that the autumn sun would do little to alleviate. Though the grass underfoot was still damp from the rain, the ground itself retained the firmness gained over the summer months. It would cause no hindrance to the coming battle.

Harold's plan relied on the Normans attacking them up the slope, so they were committed to stand and wait. But for how long? The longer Harold's army stood inactive, the more impatient they would become. Already some of the fyrdsmen to the rear could be heard grumbling. One man not far from Thurkill spoke up for the rest. "This is no way to win a fight, standing here like cattle in a field. Why do we not charge them? We should break them with our shields and spears."

Others nodded or muttered in agreement. They were not used to waiting for the fight to come to them. This was not the way Saxons gave battle. Harold must have heard the rumblings; such dissent would need to be nipped in the bud else the whole plan would crumble into dust and all would be lost. He strode out in front of the shieldwall where he turned to face them once more.

"Friends, we must stand our ground. To give up this ridge invites disaster; their horsemen would make short work of us in the open. Up here we have the advantage. They will tire their mounts charging up the hill to reach us. Do not worry, the fight will be upon us soon enough and when it is, you will be grateful for this hill, I can promise you that."

As an afterthought, perhaps conscious of the need to rouse spirits, he added. "Who here was with me at Stamford Bridge?"

Few of the fyrdsmen responded but many of the huscarls raised spear, axe and sword and roared their affirmation ferociously back at the king as if glad to have release for their pent up emotions.

Harold smiled warmly, acknowledging his warriors. "The Norsemen came to our shores in more than three hundred ships, yet we sent them home in only twenty-four, such was the destruction we wrought on them that day. I'm told the Normans have come in over five hundred ships. How many shall they need to return home?"

No one spoke. Harold's face betrayed a look of desperation, afraid that he was losing them. "What? None of you is brave enough to offer a number? Does not one of you believe that we will destroy the Norman whoresons? How many ships shall we send them home in?"

It was the grumbling solider behind Thurkill who shouted in reply. "None, Lord. Let the bastards swim home!"

Harold grinned both in relief and humour. Order had been restored. All along the line the men laughed as those that had heard the exchange repeated it to those who had not. The sound grew in volume as it spread until it morphed into a fearsome war chant, punctuated by the impact of spear shafts and axe or sword hilts rammed against shields. "Ut! Ut! Ut!"

"Look!" Thurkill shouted to no one in particular. "Something's happening."

Sure enough, one of the mounted warriors was making his way forward, the ranks of spearmen and archers parting to let him and his horse through. When he had made his way to the foot of the slope, midway between the two armies, he stopped and dismounted. Drawing his sword from its sheath, he smacked the flat of its blade against the horse's rump, sending it skittering away back whence it came. Then he turned back to face the Saxon shieldwall. To the astonishment of those watching, he then proceeded to hurl his sword into the air, catching it smoothly by its hilt each time it came back within reach. It was a bizarre display, yet unerringly skilful at the same time. He repeated the trick several times; each time the sword turned end over end multiple times and yet each time he plucked it out of the air with no more care than if it had been a stick. There was no doubting, however incongruous it might appear, that the man was a gifted swordsman.

"What kind of foolhardiness is this?" The tone of Scalpi's voice belied the respect he felt for the man's antics. "Is he going to stand there juggling all day like a fool in a king's court or is he going to try and do some damage with that thing?"

At Scalpi's prompting, a number of Saxons overcame their sense of awe and began shouting insults and jeers at the juggler. "This display is not worthy of a warrior; this is no more than a trick that you might see in any lord's hall as part of the entertainment. There is no place for this on the battlefield".

"Enough of this shit!" A huscarl a few paces to Thurkill's left had seen enough. Slinging his shield on to his back and hefting his great two-handed war-axe in both hands, he began striding down the slope towards the sword-thrower. The Saxon host fell silent as they watched, intent on the outcome. Everyone was eager to see the prancing, beardless Norman have his head cleaved for his impudence.

As the huscarl advanced, his adversary appeared to show no signs of concern; rather he continued his antics with his sword, spinning this way and that on his toes as the blade twirled above him. When the Saxon closed to within twenty paces, he began to run, lifting the heavy axe above his head as he did so and roaring a blood-curdling challenge. The blow, if it had landed, would have split any man in two, but it was not to be. At the last moment, the Norman spun a half pace to the left so that the axe swung harmlessly past him. The sheer force behind the blow caused the Saxon to stumble, sealing his fate there and then. His momentum carried him past his foe, causing him to slip on the damp grass as he tried to stop. Effortlessly, the Norman pirouetted on the spot, so fast that he was a blur, before swishing his sword down on the unprotected neck of the warrior. It was over in an instant; the head, now separated from its body, rolled a few feet away towards the cheering archers.

A collective groan rose from the massed Saxon ranks, in stark contrast to the howls of derision coming from the Norman host. *First blood to the enemy*, mused Thurkill. He hoped it was not an omen. As it was, he did not have time to consider it any further.

"Archers!"

Looking down the hill, Thurkill could see the whole front rank of the Norman army had begun to move. There were hundreds of them, crawling like an inexorable swarm of ants over the land. A knot of fear gripped at his stomach. Whilst he had not faced archers at Stamford Bridge, he knew from time spent hunting in the forests around his village just what damage they could do when they tore into exposed flesh.

"Shields up!" His father's booming voice brought him back to the moment. The cry was echoed all along the line as captain after captain bellowed the warning to their warriors. All around him men raised their round wooden shields, angled as best they could to provide most protection against the imminent swarm of deadly projectiles. No sooner had they done so than the first shafts began to fly. Moments later, the air was filled with the sound of arrow heads thudding into wood, interspersed every now and then with a terrifying scream as one of the missiles found its inevitable way through the defences.

Thurkill had no idea how long it went on for, nor how many arrows flew at them. It seemed to go on for ever. All he could do – all that any of them could do - was crouch beneath his shield and pray to God and all his saints that none managed to find a piece of him. He lost count of how many times he felt his shield take an arrow head. It was at least six, perhaps as many as ten. Glancing to his right, he caught his father's eye. He was grinning maniacally, teeth bared and eyes wide. He became aware of his son looking at him and began to laugh grimly.

"This is a different kind of rain than we're used to at this time of year, eh?"

Despite his fear, Thurkill laughed and took heart. He could endure the storm; his shield was sturdy, made of good solid willow. It could not be pierced. It was well positioned, overlapping tightly with those next to him. This storm could not go on for ever; they would run out of arrows eventually. In fact, no sooner had the thought entered his mind than the barrage ceased.

Slowly, one by one, the warriors lowered their shields and stared around them. Thankfully, it seemed that surprisingly few hits had been sustained; here and there a body lay, transfixed by one or more of the cruel shafts but, on the whole, the Saxons had emerged largely unscathed. Several of the men began to laugh, pouring scorn on the archers for their poor aim. One spearman even ran forward a few paces, turned and dropped his trousers, waving his bare arse at the enemy. Thurkill smiled. Should he survive the day, that man was assured legendary status, his exploits to be captured in verse to be celebrated round the hearth fires down the generations.

He felt a surge of confidence. The earlier duel was forgotten and they had come through a hail of arrows with few deaths and not many more wounded and they were already being dragged or led away to the rear to be tended to. Here and there one or two refused to go, claiming their injuries were of no matter. If they could still wield spear and shield they were allowed to stay, otherwise they were bundled away. The shieldwall could not allow itself to be broken for the sake of a man too weak to play his part. Even so, Thurkill found himself smiling; perhaps this would not be as hard as he had feared.

Scalpi saw him smirking and cut him down. "Don't get too cocky, lad. The rest of the day will not be so easy."

"How so, father?"

"They were shooting uphill; with our narrow ranks, we present but a small target. I fear they were just testing us, seeing how we would react; testing our mettle as it were. There's more to come, and soon. Yes, look. Now the infantry are on the move. Quick!" Scalpi shouted to those around him. "Clear the arrows from your shields as best you can and make ready."

Following his father's advice, Thurkill drew his seax and used it to hack the arrow shafts away as close to their heads as possible. He did not have time to try and prise the points from the thick wood; they were too deeply embedded. When he was done, his shield resembled a hedgehog with ten or so jagged spikes sticking out.

He was not a moment too soon; the Norman infantry was already halfway up the slope. They came on in a solid mass, bristling with spear heads pointing at the Saxons. They made no sound as they came, just the rhythmic thud of hundreds of boots hitting the ground simultaneously. It was an inspiring if not fearsome sight. Rank after rank of identically dressed soldiers, each covered from neck to knee with tapered shields. Like the Saxons, those shields bore many patterns, presumably marking out the lords for whom they fought.

Everywhere, the defenders braced themselves to face the onslaught. In their favour, they were still fresh, having so far faced nothing more taxing than an arrow storm, while the Normans could already be seen to be puffing from the effort of toiling up the slope to reach them. When they were no more than fifty paces away, Thurkill heard Harold give the order for missiles to be thrown. It was the signal for those fyrdsmen to the rear who held javelins or slings, together with the few archers that had come to the battle, to unleash their deadly cargo.

Of itself it was not enough to stop them, but it did cause a break in the enemy's cohesion. Men fell, not in great numbers, but enough to create a few gaps in what had before been a solid mass. Others found themselves encumbered by javelins embedded in their shields; giving them a choice of dropping the shield to continue or pulling back out of the line while they tried to dislodge the missile from where it had stuck fast.

The remaining soldiers continued their uphill march, closing the gaps as they came. There were still many hundreds of them advancing on a wide front, several ranks deep, spears aimed menacingly at the Saxon shieldwall. At no more than twenty paces distant, the line halted. As one, each man planted his spear in the ground, point first, before taking a lighter throwing-spear from his other hand where it had been held next to the shield grip. The resulting volley of missiles, even thrown at such short range, did little more damage than the archers had. Most clattered harmlessly off the shields. A few found their mark, and even fewer of those caused fatal wounds. Nonetheless, if the Normans were disheartened they did not show it; instead they picked up their spears and resumed their steady march.

"Brace!" Saxon captains yelled to their men to be ready to receive the attack. It was not necessary, though, as every man knew what was coming. Harold had told them that they needed to stay firm in defence. Keep the shieldwall intact and they won't break us, he had said. Now was the first real test. Could they resist these grim Norman foot soldiers? He felt the familiar churning sensation in his guts and prayed he would not disgrace himself in front of his comrades.

An image of Edith came unbidden into his mind. He wondered what she was doing right now and if she knew just what he was facing at that moment. She was agonisingly close; probably no more than a day or two's ride. Defeat could not be an option, if only to ensure her safety. Lose and the Normans would be free to rape and pillage across whole swathes of the land and their village would be one of the first they came to, especially if they rode to Canterbury, one of the biggest cities in the south.

The impact, when it came, shook him to the core. Standing in the front rank with the other huscarls, he bore the withering brunt of it. Even with his legs braced and his knees slightly bent, it still almost knocked him off his feet. If it hadn't been for the press of bodies from behind, doing their best to support the huscarls to their front, he probably would have fallen.

The strain was unbelievable. In front of him, Normans pushed forward in rank after rank, while behind him, the fyrd desperately strove to keep the integrity of the shieldwall. Thurkill found he could hardly move. His shield was locked in position, providing welcome protection, but his right arm was pinned to his side, meaning he could not bring his sword to bear in any way. Inches from his face was the snarling, sweating face of a Norman, contorted in rage but similarly impotent due to the huge numbers pressing in from behind him. Thurkill felt a wave of panic flood through him; he was defenceless, at the mercy of his enemies. At any moment someone might thrust a spear into his face and end his battle before it had even begun. Time seemed to slow down as he struggled helplessly to free his limbs sufficiently to enable him to fight. He could feel his heart racing, his breath coming in short, fevered gasps, the heat from the mass of shoving men causing rivers of sweat to cascade down his head and torso. Frantically, his mind raced for a solution. Only one answer came to mind.

With a roar that shocked him in its intensity he pulled his head back before then ramming it forward, as hard as he could in that confined space, squarely into the face of his opponent. Although well protected by his helmet, the force of the blow nevertheless shattered the man's nose and knocked the sense from him. Blood flowed unchecked as the man stood there, stupefied, unable to fall to the ground, being held in place by his comrades.

Eventually the man slid down, his legs unable to support his weight any longer. Thurkill took half a step forward into the small space that now presented itself, making sure as he did so that he stamped down hard on the man's exposed neck. He didn't want him regaining consciousness and slipping a knife into his balls as he stood over him. Although still surrounded on all sides, the sudden feeling of that little bit of freedom was almost intoxicating. Finally, he could now flex his sword arm, feeling life flow back into the muscles. His left shoulder ached from where it had been holding the shield for too long in an unnatural position, but he knew it would ease as he began the grisly business of killing Normans.

He took a moment to take stock. As far as he could see, the shieldwall was holding firm, despite the horde of howling Norman foot soldiers hammering at it on all sides. Everywhere he looked he could see swords crashing against shields and spears being thrust through gaps, looking for exposed flesh. Nonetheless the Saxons were weathering the storm well. The height of the ridge, combined with the fact that they had not had to exhaust themselves toiling up the slope, gave them the advantage as Harold had promised. To make matters worse for the enemy, the ground was still slick, making it difficult for them to find a solid footing.

"Ware!" A shout immediately to his right yanked him back to the moment. He sensed rather than saw a blur of movement to his front and managed to jerk his head to one side just in time.

It was only a small movement but it probably saved his life. The spear point which had been aimed at his eye instead scored a line across his cheek. Even the adrenaline coursing through his veins was not enough to mask the intense burning sensation he felt as his cheek open and blood pour down his face on to his mail shirt. *Damn you, boy,* he cursed himself. *Pay attention or you'll get yourself killed.*

Recovering from the shock, Thurkill was first to react. He did not have time to swing his sword so instead he punched the cross-piece into the face of his attacker followed by a brutal kick which connected with the man's kneecap with a satisfying crunch. The man next to him who had yelled the warning finished matters with a spear-thrust into his neck. Thurkill nodded his thanks; his grinning, bloodied face must have made him look almost satanic. That had been close and the lesson was not lost on him. He was not invincible; he would have to be vigilant at all times lest the next blow find its target.

The fighting went on in the same pattern for some time, as the two forces thrust against each other, trying to find the crucial breakthrough. There was none to be found though so the Normans were slowly wearing themselves out against the impenetrable mass that was the Saxon shieldwall. There was no way through. Even when they did manage to bring a man down, his place was quickly taken and the gap shored up.

After what seemed an interminable age, Thurkill became aware that, somewhere in the distance, a horn was blowing. Short blasts in groups of three, repeated over and over. Before he could work out what it might mean, the Norman warriors facing him started to pull back. There was no panic; they had not been routed. Rather it was a measured and steady withdrawal, step by slow step, never once taking their eyes off the Saxon host which remained rooted to the spot on top of the ridge. True to their word to Harold, the Saxons remained static and impassive, watching the retreating Normans and making no effort to follow.

Here and there a man stepped forward two or three paces to administer a killing blow to a wounded foe, while others helped drag their own dead or dying away from the fray. Otherwise, the rest stood where they were, silent, unmoving, watching the Normans go. No one was under any illusion that the battle might be over. This was simply the end of the opening chapter. They had survived a storm of arrows and withstood a fearsome attack by the foot soldiers, but Thurkill could not help but think those first forays had been intended to soften them up for the main event. Next they would surely face the mounted knights and only God could save them then.

SIXTEEN

14 October, Senlac Ridge

The sound was unbelievable, like a thousand thunderstorms rolled into one. He had never heard, let alone seen, so many horses in one place; the effect was mesmerising if not terrifying. Hundreds upon hundreds of mounted warriors in tightly packed ranks raked the flanks of their horses to force them up the slope. They needed little or no encouragement, though, for their blood was up; the sights, sounds and smells of the carnage making sure of that. All the riders had to do was point their heads up the hill and hold on tight to the reins as their beasts did the rest.

"Steady, steady! Hold the line and they'll not break us. You'll see. You have my word on it."

The sound of Harold's strident voice carried over the drumming of the horses' hooves and was echoed every few paces by each lord and captain. Even so, a good number of the younger warriors were still jittery, glancing around nervously as if looking to escape. Very few, if any, of them would have faced such an onslaught before and none of them knew what to expect.

The noise level was growing in horrifying intensity as the ground trembled beneath their feet with the weight of so many horses thudding across the turf. Men made the sign of the cross; prayers and supplications were offered up to all known deities, Christian and otherwise. But the fear never became a panic; the huscarls in the front ranks saw to that. Their courage was enough for those behind. Even Thurkill, as young and experienced as he was, was determined not disgrace himself or his father. No tales would ever be told about the cowardice of great Scalpi's son; that would never happen. Instead, he set his jaw as firmly as he could and ignored the voice in his head that was screaming at him to run. He took a tighter grip of both his sword and his shield and roared his defiance along with all those around him. If this was to be the end, then he would face it with his head held high.

But then the pendulum of chance began to swing back in the

Saxons' favour. On flat ground with no obstructions, the Norman cavalry could have charged straight through the shieldwall, breaking it as easily as if it had been made of twigs. But their impatience to reach the enemy was their undoing. So eager were they that they failed to wait for the retiring foot soldiers to clear their path. They began to weave and swerve in all directions to avoid ploughing into their own men. Some of the more ruthless paid no heed to the shouts and warnings and urged their mounts forward anyway, trampling several who had the misfortune to be in their way. Either way the damage was done; the cohesion of the charge was irretrievably lost. What had been begun as a single, solid mass of men and horses broke down into smaller groups, each competing with those around them to reach the top of the ridge. By the time they reached the top, their impetus had been reduced to almost nothing.

As Thurkill watched the debacle unfolding before him, he nodded appreciatively; the battle ground had been well chosen. They might be able to hold them after all. Though he had not experienced horse warriors before, he could see as well as anyone that they relied on momentum and weight to do the most damage. Without them, their effectiveness was much reduced. They still posed a significant threat, it had to be said, but a lot of the fear and menace they had posed had evaporated. Instead of crushing the shieldwall with one massive assault, they were now reduced to riding along the length of the ridge looking for weak points to exploit. Every so often, a man would stand in his stirrups and thrust his spear point through a gap between the shields, and often to good effect. The weapons they carried were longer than the infantry spear and, with the height gained from standing out of the saddle, the extra reach enabled them to pick off anyone stupid enough to leave himself exposed, while keeping the knight well out of reach of the defenders' spears.

The damage they were able to inflict was limited, though, much less than Duke William must have hoped. The terrain and the knights' own impatience had saved the Saxons up on the ridge. Though several huscarls and fyrdsmen had fallen, transfixed by Norman spears, the shields remained unbroken. And the damage was not all one-sided either; whenever one of the knights became isolated from his comrades, he was immediately vulnerable to attack. Seeing just such an opportunity, a huscarl to Thurkill's right dropped his spear and ran forward, drawing his deadly seax as he went. Cleverly, he darted round to the back of the horse, out of the eye-line of its rider, where he then slashed the sharp blade across the horse's hamstrings. The animal whinnied in pain as its ruined back legs crumpled beneath the combined weight of horse and rider. The knight had no time to react, taken completely by surprise and finding himself pinned to the ground, his right leg crushed under the horse's bloodied flank. Wasting no time, the huscarl plunged his seax deep into the man's neck, his blood mixing with that of his wounded mount. It was all over in a matter of moments; the Saxon was back in line, spear and shield at the ready once more. It was a pattern that was repeated at intervals all along the ridge.

Suddenly a great shout went up from the Normans. Thurkill had no time to turn to see what was happening, though, as his section of the wall was, at that moment, hard pressed. A group of twenty or more horsemen had surged forward, searching for openings, thrusting their spears forward as they came. They had already felled the man immediately to his left, his eyes pleading with Thurkill as he fell, the life literally draining from him before Thurkill's eyes. He was helpless though; he could offer no succour as he had to keep his own position in the wall lest the Normans sought to press home their advantage before the man's place could be taken by someone from the next rank. Before that could happen, however, to Thurkill's surprise, the horsemen began to yank hard on their reins, turning their mounts away back down the slope, trampling over the dead and wounded, comrade and foe alike, in their haste.

Thurkill felt a burst of hope, adrenaline coursing through his veins. "They're breaking. They're running"

"Stand! Stand, I say!" His father's voice roared in his ears, halting him in his tracks along with those around him who had been similarly tempted.

"Your king ordered you to stand here, no matter what. And here we stand until he says otherwise. If that means you die here on this spot, then so be it, but you must not go chasing after the enemy."

Thurkill knew his father was right. As much as he wanted to take the fight to the Normans, they had to hold their ground. The urge to run after the retreating Normans was strong, though. In every other battle he had heard of, this was the time to seize victory; now was the time to charge down the slope, hacking the fleeing enemy to pieces. Why else would their foe be running if they were not beaten? Not willing to disobey his father, though, Thurkill remained rooted to the spot.

"But what was that shout for, father? Are they not fleeing before our spears?"

"God alone knows? I can make no sense of their goddamned foreign tongue. Probably just an order to regroup for a new attack."

"It sounded more than that, though. It sounded panicked to my ears."

"And what would you know of such things, lad? You're still wet behind the ears."

A huscarl further down the line was listening to their conversation. "No, he's right, Lord. It's the Bastard; he's fallen. I swear it."

Without hesitation, Scalpi rounded on the man. "How in God's name do you know that? Speak, man. I will not have wild rumour spread through these ranks."

"My father spent time in Normandy with the old King Edward. He learnt their tongue and passed some of it on to me. I heard the words duke and dead, clear as day. I swear it on my honour."

"Look, father, it's true." Thurkill pointed excitedly down the slope. The horsemen, having retreated to the bottom of the slope, were now milling about in confusion, as if leaderless and uncertain of what to do. The whole Norman host appeared to have lost its shape. No one seemed to be in charge, no orders were being given; the whole thing was a mess even to Thurkill's untrained eye.

"We should attack now, while they are in disarray." The man who had proclaimed the Duke's death opined.

Scalpi was quick to shut down such talk, though he too could see the sense in it. "Hold fast there. We wait. We have our orders to hold this position and until that changes, we go nowhere."

Just at that moment, however, Harold himself strode forward. "Now is our time, lads! The enemy stands before us in confusion and despair. They have broken themselves against our shieldwall like so much rain off a swan's back. Gyrth! Leofwine! Take the right wing and advance. Press home our advantage while they mill about like virgin maids at a harvest feast."

Euphoric at being released from the frustration of defending the ridge, the two brothers raced away to do the king's bidding. Within moments the sound of horns reached their ears as the whole of the right flank – about a third of the Saxon army – detached itself from the main body and began marching down the slope towards the enemy. Their discipline was a marvel. This was no wild, devil-may-care charge. They strode with purpose, chanting as they went, beating their sword hilts and spear hafts against the inside of their shields. Thurkill watched in awe and not a little jealousy. "There must be the best part of two thousand men there", he said aloud to no one in particular. "They're going to send them squealing like frightened pigs back to their ships."

Within moments, however, he saw just how dreadfully wrong he was as the situation changed with disastrous results for the Saxons. Back at the base of the ridge, a knight rode out in front of the disorganised Norman host and removed his helmet. Standing in his stirrups he began shouting and gesturing with his sword, desperately trying to attract the attention of all those around him. So loud was his voice that the words carried all the way to where the Saxons stood at the top of the ridge. Thurkill could not understand them but he did recognise the name, William. His heart sank. It had been too good to be true after all; the Duke lived. Next to him, Thurkill could also see the papal banner, still held by the same dark-haired knight that had come to Harold's hall in Westminster with the monk. He was waving the banner from side to side as high as he could, helping to calm their panicked host.

Scalpi took two steps forward, a look of fear in his eyes. "The Bastard lives. Even now his warriors are reforming, confident once more. Our men must retreat before it's too late, else they will be caught in the open and massacred where they stand."

It was true. Already, a large number of mounted warriors had formed up behind the duke who had now replaced his helmet and was pointing up the hill with his sword. And then the horsemen were coming again. This time they did not have the infantry in their way and they had a clear target to aim for that was no longer on top of the ridge.

From his vantage point, Thurkill could see the danger only too clearly. His father was right. Instead of heading for the centre of the line, the huge body of knights was aiming off to the left where their right flank now stood exposed, more than halfway down the slope. The Saxons had halted, appalled by the sight of the oncoming cavalry. Thurkill could see Gyrth and Leofwine frantically shouting instructions, trying to get their men to turn back whence they had come. A good number had begun to wheel but it was excruciatingly slow. And in his heart, he knew it was too late for them.

The Normans hit them before they had even covered half the ground. And with their backs to their attackers, they were defenceless. The horsemen swept right through their haphazard ranks, stabbing and hacking at the exposed necks, heads and backs as they went. It was a slaughter. Man after man went down; bodies impaled on spear points, limbs and heads severed from bodies. All around Thurkill, men – himself included – howled in impotent rage. They were desperate to go to their aid but Harold refused to allow them. He knew that were they to break ranks too, all would be lost. Even so, the sight of so many of their comrades being so cruelly killed was more than many could bear; several looked away or cast their eyes down to the ground, unable to watch the unfolding tragedy. It was as bad, if not worse, for Harold; not only were his precious warriors being hacked to pieces, but two of his brothers were in the thick of it, in mortal danger.

Thurkill could not drag his eyes away, though. He forced

himself to watch as the devastating attack played out. The impact of the charge had split the fleeing Saxons into two almost equal parts. For those nearest the king's position, there was a chance for deliverance and many of them were able to regain the ridge and the safety of the shieldwall. For the others, however, there could be no salvation. Cut off from the rest of the army, their fate had been sealed and most were cut down where they stood. A few – probably no more than two hundred, with Gyrth and Leofwine among them – fought their way to a small hillock not far to the west. There they readied themselves to make a last stand, their efforts at forming a solid shieldwall hampered by the numerous gorse bushes that were scattered across the summit.

They were surrounded and vastly outnumbered. Again and again the Normans charged the ever-dwindling defenders, each attack accounting for more and more of the terrified Saxons. In the middle of the encircled group, Thurkill could still see the two brothers, fighting bravely and shouting at those around them to hold the line and keep their shields up. They must have known it was futile, that there was no hope of rescue, but there would be no thought of surrender.

Then, inevitably, Gyrth fell, pierced through by a javelin thrown from a distance of no more than ten paces by one of the circling knights. He pulled at the shaft, determined to fight on, but as the point came free, great gouts of blood gushed forth from a ruined artery. He sank to his knees, unable to support his own weight any longer.

Leofwine, seeing what had happened, rushed to his brother's side, howling in anguish. There was nothing he could do except cradle his brother's head as he lay dying. All around them, their huscarls continued to fight on, defending the body of their fallen leader as best they could. It must have been clear to all that death was upon them, but that did nothing to slacken their resolve. They hacked and parried in all directions, making the Normans pay dearly for every life they took. But every charge by the Normans reduced the perimeter of their shieldwall that little bit more. Huge gaps began to appear in the wall; there were no longer sufficient uninjured warriors to plug them. Realising that all was now lost, Leofwine roared in anger, grabbed a discarded two-handed battle-axe and ran wildly towards the nearest knot of horsemen. It was a brave but useless show of defiance and he was cut down before he had managed a dozen paces, assailed on all sides by sword and spear points. Blows rained down on him long after he must have been dead, causing fury among the surviving warriors.

With their leaders gone, the end came swiftly for those that remained. Though they gave a good account of themselves, they could do nothing to prevent the inevitable. Again and again, the horsemen wheeled and turned, hacking down on all sides until not a single man was left standing. The whole thing could not have lasted long, but for the rest of the host watching helplessly on the ridge, it had seemed an eternity. Harold had maintained a stoic serenity throughout, despite watching his own kin dying before his eyes whilst knowing that it had been his bold order that had sent them to their death.

Thurkill could only imagine the pain he must be feeling. He had lost three brothers in as many weeks. Even though Tostig had stood against him at Stamford Bridge, he was still family. They had grown up together, played together, fought together, laughed together. Those memories could not be discarded easily. With tears in his eyes, Thurkill found himself thinking of his own family. He knew to lose them would be devastating. He knew he had to survive, if only for their sake, but he could do nothing but trust in God to deliver him safely through to the end of the battle. But hope for Harold and the Saxon host was fading.

SEVENTEEN

Afternoon, 14 October, Senlac Ridge

An uneasy lull fell over the battlefield in the aftermath of the slaughter. It was as if both sides had somehow agreed to pause the hostilities, perhaps shocked by their intensity. The horsemen had swept away back down the hill, rejoicing in their victory as they went. Behind them they left only the dead and dying. The screams and moans of the wounded carried across the wind to where Harold stood with the remainder of his army. Though they were much weakened their numbers were still formidable and, for the most part, largely untested.

Perhaps conscious that his followers still looked to him for leadership and direction, Harold refused to show any emotion at the reverse. To appear downcast or defeatist now would, Thurkill surmised, send shockwaves through the ranks, stripping the men of their courage and their will to fight. Appearing as calm as he could, Harold called for Scalpi to attend him.

"Take as many men as you need and bring my brothers back to me. I would have them here beside me where we may keep them safe from any further despoiling."

Scalpi nodded wordlessly and trotted away, grabbing Thurkill and a dozen or so other huscarls as he went. It did not take long to reach the bodies, but once there, they had to slow down to be sure not to tread on the fallen. So many were they and so close knit had been their last stand, that there was little space to step between the bodies. It was a scene of devastation far worse than anything Thurkill had seen before. Steeling themselves to deal with the horrific sights before them, the small group of men soon located the bodies of Gyrth and Leofwine. They were well known to all and their features were mercifully unblemished, making their identification a matter of no difficulty.

Their quarry found, Scalpi urged the group into action. There was no way of knowing how soon the Normans might resume their attack. "Grab a couple of those long shields, lads; use them to carry the bodies. Also, find a couple of good cloaks so that we may hide their wounds."

The Norman shields were about the right size for the purpose, though some care was needed to ensure the bodies did not slip off.

"Do it gently, boys. Treat them with the respect they deserve, for pity's sake. Come on, lads. The king watches us; he will mark how well we handle his kin."

The men were not being clumsy or slow; Scalpi just needed something on which to focus to help disguise his sorrow. Shouting at the men, whether justified or not, helped distract from the hurt that threatened to engulf him. As he laboured with the others to manhandle the two bodies on to their makeshift stretchers, Thurkill could see his father's cheeks were wet with tears, shed for his fallen companions.

Thurkill had not known them for as long as his father but they had always treated him kindly, especially Gyrth. Yet he too was struggling to hold back the tears as he dragged the shields back over the body-strewn ground, towards the Saxon shieldwall on top of Senlac ridge. When they arrived, they halted in front of Harold and bowed their heads in respect. The king said nothing, but stared sadly at the bodies of his two younger brothers. Abruptly he waved them away, gesturing for them to be taken to the back of the shieldwall, before turning on his heel and striding back into the centre of the front rank to await the next attack.

***

He didn't have long to wait. And when it came, it hit them with a hitherto unparalleled ferocity. Whether the enemy knew the identity of the two slain leaders or not, the boost those deaths had given to their morale was immediately evident. Wave after wave of horsemen charged their shieldwall, hurling javelins, probing for gaps or weaknesses to exploit. Yet still the Saxons refused to break. Even though they had seen the loss of so many of their number, they would not allow their heads to drop. They were fighting for their king, for their country, for their very lives. Thurkill realised now that, whether intended or not, Harold's decision to bring his brothers back within the confines of the Saxon lines was inspired. The shieldwall was determined to protect from further harm. They were not about to allow them to fall into Norman hands.

As the afternoon wore on, the intensity of the fighting, if anything, increased as the Normans became more and more desperate to bring the battle to a successful conclusion before nightfall. They knew that, once the sun went down, Harold could use the cover of darkness to slip away back to Lundenburh where reinforcements would await him.

In a break between attacks, Thurkill asked his father whether he had noted the same. Scalpi nodded, mid gulp, emptying yet another water skin to slake his burning thirst.

"They seek to finish us before the day is done. But though we've lost many over on the right, I think we can still hold on 'til nightfall if we don't do anything silly. What's more, I think there is a fair chance we may see fresh warriors arrive tonight. It's no secret that many of us wanted Harold to wait longer in the city, as so many more were still expected. Those same men could be on their way here as we speak... Watch out! Here they come again."

The warning came not a moment too soon for another wave of horsemen was fast approaching. All around them, javelins were flying, some sailing harmlessly overhead, others thudding heavily into wooden shields, but yet more finding their mark in many a warrior's soft flesh. Their numbers were such that the horsemen spread across the whole length of the fore-shortened Saxon line, threatening to swamp them. Right at the centre of the attack came a group of twenty or so riders, every one clad head to toe in armour and mail. They rode knee to knee in a wedge shape, hunched down over their horses' necks and hidden as much as possible behind their shields. The papal banner flew high and proud over their heads. They came on fast and true, wavering neither left or right, aiming for the centre of the line where Thurkill stood with his father in front of the king and his wyvern banner.

The impact when it hit them was worse than anything that had gone before. But there was no way to avoid it; He had no choice but to stand tall and hope to survive. It was useless though. The first horse missed him by no more than a hand's breadth; its bared teeth and hot breath flashing past his eyes as it crashed through the shieldwall, the Saxons too exhausted from many hours' fighting to resist. The beast to its left, however, hit him full on. He had no time to marvel at the strength and courage of the animal, willing as it was to charge into a line of men each wielding wickedly sharp blades, as he was thrown backwards by the force of the blow. The only thing that saved him was the fact that the horse had hit him with its shoulder rather than full on, knocking him sideways rather than backwards thereby stopping him from being trampled underfoot.

Even so, the situation remained dire. The shieldwall had been fractured right at its centre. The whole fate of the army hung in the balance and there was nothing Thurkill could do. He was lying dazed and winded on his back, praying to God with what consciousness remained to him that he be neither skewered nor bludgeoned while he lay there. Around him was a heaving mass of hooves and feet as the battle raged on intensely; the defenders desperate to stem the tide created by the surge of horsemen through the wall. Despite his blurred state, he was reassured by his father's voice, calmly directing those around him, plugging gaps where he could, encouraging everyone to keep fighting.

"They come for the king's banner. Stand firm; we must protect the Dragon of Wessex."

Thurkill marvelled at the strength and courage of his father. All day he had been like a beacon of hope and light for all those around him, lambasting and praising them in equal measure; exhorting and cajoling everyone to dig deep into their souls to find the will to resist. As Thurkill lay there, a tear came unbidden to his eye. If he could be but one half the man Scalpi was, he might yet do his father proud.

Yet despite his father's example, the bravery and strength of the defenders was not enough as, one by one, they were being cut down by the merciless blades of the rampaging knights. The Normans were getting ever closer to the banner and showed no signs of slowing their relentless attack. Not one Saxon fell without taking at least one foe with him before he died, but there were always many other willing horsemen to take their place. Eventually, there was no one but Scalpi left between them and the banner of Wessex. Although the Normans had lost well over half their number in the attack there were still far too many of them for the old Saxon warrior to resist alone.

But still the old huscarl did not panic; the first man to make a lunge for the banner was dispatched with calm efficiency, his sword thrust taking him in the armpit where the mail shirt offered no protection, just as he was in the act of reaching out to grab the shaft from which the banner still fluttered. The man fell screaming to the ground, writhing in agony and clasping his opposite hand to the wound in a vain effort to stem the flow of blood. The next two met similar fates, unable to learn from or better the experience of their comrade. Those behind, however, were not so foolhardy. They pressed in, attacking Scalpi on all sides, prodding at him with their spears, swarming him so that he could not defend against them all and was unable to wield his sword to any real effect. He fought desperately against the odds but it was hopeless. One more fell, then another, but fate was inescapable. In the act of lunging to kill the fifth man, Scalpi was caught from both sides on the savage points of two Norman spears. The blades bit deep into his flesh, tearing his internal organs to shreds as they lanced through him. He sank to his knees, unable to stay on his feet for a moment longer, coming face to face with his son who remained unable to stand.

Time stood still for Thurkill as he stared into his Scalpi's eyes, grief stricken at the sight of his father's face contorted with pain. His whole world shrank until he could see nothing else, blocking out all other sights and sounds. His ears were filled with a whooshing noise that drowned the noise of the battle. He was helpless; there was nothing he could do now to help; nothing he could say to comfort him as his father's life ebbed away before him. Images of his childhood flashed through his head: days spent hunting in the forests, long hours spent learning to be a warrior, his father laughing at his first clumsy efforts to hold a shield. The thoughts and pictures jumbled together in an addled mess that overwhelmed his mind.

Scalpi slumped forward, his head hitting the soft earth with a sickening thud. He was just moments away from starting his journey to the afterlife, but in his final moments he reached out to grab his son's hand. Gripping it with what strength remained to him, he pulled Thurkill close to him so he could speak and be heard. The words, when they came, were nothing more than a whisper.

"Save your king."

***

"No!" Tears blinded Thurkill's eyes as he lurched painfully to his feet, finally galvanised into action. Both his sword and shield had been forced from his hands in the fall but he did not care. He had no thoughts of defence now, only to kill. Kill those who had taken his father from him. The great battle-axe, the one that Harold had given him after the battle at the bridge, the same one the Viking warrior had used to kill so many brave warriors on that day, was all he had, strapped to his back. It would serve his purpose well enough. The leading Norman knight had now reached the banner, a look of triumph on his face as he prepared to grab it. His expression quickly changed to one of confusion and pain, though, as Thurkill swung the axe with both hands, using all the strength he could muster from the exhausted muscles of his shoulders and back. The immense power and momentum brought the heavy blade down on the knight's forearm so hard that the limb was severed clean in two. The stricken knight could do no more than stare aghast as his amputated arm fell to the ground, blood spurting from the stump where once it had been. Thurkill left him no time to react, continuing his attack by ducking his head and using his bull-like strength to butt the man in the face with the point of his conical helmet.

Away from the confines of the shieldwall, Thurkill felt an incredible freedom that had been denied him all day. His body ached dreadfully from where the horse had smashed into him and his muscles screamed in protest as he continued to swing the axe in wide, sweeping arcs. But his mind paid no heed. Either he would rest later, or he would be dead anyway. At that moment, it mattered not to him either way. Even his father's last words, even the thought of his sister, could not break through.

His rage was as blinding as the low sun on a bright winter's morning.

Having dispatched one, he swung round to face the others, standing squarely in front of the banner, shouting insults, spitting at them, daring them to come and take it. Two of them immediately obliged, kicking their heels into the flanks of their mounts, urging them forward. They had lost their spears but both were still armed with long, deadly swords whose blades were streaked with the blood of his comrades.

Without hesitation, he buried his axe in the skull of the first horse. Its legs gave way instantly, throwing its rider who landed heavily on his back. Thurkill took a step forward, stamping down hard on the man's balls to disable him while he focussed on the next assailant. He ducked just in time as the knight's sword swished through the air, glancing off his helmet with a loud metallic clang. As the knight swept past him, Thurkill rose up, twisted on his heels and launched the axe blade in a horizontal arc, catching the rider squarely in the back, snapping his spine in an instant. The rest of the party, just three of the original twenty, including the dark-haired knight with the papal banner, had seen enough. As one, they pulled on their reins to turn their mounts' heads round and spurred them down the hill, away from the berserk, axe-wielding fiend. As a parting gesture, the scar-faced knight stood up in his stirrups, pointing his sword at Thurkill, as if promising him a future encounter. The young Saxon had no energy to respond, however; Instead he sank to his knees, exhausted by the fight and the maelstrom of emotions that flooded his brain.

EIGHTEEN

Evening, 14 October, Senlac Ridge

Thurkill had lost track of time. He knew it must be getting late as the sun had dipped low in the sky, the shadows around him lengthening all the time. Still they held out on the ridge; still they resisted the furious onslaughts of the Norman horsemen. Since repelling the last of the raiders who had so nearly seized control of the wyvern banner, the Saxon line had once again been shored up, though it was weaker now than it had ever been. More men of the fyrd stood in the front rank, filling the gaps left by fallen huscarls, and there were fewer ranks behind with which to make good any further losses. The fyrdsmen were brave enough but they did not have the same skills or strength as the trained warriors who made up the elite of the Saxon host.

Thurkill leaned on his heavily pitted shield, taking advantage of another lull in the fighting; another pause in which both sides attempted to recover their strength and regroup. He was blowing hard, his cheeks puffed out as he sucked much needed air into his lungs. He had no idea how he was still standing as exhaustion had long since crept into every muscle and sinew. He glanced at the horizon, willing the sun to go down, willing an end to the day. It was clear now they could not win this fight. Their numbers were too few and their strength too depleted to have any hope of success. All that remained was to steal away in the darkness, back into the woods behind them, whence they had come. This was the only path to salvation, to the chance to fight again another day when the northern fyrd would be available to them. They had the whole country to fall back on, whereas the Bastard of Normandy had only those men who had sailed with him and who stood with him on this field. His strength was surely nothing compared to the resources that Harold could muster. If only they could survive the last hours until the sun went down.

"Here they come again." Everywhere, captains shouted orders, jostling and cajoling weary warriors to prepare themselves once more. Thurkill hefted his shield back into place, its weight pulling hard on tired shoulder muscles. *One more time*, he told himself, *just hold them off one more time.*

The horsemen charged up the slope once again, hurling javelins as they came within range. It was the same pattern as before, the same threat that they had endured all afternoon. They could survive this, he thought, just as they had survived all the others before.

"Ware! Ware! Arrows."

Thurkill glanced quickly up to the sky, a cold finger of fear running down his spine. Sure enough, the air was once again filled with hundreds more of the deadly shafts arcing towards them. Unbeknown to them, the archers had followed the cavalry up the hill unseen, in one last desperate attempt to turn the tide. From that closer range the missiles could be deadly to friend and foe alike, as closely packed together as they were. William must have decided that he needed to gamble to gain his victory; he had to try something different to make the breakthrough he craved before nightfall.

The desperate defenders were now caught between two devils. Before them, the horsemen thrust viciously at the front rank, aiming to bludgeon gaps in the shieldwall through which they could pour. Above them, death rained from the skies. Those in the ranks behind did their best to protect themselves and those in front with their shields, but they could not completely stem the tide of devastation that now fell upon them. Hearing the screams of the dying all around him, Thurkill knew it was all over. They had withstood attack after attack all day but there was little they could now do but to die with honour.

As the arrows thudded into shield and flesh on all sides, Thurkill hoped that the end, when it came, would be swift. He had seen enough men lying wounded, bleeding out slowly in agony, to know that it was a fate best avoided. Better a clean thrust from a sword or spear than an arrow that failed to finish him. Despite the imminent inevitability of his own demise, however, he was surprisingly calm. He knew he would be reunited with his father soon and the excoriating pain of his loss would be expunged. In fact, his only burning regret was that his sister and aunt would no longer have their protection. With luck, though, Edith would soon marry a good Saxon man who could take on the village and look after her, Aga and the land. He hoped she would never forget him but she would be alright, he told himself; she would be well cared for. It was the way of things; life would go on. There was no need to be concerned; he could die in peace.

"The king. The king!"

The panicked tone of the voice ripped into his thoughts. Ignoring the horsemen in front of him, he spun round to try to see what was happening. Unable to see clearly past the heaving melee, despite his height, he began pushing his way through the ranks to where Harold's banner stood. The sight that greeted him filled his soul with terror. The king lay on the ground, propped up on one elbow. The shaft of an arrow protruded from the place where neck met shoulder. Less than half of its full length was visible, though, indicating that the rest of it was buried deep within his flesh. Though there was blood, it was no great amount. Perhaps the wound was not as bad as he first feared? Harold seemed dazed but otherwise alert and aware of what was going on. His teeth were bared in a grimace that betrayed the pain he felt, yet he did not cry out.

As Thurkill drew closer, one of those surrounding the king knelt by his head and took hold of the shaft, preparing to draw it from his neck.

"Hold!" Another warrior rushed forward and took a grip of the man's shoulder.

"Why? We need to remove the arrow to treat the wound."

"I have knowledge of wounds such as these. If you pull the shaft out, you could release his life blood, killing him in moments. I have seen men survive with an arrow in the neck for some time, but if you pull it out now without the proper care, he may bleed to death before our eyes."

"Well we can't leave him here," Thurkill shouted. "We have to get him away to safety."

The thegn who had been prepared to remove the shaft rounded on him immediately. "If you can manage that, boy, then you are a better man than me. Perhaps you might ask the

Normans to stop shooting arrows at us for a moment while we carry him off the field?"

Thurkill felt his face redden, conscious of his youth and the fact that he no longer had his father around for support. "Well, we have to do something."

The man nodded, more sympathetically now. "We don't have many options left to us, lad. But all of us here know there is nothing more honourable than dying in defence of one's lord. I suggest we all prepare ourselves to do just that. Perhaps the Normans will spare the king in the end. But before they have the chance, we must make them pay dearly for every one of us that stands between them and Harold."

Several grunts of approval greeted the thegn's words. In his heart, Thurkill knew the man was right. There was no hope now. There was nothing to do other than to defend the king, giving their lives in the process if need be. There was no finer death that a huscarl could wish for. As he stood there, with the fury of battle still raging around him, he was comforted by the thought that their names would live on in song; celebrated as those that had stood by Harold to the very end. The thought gave him courage; it lent strength to his sword arm and it helped keep the fear of death at bay.

Still the arrows kept falling. Still they kept picking men off at random. One minute the man next to you was hacking at a Norman horseman, the next he was spiralling downwards, stuck like a pig by one or more arrow shafts. Soon there would be too few of them to form a solid shieldwall. When that moment came it would all be over. Yet there was no thought of retreat; no thought of surrender. The sight of Harold lying wounded a few steps to their rear gave them purpose; a reason to keep on fighting. Four of Harold's personal guard had stayed close to him; they crouched around his prostrate form, holding their shields above him to protect him from the arrow storm. Still he would not moan or complain of the pain but, rather, he bore the wound with a grace and stoicism that Thurkill found inspiring. Those huscarls that remained, with Thurkill among them, formed up in front, ready to make their last stand.

Though the Normans could not know that Harold had been

gravely injured, they could sense a change in the mood of the Saxon defenders, as if a great sadness had come over them. Their blood was up; they had the taste of victory on their tongues. The scent of glory was in their nostrils and so they strove yet harder for the final breakthrough.

It was too much for what remained of the Saxon host to bear. That one last great charge saw the shieldwall splinter at last. A huge phalanx of horsemen rode through the broken line, chopping down on all sides as they went, wreaking great swathes of destruction through the once proud and resilient army. With their defensive line destroyed, many of the fyrdsmen took flight, flinging away their shields and running for the safety of the woods, pursued closely by mounted warriors. Several did not make it, but those that did would not stop running until darkness fell, in their eagerness to be away from the slaughter.

But the huscarls did not flee. They stood their ground, clustered around the wyvern banner, still defiant, still cursing the enemy, daring them to come taste Saxon steel. Thurkill stared grimly at the carnage around him. Bodies were strewn all over the ridge, friend and foe mixed together in deadly embrace. He had had his fill of battle; death would be a welcome release now to put an end to the suffering and the misery that lay before him.

"Come on!" He yelled, tears of frustration welling in his eyes. "What are you waiting for? Come and finish the job. Kill me now so I may haunt you for eternity." He did not care that they would not understand his harsh Saxon tongue; he did not even care if none of them heard him. It made him stronger; hardened his heart so that he was ready to meet his end. He squared his shoulders, thrust his chin forward and planted his feet firmly shoulder-width apart. He slung his shield, with three new arrow shafts embedded, over his left shoulder, freshened his grip on the shaft of his battle-axe – its blade now notched and blunted through use – and began to swing it slowly in ever widening arcs.

It did not take long for his challenge to be answered. Out of the gathering gloom, another tight-knit party of horsemen charged straight towards him. With so many fallen and so many now running for their lives, Thurkill had no chance of stopping them, no chance of defending his king any further. All he could do was take as many of them with him as possible.

They came on at a fear-inducing pace, hammering across the churned up turf. They were confident of victory now, disdainful of what pitiful resistance remained. They came to bring the battle to a close and, for that, they needed to kill or capture the Saxon king. Lances pointing forward, the knights crouched low over the heads of their horses, their shields held high for the greatest protection. The first man swept past Thurkill, beyond his reach, but the second was heading straight for him. Just before the moment of impact, he took a step to the right and swung his great axe, using his last remaining strength to deliver as hard a blow as he could muster. The knight's sword slashed down, uselessly hitting the spot where his head had been just moments before. But Thurkill's axe connected with his leg, landing with a sickening, yet satisfying ,crunch as the bone shattered.

There was no time to admire his work, though, as the next wave was already upon him. Thurkill raised his axe once more, but he was too late. Fatigue had taken its toll, making him too slow to react. The sword caught the axe mid-way along its shaft, numbing his hands and causing him to drop the weapon. Before he could move, though, the next knight hacked at him. He felt an intense pain as a hand's length gash appeared on his left forearm. His vision blurred as he stared dumbly at the blood welling up along the wound. Shaking his head to recover his senses, he cast around for a weapon. Exposed and defenceless as he was, he could do nothing to protect either himself or Harold.

As he scrabbled amidst the gore and debris, he failed to see the killing blow when it came. Reaching down to grab a discarded sword, his head exploded in pain. The sword caught him on the side of the head a finger's breadth above the rim of his helmet, from where the blade then slid down, taking his ear. Only the fact that he had stooped at the precise moment of impact the saved his life. Had he been upright, it would have taken his head. Nevertheless, the weight of the blow, launched from a charging mount, knocked him off his feet. As he lay on the ground, unable to move or even speak, the last thing he saw was a group of dismounted knights, gathered around Harold, stabbing and hacking away at his already lifeless body. It might have been a trick of his addled brain, but he could have sworn that one of them bore a scar across his cheek. That same knight then reached down towards the king, his dagger gleaming in the last rays of the sun. Moments later, he rose once more, lifting his hand for all to see. Blood dripped down his forearm from his hand where he gripped the severed remains of England's manhood.

Thurkill cried out in anguish but no sound came. He felt his eyes closing despite his straining every sinew to remain conscious. His king had been killed, mutilated, and he was powerless to avenge him. With his last conscious thought, he swore vengeance on the man who had so dishonourably defiled Harold. He swore he would find him and he would kill him for what he had done.

NINETEEN

15 October, Senlac Ridge

Thurkill regained consciousness in complete darkness. *Is this what heaven is like?* was the first thought that entered his mind. *It's not like how Father Wulfric described it.* He recalled how the local priest had talked of a bright and sunny garden with angels singing hymns and psalms. But this was different; this was dark, cold and decidedly damp. If it were not heaven, it could not be hell either as Wulfric had scared him with tales of insufferable heat from huge fires stoked by the devil's minions while foul-smelling sulphur assailed the nostrils.

As he recovered his senses, he slowly became aware of his surroundings. His head throbbed intensely; it felt as if his head was the anvil on which a blacksmith was hammering a piece of metal. Fighting the pain in his head for supremacy was a burning sensation from the side of his head and another from his left arm. Gingerly, he lifted his right hand to touch his face, confusion filling his mind until he recalled how the sword blow had severed his ear. He winced in pain; the wound was still raw but, from the feel of things, it was no longer bleeding. The surrounding skin was crusty where it had dried, cracking and flaking away under his probing finger tips.

Next he reached for his forearm, fearful of what he might find. It was still wet to the touch, but appeared to be no more than seeping. He gave thanks to God the cut had not been deeper or he might already have died. Though his wounds did not seem too grievous, he knew they'd need treating soon. He'd seen many similar injuries succumb to evil humours that would penetrate exposed flesh, giving rise to a fever from which he might not recover. The same had happened to Aelfric last summer after he slashed his foot on a scythe that had been carelessly left lying in a field. He had laughed it off at the time, but within days his leg had swollen to twice its normal size and he was thrashing about, driven mad by the pain. The priest had been unable to help, blaming demonic possession, and Aelfric had died within the week.

Putting such frightening thoughts to the back of his mind, he continued to probe his body as best he could, looking for any other cuts or injuries. As he did so, he began to recall the last moments of the battle. The knights who had led the final charge, the one who had cracked his head with his sword, putting paid to his ear in the process, and especially the truly evil scarred bastard who – he remembered with an involuntary sob – had attacked the king, slaughtering him in cold blood before hacking off his penis.

Waves of sadness flooded over him, forcing torrents of tears from his eyes. A day ago they had awaited the dawn with quiet confidence, eager to put the Norman invaders to flight. Now all lay in ruins. Harold was dead; his army slain or routed. He had lost his father and he had no idea what had become of the fyrdsmen who had come with him from Haslow. Most likely they were all dead too. His body heaved with uncontrolled sobs, the tears tracing narrow tracks through the blood and grime encrusted on his face. He was grateful for the darkness so that none might see his shame. In his self-pity he longed to go back to the simpler times of his childhood, before the slaughter and horror of the previous day.

Thoughts of home brought him back to the present. He could not lie here forever; there were others that had need of him. He had no idea where the Normans might go next, presumably to Lundenburh or Wintanceastre, or both. Either way, he did not doubt that they would be laying waste to everything in their path and that could very well mean his own village was in danger. His own? Well, he supposed it was his now, though there was no king to confirm the transfer of title. Nevertheless, it was now his duty as the new lord to protect the people of Haslow.

He tried to move but yelped in pain, the sound immediately dying on his lips in terror. Through the black of the moonless night, he could see a number of torches illuminating the faces of several groups of men picking their way across the body-strewn field towards him. As they walked, they stopped every now and then to examine a body, after which an arm would thrust out, followed by a blood-chilling scream. *God preserve me,* Thurkill prayed fervently. *They're finishing off the wounded. If they find me here, I'm lost for sure.*

He could not risk moving, however. Despite the darkness, the nearest group were close enough that they'd spot him as soon as he did. There was nothing he could do but lie there, eyes staring blankly into the night, and hope that the blood and the dirt that covered his face was enough to convince them he was already dead. He did his best to slow his breathing, as difficult as that was with his heart pounded furiously in his chest. The sound of it filled his ears, making him feel certain that the Normans would hear it too. He yearned to cry out, to throw himself at them in cold fury. But he was so weak from pain and exhaustion that he knew it was hopeless.

The nearest man was almost upon him. He had paused by a man two or three feet away from him, stabbing him in the throat for good measure. Thurkill had not even realised that he had been alive. With a sudden pang of fear, he wondered whether they were stabbing everyone – alive or dead – just to be certain. Every part of him screamed at him to move, to run far from that place, but he dare not, could not. His only hope was to remain still and trust in God to deliver him from evil.

As he stared glassily upwards, his vision filled with the huge, dark form of the Norman soldier. By the light of his torch's flame, Thurkill could see the man was staring down at him. He was grim-faced with wide, cruel eyes either side of an immense, hooked nose. Would he pass him by and leave him unmolested? He seemed to be lingering forever; why does he not move on? *Sweet Mary, mother of Jesus,* Thurkill thought, *he thinks I'm alive. That's the end of me!* He did not even dare reach for his seax.

Just then, a shout from the next group a few paces away caused the Norman to turn his head. A second, more urgent shout had him running along with all the others who were within earshot. The soldiers gathered at a spot about twenty paces away, forming a ring of torches to shed more light on whatever it was that had caught their attention, yelling and gesticulating wildly.

With a jolt, Thurkill realised they must have found Harold's body; a great prize which no doubt promised great reward for the men that conveyed the fallen king to Duke William. As he lay there helpless, he was struck by the irony of the moment. Where he had failed to save Harold's life, his king had now just spared his. Even in death, Harold had saved him. The discovery of Harold's body meant that the remaining wounded were now forgotten – at least for the time being – as the Normans squabbled with each other to decide who should be the one to gain the glory of presenting the prize to the duke.

As the sound of the soldiers receded into the distance, Thurkill knew he had to take advantage of the precious time he had been given. Who knew when they might return? Shutting out the pain in his arm as best he could, he rolled over on to his side, slowly and carefully, so as to make as little noise as possible. When he was sure there was no one in earshot, he pushed himself up on to his hands and knees. In doing so, he could not prevent a gasp as he felt the gash in his arm split further and blood begin to flow freely once more. He knew had to get help soon or he could bleed to death.

He rested for a moment on his haunches, squeezing his arm tightly to try to stem the flow. He felt himself sway, as if he were a new born foal trying to take its first steps, until he put a hand down to steady himself. He had little idea of his bearings; there was no moonlight to help orient him. He knew he was still on the ridge and he thought he could feel the ground sloping away in front of him; but much more than that was impossible to discern. As he contemplated his next move, he became aware of a faint glow on the horizon, off to his left. Were more Normans coming with torches? No, it couldn't be. The light was spreading all the way across the skyline now. It was the dawn of the new day. This told him two things: he was facing south as the sun was rising on his left; and he must move now before the growing light left him caught him in the open.

Clamping his lips together to stifle any further cries of pain, he rose to his feet. Turning so that the dawn's light was on his right, he set off north, crouching as low as he could. After a few paces he stooped to grab his war-axe, marvelling at his luck in finding it once more. He still had his seax tucked into his belt but he felt better gripping the worn wooden shaft. He doubted he had the strength to use it in anger, but it might at least give pause to anyone he might encounter.

After a short while, he became aware of dark shapes looming up ahead of him. He allowed himself a brief smile; his sense of direction had not let him down. It was the forest through which the army had emerged on to Senlac ridge the previous morning. Reaching the first tree, he leaned against the gnarled bark of its ancient trunk to catch his breath. He hadn't gone far but the effort had weakened him still further. He knew he could not wait here, however. He had to keep going, to put distance between him and the battlefield. He pressed on, aware also of a growing hunger and thirst. Food would have to wait, but hopefully he would happen upon a stream sooner or later.

After stumbling and shuffling his way through undergrowth and leaves for a few hundred paces, he knew he could go no further. The sky had lightened considerably now, though it remained gloomy under the thick canopy of trees. He would have to take a chance; he had to rest. The pain from his arm was excruciating. A short way in front of him he spotted a slight hollow by a couple of huge oak trees. He staggered over and sank gratefully to the ground, careful to keep the weight off his arm as much as possible. He was asleep almost as soon as his head touched the thick carpet of leaves.

**

He woke with a start and immediately made a grab for his seax, wincing in pain as the sudden movement reawakened the tortured nerves in his left arm. Before he could reach the hilt, though, a powerful hand pinned his wrist hard against his body while another clamped tightly over his mouth. He could feel hot breath on his cheeks, but could not tell whether the face that was poised just inches from his own belonged to friend or foe.

He wanted to struggle, to fight off his assailant, but he was too weak. Every inch of him ached. His arm was agony once more. To make matters worse, his body cried out for food while his mouth was as dry as the hay barn on a summer's day. Only his eyes retained any strength of character.

"Quiet, you whoreson!" the mouth hissed into his ear.

Thanks be to God, he's English! Thurkill let his body slump back into the earth. His throat was not about to be slit; well, not yet a while.

"There's Norman scum everywhere. I am amazed they have not found you, lying out here in the open without a care in the world."

Slowly, the hand was pulled away from his mouth and then the other eased off his wrist. The man then slumped down next to Thurkill with a thud and a great exhalation of breath. Thurkill turned his head to stare at the newcomer. He was not much older than him and, by the looks of him, he too had been in the thick of the battle. His face and neck were streaked with blood, with even more matted in his straggly blond hair; none of it seemed to be his, though, from what he could tell. Two green eyes shone out from the shadow of a heavy brow, still betraying the horror and pain of the previous day. He wore a padded leather jerkin in place of a byrnie, suggesting he was a man of the fyrd, but he did carry a sword at his waist. Whether it was his or whether he had plundered it from the field, Thurkill could not say.

"You were there, right?" Thurkill spoke with a low voice to avoid the sound carrying far.

The man did not speak, but merely nodded, as if unwilling to speak further of the horrors that he had seen.

"Who was your lord?"

"I stood with the men of Sussex under ealdorman Aelfwin. Not one week ago I was bringing in the harvest with my fellow villagers. Now they all lie dead, slain by my side." His voice cracked with emotion as he spoke, his body shaking with barely supressed sobs.

Thurkill smiled empathetically. "It was your first time?"

"Can anyone ever do that twice?"

"It was my second battle; it doesn't become any easier. I was with Harold at Stamford, near Eoforwic, not three weeks since."

The man scoffed in surprise. "You don't look old enough for one battle, let alone two."

Despite his weakness, Thurkill bridled at the perceived slight. "Don't be confused by the lack of beard, friend. I know how to handle a sword and shield better than most!"

Something in Thurkill's voice and demeanour gave his

137

companion pause. "I beg for your pardon. I had not meant to suggest…" His voice tailed off, as if embarrassed and unsure how to proceed. Aiming for firmer ground, he continued. "Who did you stand with?"

"I fought with my father, Scalpi, who was himself one of Harold's own huscarls. I saw my father cut down and was with the king to the end."

"Harold's dead?"

"Aye. He was wounded by an arrow in the final attack, so that he could no longer defend himself. We tried our best to protect him but the enemy were too strong by then and there were too few of us left. I was knocked unconscious but the last thing I saw was a group of the murdering bastards hacking at him like a piece of meat. There was no honour in it."

There was a silence between them for a few moments as each considered the import of Thurkill's words. Eventually the man spoke once again.

"My name is Eahlmund, son of Ealdric, and I am sorry for your loss."

"And I am Thurkill, son of Scalpi and I, too, am sorry for yours. Now that is done, we must be away. We cannot lie here all day, as comfortable as it may be."

Eahlmund chuckled, pleased for the mood to have lightened somewhat. "Well, there I can be of some small service, I think. My village is no more than a day's walk north of here. There's a woman there who has some skill as a healer. She will have your arm as good as new in no time."

TWENTY

15 October, Brightling

It was almost dark when Thurkill and Eahlmund arrived at his village. It was a modest affair: a small wooden church at its centre, around which were grouped about a dozen thatched houses of varying shapes, sizes and states of repair. It was situated at the junction of two roads, one heading roughly east to west and the other branching off to the south, whence they had come. Although the distance from Senlac had not been great, the going had been slow, partly because of Thurkill's wounds, but also because they had shunned the main paths and roads, to reduce the risk of discovery.

For Thurkill's part, although he could walk unaided, he had so little strength that Eahlmund had to help him as best he could, allowing him to drape his uninjured arm round the farmhand's broad frame. Eahlmund was half a head shorter than him so his shoulder acted as a crutch, nestling into Thurkill's armpit, helping to support his weight. His left arm was bound up with a strip of cloth cut from a cloak they had found discarded a short distance from their resting place. From the blood stains it looked as though its former owner had met a sorry end, but it was the best they could find. Using a cleaner part of the garment, Eahlmund had managed to fashion a sling to hold Thurkill's arm firmly in place against his chest, bent up at the elbow so that the blood flow was lessened somewhat.

As they walked, Thurkill had told him about the battle in the north; the forced march which had caught the Vikings off guard and the slaughter that had followed. He left off the part about the lone axe-man on the bridge as memory of it still brought him some embarrassment, both from the gifts that Harold had bestowed on him and the dishonourable way in which he had killed the man. Nevertheless, Eahlmund had listened in awe to the stories, finding a new level of respect for his companion. He had even laughed out loud at the thought of the Norsemen going home in just two dozen ships, having come in more than two hundred. Thurkill had also told him about his sister and aunt, alone in their village in Kent, and how desperate he was to get there as soon as possible before the Normans could despoil the place, or worse.

Eahlmund had shaken his head ruefully. "You're no good to anyone in this condition, Thurkill. We need to get you mended first. Until you can hold a shield with that arm properly, you wouldn't last a moment in a scrap."

By the time they arrived, Thurkill was almost dead on his feet. More and more he was having to lean on Eahlmund who, despite his continual moaning, showed no signs of flagging. He longed for a bed or even a barn filled with hay come to that; anywhere he could rest in some comfort and warmth. Since the sun had gone down, the air had turned cold once again; the clear skies providing no insulation to keep hold of the thin warmth of the autumn sun. The sight of the village appearing out of the gathering gloom as they broke through the tree line, though, lifted his spirits; he even managed to straighten up a little, relieving his new friend of some the burden.

"That's odd."

Thurkill barely lifted his head; he was too tired to care, too tired to sense danger any more. "What is?"

"I know it's nearly dark but you'd think someone would be around. There's usually still folk wandering about at this time. I can't see any light coming from any of the houses either."

"Maybe everyone's had an early night?" Thurkill was wishing for nothing more for himself at that moment, and was not happy at the thought of anything get in the way of it.

Eahlmund snorted, disbelievingly. "Come on. I'll take you to my parents' house. They will know what's happening."

Eahlmund led them to the second house on the left beyond the church. He pushed against the door but found it to be barred. Raising an inquisitive eyebrow in Thurkill's direction, he tapped quietly against the wooden slats. There was no reply. Eahlmund tapped again, louder this time, nervously looking around him as if worried someone would hear him. Eventually, a quiet querulous voice answered.

"Who's there?"

"Father. For the sake of our Lord, let me in."

They heard some stifled muttering followed by the sound of something being dragged across the floor. Moments later the door opened a crack to reveal Eahlmund's father. He was shorter than his son by some margin, but was broad-chested with powerful limbs; the result of a lifetime of toil in the fields. His eyes were nervous, though, darting around either side of his son, as if checking to see who else might be outside. When he caught sight of Thurkill, he gasped with fear. The sight of the huge bloodied warrior still in his full armour took his breath away. From behind him, though, a woman's voice hissed at him.

"For pity's sake, Ealdric, let him in and get that door closed!"

Accustomed to following his wife's instructions, Ealdric wasted no time in pulling the door open wide enough to let the two men in. "Alright, Estrith, give a man a chance eh?"

Eahlmund pushed his way over the threshold and led Thurkill over to a straw mattress in the corner where he helped him lie down. All the while, his mother fussed and flitted around him, clucking like a hen, overjoyed to have her son safely back under her roof.

"Thank God you're alive, Eahlmund. We heard the battle had been lost and we feared the worst. There's been soldiers on horseback riding through the village on and off all day, looking for fugitives no doubt. When you didn't come home, we assumed you must be dead." An involuntary sob escaped her as she pronounced this word. Her eyes, already red from a day spent crying, quickly filled with tears once more.

Ignoring his mother's distress, however, Eahlmund froze at the mention of soldiers. "How long ago was the last time you saw them, mother?"

Estrith sniffed and wiped her sleeve across her face. "Oh I don't know; a couple of hours now, I think. The last lot were heading south back down towards the coast. Either way, we were taking no chances. Half the villagers have already fled into the forest, while the rest of us decided to sit it out. So we barricaded our door and put our faith in God. We've got nothing for them to take anyway, unless they want our scythes or ploughshares."

"Or old Bebba the pony."

Estrith rounded irritably on her husband. "And what, pray tell, would they want with old Bebba? She's barely got the strength to pull a cart these days, let alone carry a man into battle."

"I don't know, Estrith, I just thought…"

"Thought you say? Well I suppose there's a first time for everything."

The bickering was making Thurkill's head hurt even more and before he could stop himself he groaned out loud.

The noise was enough to remind Estrith that she had a guest in her house. "And who's this fellow? One of ours by the looks of him."

"Mother, this is Thurkill, son of Scalpi, huscarl of the house of Wessex. He was at the battle, defending our king to the end. He has wounds that need care and he needs time to rest and recover his strength. It is the least we can do to offer this brave warrior our help in his time of need."

"I don't much care if he is brave or otherwise, if the Normans find him here they'll kill the lot of us." She paused, as if considering further. "He can stay the night but tomorrow I want him gone."

"But, mother, he's in no fit state to travel."

"That's as may be but I want him out of my house tomorrow and that's an end to it."

"Whose house is this that you speak of, woman?"

Eahlmund turned to Ealdric in surprise. His father was normally such a timid man, often cowed by his far more intimidating wife. In fact, he could not recall him ever standing up to his mother before.

"Last time I looked, I was head of this house; it is our duty to offer hospitality to our guest, Normans or no. It is a tradition that goes back to the earliest times and I will not be the first of my line to abandon it. The boy stays as long as he needs to and you will be civil to him while he is here, or you'll feel the back of my hand."

Estrith was shocked to silence. Rather than be angry, however, Thurkill could have sworn he saw a playful smile flit across her features as she turned away. Perhaps her husband's uncharacteristic display of strength had pleased her in some way.

Emboldened, Ealdric took control of the situation. "Son, rouse Switha; see that she brings her healing bag with her. Wife, fetch up a bowl of that broth we had earlier and some bread for our guest. I'll wager he needs a good feed after the day he's had."

Thurkill was gratefully mopping the last of the vegetable soup out of a deep, wooden bowl with his hunk of bread when Switha arrived. The bread was a little stale but it softened wonderfully in the thick soup. It might not have matched the quality of the king's own cooks but it was far and away the best meal he'd had for a long time. He was keenly aware that these were poor folk; they would not have a lot to spare so for them to share their food with him, willingly or otherwise, was a great sacrifice.

Switha swept into the one-roomed house with bustling efficiency, directing Estrith to clear the table and Ealdric to build up the fire. Thurkill couldn't help but stare; he wasn't sure he had ever seen anyone as old as her. Her hair was completely white and was, in places, thinning to the extent that patches of her scalp were visible, shiny in the light of the fire. Her face was so lined that she seemed to have wrinkles on top of her wrinkles. Despite her age, however, she stood proud and strong and spoke with a forceful, assertive voice; one that was used to giving orders. Age had most definitely not dimmed her vitality. Thurkill relaxed back in his chair. He felt safe in her hands, safe for the first time since before the battle.

Switha dealt with his wounds with a calm authority. She quickly identified that the wound to his ear was superficial, in need of nothing more than to be cleaned and wrapped in a strip of cloth to 'keep dirt and creepy crawlies out', as she put it. She also pronounced that the wound had already begun to close of its own accord and would give him no more trouble. With a cheeky smile, she recommended he keep his hair long to hide what she called the unsightly blemish, in case it were to spoil his chances of finding a bride in future. Thurkill blushed but merely nodded, dumbly, in agreement.

She was more concerned by his arm. It was a nasty cut and, although it had finally stopped bleeding – thanks to Eahlmund's bandage, she said – it had, however, been exposed to all manner of harmful things over the last several hours. There was a chance that fever might set in, she said, and that he might die as a result. She spoke matter-of-factly, talking about him as if he were a lamb or calf, oblivious to his feelings or worries.

In a state of some nervousness, Thurkill's voice wavered. "You can help me, though?"

"I will do what I can; I can promise no more than that. After that you will have to trust in the gods."

"The gods?" Thurkill was incredulous; surely no one still clung to the old ways? Before he could say any more, however, he caught Eahlmund's eye. He was standing behind her, holding his hands up and shaking his head as if to say 'Let it be'. *My God,* Thurkill thought to himself, *I'm in the hands of one of the old people. She still holds to pagan ways.* He'd heard his father talk about such people before and it was always with a sense of warning and distrust. Some said that they were in league with the devil, that their healing magic could only come from him. Still, he had no choice; there'd be no other healer for miles around. He would have to put his fears to one side and let her do her work and trust that God would forgive him when judgement day came.

The old woman worked quietly, her nimble fingers dancing like a spider around his arm. She used a cloth soaked in hot water to clean the wound and, although she was not overly rough in her actions, Thurkill still winced at the touch of the material around his savaged forearm. Swijtha merely shook her head, tutted as if he were some particularly pathetic child, and continued with her work. Shamefaced, he resolved to grit his teeth and make no further sound.

Having finished her cleansing, she then inspected his arm more closely, frowning as she did so. Then she leaned in so closely that he could have sworn she was actually now sniffing his flesh, her nose almost touching the broken skin.

"Well, it seems clean enough and there is no smell of pestilence as yet. With luck you will not lose the arm."

"What?" Embarrassed, Thurkill realised he had shouted.

Switha smiled as if she had seen it all before. "Calm yourself, dear. I only say that it is a possibility. I have seen wounds like these before. The worst ones start to smell, worse than a rotting, dead cow on a hot summer's day. Then they go green and swell up, filled with all manner of evil, foul-smelling demons. If that happens you will die if left to your own devices. Or if you come to me, you might survive, but only if we cut off the limb before the demons make their way to the rest of your body."

Thurkill found he was shaking with fear again. "Without my arm, I am nothing. I only know how to fight and if I can't hold a shield then even that will be taken from me."

"Well, there is a good chance you won't lose it so stop bleating about what you can't control. In all my years I've never heard such whining; you're worse than an infant. As I say, there is no smell as yet, but we'll know more in a few days. Until then you must rest and regain your strength. The best healer I know is the body itself, if you give it a chance. I am certain you will live to do more killing," the disdain in her voice showed what she thought of the practice, "though I do not know who you will fight for, as I hear our king is dead. Perhaps you will fight for this new one from overseas?"

"Never!" Thurkill had shouted again. "I would give my life to kill the Norman Bastard, just as soon as I have made sure that my kin are safe back home in Kent."

Switha chuckled. "Well, you're going nowhere for a while, dear boy. Not with this arm." With that she set about her work, dipping into her sack to draw out a mixing bowl and handfuls of various types of herbs and other plants. With a practised hand she worked them into a paste, using more of the warm water and other, unknown substances. When it was ready, she took a handful of the pungent mixture and carefully smeared and pressed it over the open wound before binding it as tight as she could with more strips of cloth.

Thurkill forgot his earlier promise to himself and yelped as she pulled hard on the cloth, as she wrapped it around his arm several times. "Does it have to be quite so tight? It feels like my arm will drop off by itself."

"Ach. All this fuss over a little cut. It has to be thus," she explained patiently, "so that the two sides may be pulled together to help the wound to close properly. You can't go around with half your arm hanging out now, can you?

"There," she said, packing the bowl and leftover herbs back into her bag, "I will come back in two or three days to check the wound and put a new poultice on. Try to keep out of mischief until then and don't get in Estrith's way." With that she strode from the house, laughing at her own joke as she went.

TWENTY-ONE

22 October, Brightling

In the week that followed, Thurkill could feel himself improving with every day that passed. As promised, Switha had come back after three days to redress his wounds. She had removed the cloth strips from around his head altogether, content that no more need be done as far as that wound was concerned. It was still sore, and he could not yet lie down to sleep on that side at night, but other than that it was no more than a minor irritation.

She'd been far more worried about his arm, carefully unwrapping the bindings before gently wiping away the remains of the herb poultice. Thurkill had steeled himself for the worst. The wound had been throbbing almost incessantly, so much so that he had convinced himself that it must be diseased and would have to be removed. After a couple of sleepless nights, he had begun to resign himself to a life with just one arm, assuming – of course – he survived its removal. He knew not what he would do, but he was determined he would not let it be the end of his life, whatever happened.

As soon as the bindings had been removed, he could not help but sniff the air, as Switha herself had done that first night, trying to assess whether he could smell putrefaction. The old woman had smiled kindly, understanding his fear. Taking his arm gently in her hands, she'd raised it to her nose and inhaled deeply. Watching her face intently, he'd searched for a sign – good or bad – in her expression, but to no avail. Just when he'd been about to demand answers, she had let go of his arm and pronounced curtly: " There's no decay."

Thurkill had let out a huge sigh of relief. He would remain whole after all; he would not surrender his shield arm just yet. All those thoughts of what would become of him had faded into the back of his mind. Closing his eyes, he'd raised his face to the heavens and prayed aloud: "Thank you, Lord, for my deliverance".

Switha had chuckled but said nothing, causing Thurkill to

blush, remembering her supposed lack of faith in the Christian God. Still, she had not seemed offended. *No harm done*, he'd told himself with a grin. Switha, meanwhile, had continued to inspect his arm. The wound was healing well; the skin already starting to knit together to close over the wound and some of the swelling had reduced. The flesh around the wound was still an angry pink and painful to the touch, but at least it looked healthy to his untrained eye. Indeed, Switha had soon pronounced herself satisfied with the results of her work and had finished off by applying a new poultice and re-binding the wound with fresh, clean strips of cloth.

Soon after, Thurkill felt strong enough to venture outside for the first time. Since his arrival he had been confined to a bed, hastily thrown together by Estrith, in the opposite corner of the room from the rest of the family. He had been acutely aware of the fact that Eahlmund's mother would rather he were not there, not least because he was rapidly eating her out of hearth and home now that his appetite was back with a vengeance. It was another sign that he was on the mend, and his huge frame needed a lot of food to fuel it. He'd gladly given them what few coins he had in his pouch but he knew it was not enough compared to what they were doing for him.

Eahlmund lent him some of his clothes; his own had been beyond the pale, being blood-stained and ripped beyond repair. Estrith had taken them off him without a word, before burning them without ceremony behind the house. His mail shirt, axe and shield, however, he had carefully hidden, wrapped in the remains of his cloak, in the rafters of the hamlet's communal barn just behind the church. He felt sure he would be needing them again before too long.

It was wonderful to be out in the fresh air once again. It also meant he could finally contribute towards his keep, though his arm was not yet strong enough to allow him to do anything other than the least manual jobs. But it felt good to be part of a community once more. The last few weeks and months had been a time of turmoil and upheaval as they had waited for an invasion that they knew would come sooner or later. Now he was back doing what he had grown up with and it felt very much like home. The memories of the horrors of battle, the loss of his father, were receding bit by bit as he rediscovered the joys of working the land. The villagers had welcomed him with little hesitation; there was always work to be found for another willing pair of hands especially since only Eahlmund and one other had returned from Senlac. The fact that he had stood with the king 'til the end lent him a status and measure of respect that he felt he ill-deserved. Nonetheless, there was no doubt it had helped his acceptance.

One in particular seemed more pleased than most at his arrival; a girl of roughly the same age who went by the name of Hild. He hadn't noticed her at first, and only became aware of her a day or two later when they were working in one of the barley fields. Eahlmund had nudged him a little too sharply in the ribs, smirked and nodded, directing him to look over to his left. Glancing over, he found himself looking at a girl with flowing blonde locks that framed a face as round and as bright as the sun. His mouth formed an involuntary O shape as he stared for her beauty was striking. She was standing in the middle of a group of three other girls and it was immediately obvious that they were talking about him as they were throwing what they took to be secretive looks in his direction, giggling and whispering behind their hands.

Thurkill blushed furiously and immediately jerked his head back to his front. Focusing on his work, he dared to hope that she'd not seen him looking at her, but to no avail. The four girls burst into peals of laughter before scampering off back to the hamlet. He had stood dumbfounded for a moment, the fleeting image of her face etched indelibly in his mind like the bright sun burns its image in your mind when you close your eyes. As nonchalantly as possible, he had resumed the back-breaking work of tying down the remaining stems of the recently harvested crop. If he had thought he was going to get away with it, however, he had been sadly mistaken.

"I think she likes you, my friend." Eahlmund laughed, unable to conceal his delight at his friend's obvious embarrassment, laughter that was echoed around them by every other farmhand in earshot.

Thurkill had not thought it possible for his face to burn any more than it already was. To hide his discomfort, he laughed along with the others as if pretending that he was not bothered by such things. Cries of "She'll keep you warm on a cold night, son" and "I'll wager she can handle a sword," only served to make things worse, but he bore it in good part all the same. Sometime later, when the conversation had moved on to other matters, he had turned to Eahlmund and asked as casually as he could. "So, what's her name then?"

His friend smiled knowingly, but thankfully refrained from starting another round of ribald jesting. "Now that, my friend, is Hild, daughter of Nothelm, the headman of Brightling. There's many a lad here that's taken a shine to her but, as yet, she has never shown interest in any of them. Perhaps you might finally be the one to unlock her door, as it were."

Thurkill chuckled, "Is that so? It must be my handsome good looks that does it. She clearly has me marked out as a cut above you ugly, sheep-rutting bunch."

"That or she's the type to be impressed by big dumb warriors with huge swords. I assume you do have a huge sword to go with the huge rest of you?" More laughter ensued following Eahlmund's crude observation.

"Well, it's slain a few in its time and doubtless will serve me well now." He chose not to mention that he had lain with only one woman before, and that just a few weeks ago.

"Well, whatever the case, make sure you keep that weapon of yours sheathed when Nothelm is around. He's fiercely protective of his little girl and he will break it in half for you if he catches you with her. There's a few here that can vouch for that."

No more was said about Hild for a day or two. But he found himself thinking of her more and more, especially at night when her face – as radiant as the full moon above – would come unbidden into his mind when he closed his eyes to sleep. Without even having spoken to her, he realised he was already besotted with her. He knew that nothing could come of it, though – not so much because he feared what her father might say or do, but rather because he knew he could not be stay here long. As soon as he was strong enough, he knew he had to head home. He was already consumed with worry for his sister and aunt. Who knew if they were safe, or even alive? While he was wasting time working in the fields and being a love-sick puppy, anything could be happening to them. He had to put Hild from his mind and focus on getting better.

**

His good intentions did not last even a day. Thurkill rose with the dawn and made his way down to the stream that ran past the hamlet on its way down to the coast. The night had been cloudless so it was a crisp morning. His feet crunched their way across the meadow as the blades of grass, made stiff by the first frost of the season, protested beneath his leather boots. He'd always loved these autumnal early mornings; the sunlight glinting off the wet ground made everything shimmer and sparkle as if imbued with a dusting of ancient magic. He loved to see the fog forming in front of his mouth as he breathed. What could be finer than being surrounded by nature on a day like this, he asked himself.

Reaching the water's edge, he made his way upstream to where a clump of rocks and bushes shielded him from any who might happen to be drawing water down by the hamlet. Then he removed his boots, cloak and tunic and waded out into the clear, blue water. He gasped at how cold it was; already his feet were tingling as the numbing sensation of the icy stream permeated his skin. He knew he would not be able to stand it for long, so he forced himself further out into the current until he was up to his waist. Once there, he took a deep breath, prepared himself for what was to come and fell backwards so that he was fully immersed in the water. The shock was like nothing else; an incredible sensation pain mixed with vitality as the freezing water engulfed his torso and limbs. His arm, still in the process of healing, burned as tiny spears of intense cold poked at the tender flesh. Pain soon turned to pleasure though as the cold slowly numbed the feeling in the wound, leaving him with a delightful sensation.

He stayed under for as long as he could hold his breath, before lurching to his feet and wading as quickly as he could back towards the shore. It was slow going, though, made worse by the weight of his saturated braies which had caused them to sag down around his thighs, exposing his backside and everything else to the cold air. Just as he reached the shallows, insult was added to injury when the sodden garment became tangled around his knees. Another step found him falling head first into the water, arms flailing in all directions to break his fall.

At least the cold is not so bad this time, he grinned as he struggled to his hands and knees, his bare arse pointing skywards. It was then that he became aware of the laughter, the pitch of which told him all he needed to know. In a panic he rushed to pull his braies back up and tie them firmly in place.

"Who spies on me? Show yourself."

The laughter continued unabated. "I think there has been quite enough showing for one morning, don't you?"

He still couldn't see his tormentor and by now his embarrassment was turning to anger. "It is not seemly to watch from the shadows as a man bathes. You should be ashamed of yourself."

"I beg for your pardon, noble warrior. I confess I had heard tell of some great and terrible weapon in your possession and I wanted to see for myself. Yet, I find I am not so impressed when confronted with it." More unrestrained giggling accompanied these words.

Thurkill blushed and moved his hands protectively in front of his groin, even though he was no longer exposed. "The air is cold and the water even more so. These things don't help."

At this moment, Hild chose to reveal herself, stepping out from behind the bush where she had been hiding. She walked towards him, with a face that showed what he took for genuine remorse, though a playful smile still flitted across her lips.

"Forgive me, Thurkill. I had not come here to spy on you or mock you. It is chance that finds us here at the same time. I like to come here to watch the colourful birds catching fish as they swim upriver. I had meant to call out sooner but when you entered the water I was struck dumb, too embarrassed to speak out until you fell over. It was so funny I could not help but laugh. You must hate me."

In truth, his shame still made him want to chide her but he found that he could not. The way she held her head to one side was the very picture of ardent contrition; it was so effective that it made him want to reach out and hug her. He had no idea whether her apology was genuine but he was not sure it mattered at that moment. Her beauty was too mesmerising for him to care. Despite her sombre expression, though, she still retained a cheeky glint in her eye that made him weak at the knees. There was no two ways about it, he was smitten.

"I have nothing for which to forgive you, Hild. It is your river as much as mine and you have every right to be here whenever you like whether or not you find a hulking oaf splashing about with his braies around his ankles."

The grin was back. "True, but some visits here are better than others, especially the ones with the hulking oafs."

Thurkill joined in with a grin of his own, his embarrassment forgotten as he basked in the warmth of her smile. Before he realised what he was doing, he blurted out, "I would like to see you again, Hild. Would you allow it?"

"I would like that very much, Thurkill, but I cannot say the same for my father."

He hoped his face did not appear as crestfallen as he felt inside. "Would he have to know?"

"It's not the sort of thing you can hide easily in a place this small." Catching sight of his expression, Hild rushed to assuage his disappointment. "But listen, tomorrow I have to go into the woods to gather mushrooms. If you happened to be there, hunting perhaps, then it would not be beyond the bounds of probability that we might accidently happen upon each other?"

Thurkill nodded knowingly. "I was only saying to Estrith, last night, that a nice rabbit or two would help liven up her broth."

***

The next morning, Thurkill could not contain his excitement. He was up and out of the house before anyone else had even stirred, determined not to waste the opportunity he had been given. He took with him some snares, a bow with a sheaf of arrows, a spear and his trusty seax, together with Eahlmund's forage sack. Having told Estrith the night before that he was off hunting, he knew he ought to look the part and would need, he supposed, to at least try to catch something at some point during the day.

Eahlmund had suggested accompanying him, causing him to panic for a moment as he frantically searched for a valid reason to say no. Before he could do so, however, he was rescued by Ealdric who said he had need of his son's help in the fields. Thurkill only hoped that the relief on his face had not been too obvious. Eahlmund had seemed to give him an odd look which had seemed to morph into a sly smirk, but he could have been mistaken. Perhaps his mind had been playing tricks on him.

It was another cold day, and the wind was whistling through the tops of the great oak trees that grew around Brightling. Many still stubbornly held on to their last few leaves as autumn moved inexorably towards winter. It had rained overnight too. Though it had stopped now, the sky remained leaden-grey with unbroken cloud in every direction. The ground was slick and in places gave way to glutinous mud where the moisture had failed to drain away. Several times he felt his feet slip from under him in his haste, but each time he managed to save himself by grabbing the nearest branch. Nevertheless, his boots were well-worn and almost threadbare in places and his feet were soon sodden and bitterly cold. Unperturbed, he strode on at pace; the strenuous exercise generating at least some warmth that he hoped would seep down towards his toes.

Soon enough he arrived at the appointed place, a patch of thankfully drier ground under a thick canopy of evergreen foliage where clusters of mushrooms grew by the dozen. There he was able to kick and scrape the worst of the mud from his boots against a tree trunk and stamp his feet a few times to force some feeling back into his toes.

It wasn't long before he heard the sound of singing. Without thinking, he straightened his tunic and brushed what dirt there was off of it as best he could. He even ran his fingers through his thick unruly mop of hair to try to untangle the worst of the knots. Guiltily, he realised that it had been a few days since he had last fought it to a standstill with an actual comb. He was still struggling with it when Hild came into view about twenty paces or so away. He dropped his arms to his side, grinning sheepishly as he did so.

She was wrapped up warm against the cold: a green woollen cloak, the colour of which, he noticed, matched her eyes, was pinned at her shoulder with an ornate silver brooch inset with a piece of amber. She had pulled its hood over her head for warmth, the folds perfectly framing her face with ringlets of blonde hair escaping on either side. To Thurkill she looked more beautiful than ever and he was at a loss for words. Hild seemed to be aware of his awkward gaze and delighted in it. She stopped a few paces away from him, and stood expectantly with her hand on her hip and her head tilted coquettishly to one side.

"Good morning, Hild, I trust you are well?" Thurkill stammered. He knew his words were clumsy at best and he cursed himself inwardly for it. *How can I stand and face a screaming enemy horde intent on killing me and yet be struck dumb in front of a solitary woman, however damned pretty she might be?*

She laughed, but with no trace of malice. To ease his discomfort, she crossed the gap between them before lifting her face to place a delicate kiss on his cheek. She was by no means a short woman but she still had to stand on the tips of her toes to reach. Then she deftly linked her arm through his and turned him back towards the direction whence she had come.

"Walk with me while I collect some mushrooms."

Thurkill nodded dumbly, holding out his hand to take her basket. For a few minutes, they walked in companionable silence as Hild moved among the trees, stooping every now and then to select the best-looking specimens which she then placed carefully, so as not to bruise, in the basket that Thurkill held out for her. It reminded him of his childhood as he had often accompanied his aunt or sister for the very same purpose. The thought brought the same feelings of guilt flooding back; here he was idling his time away picking mushrooms with this beautiful woman when he needed to be at home to care for his family. He felt much stronger now; surely, he was ready to go?

But then what about Hild? Though he had only just met her, he didn't want to leave her so soon. Perhaps he could persuade her to come with him? As soon as the thought entered his mind, however, he realised how futile it was. Why should she leave her home to go with someone she hardly knew? And besides, her father would never allow it.

Suddenly, he was conscious that Hild had stopped and was looking at him expectantly. *Oh God! She's asked me a question and I was too wrapped up in my own thoughts to hear it. She must think me a complete fool.*

He resolved to be truthful. "Your pardon, Hild. I was thinking of home. What did you say?"

She tutted admonishingly but without rancour. "I am sorry for I had not realised my presence to be so uninteresting." The glint in her eyes told him she was joking but nonetheless he resolved to hang off her every word from that point on. It didn't pay to make the same mistake twice, his father had always told him – especially where a lady was concerned.

"I was asking how it felt to be in a battle," she continued. "Such things have not, until now, affected us in our little village, and I am curious to know how a man can summon the courage to kill another."

Thurkill sighed before replying, as if unwilling to bring back to mind the horrors he had experienced. "You don't have time to think, Hild. The man in front of you is swinging a sword at your head. You either kill him or he kills you. It really is as simple as that."

Hild shuddered. "I still can't imagine what it must be like, actually killing someone."

"The first time was horrible – I could not believe what I had done – but you become accustomed to it. You have to. The shieldwall is so tightly packed that as soon as you kill one, there is another there to take their place straightaway."

"How does it ever end? How in God's name does anyone survive?"

Thurkill was determined to spare her the worst of the detail. "To be honest, with everyone packed so tight together, there's not a lot of room for much actual killing for most of the time.

It's mainly a lot of pushing and shoving in truth. That said, it was different with the Normans; many of them were on horseback with long spears. They could reach over the top of our shields with ease. It was that, and their archers, which did for us – especially once they broke our right wing."

He stopped for a moment, reliving the final moments of the battle in his mind, remembering his father being cut down and being unable to stop it. He had not really stopped to mourn his father's passing since that day. As he stood there, memories flooding through his mind, the tears finally came, welling up in his eyes before streaming down his cheeks in what felt like a torrent.

Hild said nothing, knowing no words were needed. Instead, she simply reached out to him and enveloped him in her arms as far as her slight frame would allow. The strength of his emotions astonished him and it was a while before the feeling passed. The loss of his father, the death of his king, his own inability to prevent either of those two events and, on top of everything, the destruction of the army had been weighing on his mind, searching for an outlet. As she released him from her embrace, Hild voiced the same thought that was coursing through his mind.

"So, what now with Harold gone and his army beaten?"

"I don't know, Hild. Truly I don't. His brothers were also slain at Senlac. I don't know who else could take up his mantle."

"Who then will take the throne? Who will lead us now? Is there no other?"

Thurkill wished his father were there. He would surely know. He vaguely remembered stories Scalpi had told him around the hearth some months back; it was shortly before the old King Edward had died. He had asked his father who would be king after Edward once it became clear that the old man's days were numbered. The answer had been so long and detailed that he had fallen asleep before the end, earning himself a cuff round the back of the head and a boot up the arse as he retreated to his bed. He smiled to himself at the memory, as he tried to pull the key threads together to answer Hild.

"I remember my father saying that Edward had a half-brother; Edmund, I think his name was. He died fighting the Danes in the same year as their father, King Aethelraed Unraed. Anyway, this Edmund had a son – but I can't remember his name. It might also have been Edward. I do know, though, that he was sent into exile when Knut took the throne."

He could see that Hild was beginning to lose interest and hurried to end the story. "So when King Edward was getting old and had no children of his own to follow him, men were sent east to bring back this son of Edmund. This was about ten years ago, I think."

"So where is he now then and why did he not become king after Edward?"

"Well… if I remember right, he died soon after returning to these shores. Murdered, I shouldn't wonder."

"Oh. So what was the point of telling me about him, then?" She was trying to follow but was growing impatient.

"Ah… but he had a son."

"But you don't know his name either?"

"No, I do!" Thurkill asserted. "His name is Edgar. That much I do know. He's younger than me, I think, though I don't know by how much. But, nevertheless, he should be the rightful king as the last male heir of King Edward's line."

"A king who is not much more than a boy? That does not sound like a great idea. If Harold – a grown man and seasoned warrior - could not beat the Normans, what hope does this Edgar have?"

"There is no one else, though. Unless we look to the northern earls, Morcar or Eadwine. But who would follow them after they were beaten so easily by the Vikings at Eoforwic?"

Hild nodded, pensive, before skipping ahead. "Come on; my bag is full of mushrooms now and you need to catch some rabbits in case anyone wonders what you've been up to. Can't have the mighty warrior going back empty-handed – what would people think of you and your fearsome weapon?"

He saw the sparkle in her eye and realised she was thinking back to the river. "Why you little…" He roared in mock anger as she scampered away, half screaming half laughing, with him bounding after her.

TWENTY-TWO

23 October, Brightling

They were still some way from the village when they heard the sound of screaming, shouting and many feet crashing through the undergrowth. Moments later, Thurkill spied the first villagers running towards them, darting in and out of the tree trunks as they fled. Any concerns about being spotted with Hild were forgotten immediately; something was horribly wrong.

"What's happening?" The fear in Hild's voice echoed his own.

Thurkill's jaw was set in a grimace for he feared the worst. "I don't know for sure, but I'll wager it has something to do with our new neighbours." Without his mail shirt and axe he was next to useless, but at least he had a bow and spear. But, then he was just one man and who knew what awaited them in the village?

Just then, he recognised one of the men rushing towards them; one of the lads he had worked the fields with not two days since. "Hey! Brithnoth. What news?"

But Brithnoth showed no signs of slowing let alone stopping. Fleeing Brightling was all that was on his mind, until Thurkill stepped into his path to grab his arm, almost wrenching it from its socket in the process.

"Unhand me, you fool. The Normans are right behind us. You'd run too if you knew what was good for you."

"I'll let you go when you tell me what's happening and not before."

Brithnoth struggled to free himself but Thurkill's grip was too tight. He seemed to think about throwing a punch, but then, perhaps wisely, thought better of it. He was not about to fight someone far taller and bigger than him, Normans or no Normans. Instead, his shoulders slumped. "A group of about five horsemen rode into the village a short while back. Armed to the teeth they were."

"What do they want?"

"I don't know but they have taken Eahlmund. Perhaps they are looking for fugitives from the battle. Men like you," he spat contemptuously to one side as if blaming Thurkill for their predicament.

With his friend's safety at stake, anxiety took hold of Thurkill's mind. "What have they done to him?"

"Not much as far as I could tell. Well, not up to the point where we all ran for it anyway."

"What do you mean, man? Piss or get off the pot for God's sake."

In his eagerness to be away, Brithnoth gabbled his words. "First, they roughed him up a bit, gave him a slap or two. Then they accused him of having fought against them and of helping some of Harold's own men to escape. Well, then his old dad, Ealdric, tried to intervene. He was having none of it, you see? So, he rushed at them with nothing more than a scythe."

"By almighty God, what was he thinking, the fool! Is he dead?"

"He managed to put one on his arse – stabbed him in the leg, you see - but the others put an end to it. It was quick but it was gruesome all the same. As soon as folk saw that, they ran for it. All except Estrith and your father, Hild."

Thurkill hadn't known Ealdric for long but he felt a stab of grief at his death all the same. The old man had been kind to him when he had arrived and now he had paid the price for his hospitality. He also felt sorry for his friend. He knew what it was like to watch your father die in front of you and be unable to stop it. This time, however, perhaps he could do something to help.

"My thanks, Brithnoth. I have one more favour to ask you, however. Will you come back with me now to help Eahlmund? We can't leave your friend to the mercy of these scum."

Brithnoth looked miserable. Torn between a desperation to run and fear of this hulking warrior with reputation to match who towered over him. Then there was Hild. She was looking at him in that way she always did, the way that all the men in the hamlet found impossible to resist. He blushed and looked down at his feet, unable to look either of them in the eye.

"But, I have no weapon."

"That's soon sorted; you can have my spear. You know how to use one, right? You have trained with the fyrd in the past, I assume, even if you were not called to fight this time?"

Brithnoth nodded slowly. His face had now turned very pale; he looked as if he were about to vomit, which Thurkill considered quite likely in the circumstances. So as not to give the poor man any further time to object, he took control of the situation

"Right, that settles it, then. The three of us will head back to the village and see what we can do about rescuing Eahlmund, Nothelm and anyone else that they might have there."

***

By the time they arrived at the edge of the treeline, close to the first of the houses, Brithnoth was shaking with fear. Thurkill seriously doubted how much use he would be if it came to a fight, but at least he might look like he was a threat and distract some of the soldiers away from him for a short while.

On a more positive note, he did have Hild. She had already grabbed the bow off him, claiming to possess some skill in its use. Her father had been denied the son he'd always wanted, she said, and so he had been determined to teach his daughter to use a bow, both for hunting and for self-defence. She swore, with no small amount of pride, that she could take down a squirrel from fifty paces nine times out of ten. Even so, it was not the most powerful bow he had ever seen and he doubted it would be much use against mail, but she might get lucky. More encouraging, though, was her demeanour; her fierce determination was about the only thing holding Brithnoth's resolve in place. Thurkill could not have been more impressed to find that her fair exterior masked a warrior heart that matched his own.

Hild had guided them to the point nearest to Eahlmund's house. Having given away the spear and bow, Thurkill now only had his seax which was too short to be much use in a hand to hand fight against trained warriors. He needed his war-axe and that meant getting into the barn next door to retrieve it from the rafters where he had hidden it the day after his arrival. Only then would the odds be tipped a little more in his favour. He just hoped his strength had returned sufficiently to enable him to make a decent fist of what was to come.

From his vantage point, he had a good view of what was happening in the village. But for the five Norman soldiers and Eahlmund, the place looked deserted. His friend looked terrible, though. He was kneeling in the middle of the village square, his head bowed and his face bloodied from what looked to have been a savage beating. Not far from him lay the prostrate form of his father, a dark patch spreading away from his chest where the fatal wound had struck him. The only other person in sight was the village headman. Nothelm was standing on a small barrel that had been positioned beneath the roof beams of the church, from which a rope dangled, the end of which had been looped around his neck. Thurkill glanced sideways at Hild to see she had also noticed her father's predicament. Though her eyes burned with hatred, she showed no other signs of reacting.

Nodding empathetically, Thurkill turned back to assess the strength of the enemy. One of them seemed to be out of action. Sitting with his back against the church wall, his leg bound with bloodstained strips of cloth, he looked pale and listless as if not long for this world. Thurkill allowed himself a wry smile; *at least the old boy had not died in vain.*

His survey complete, he whispered his instructions to his companions. "We need to move quickly. There's no telling how long we have until they decide to bring matters to an end. But first I need you to wait here while I get my axe. Then, when I give the signal, we attack."

"What will be the signal? How will we know?" Brithnoth's voice cracked as he spoke.

"You'll know, my friend. Trust me." He put a steadying hand on the other man's shoulder, fixing him with a firm glare. As he did so, he noted with no little satisfaction that the farmhand seemed to calm himself a little. Confronted with the sight of Eahlmund, he had found a hitherto unknown reserve of courage. Whatever the reason for it, Thurkill was grateful, feeling his own spirits rise as a result. Perhaps they did have some small chance of success after all.

As he watched, however, things took a turn for the worse. At a word from the man who seemed to be in charge, two of the soldiers strode over to the blacksmith's house, where each of them grabbed a burning log from the forge. Holding the firebrands at arm's length, they headed towards the far end of the village where they proceeded to set fire to the thatch. Even though the straw was damp from recent autumnal showers, it did not take long to burst into flames.

"That changes things," Thurkill sighed. "But at the same time, it might help. Now, two of the bastards are otherwise engaged and may take a moment or two to react. Let's delay no longer. Be ready for the signal."

With that he stole away, seax in hand, half crouching, half running behind the row of houses until he had reached the rear wall of the barn. There he stopped, holding his breath and listening for any sign of his having been detected. Hearing nothing, he allowed himself to exhale slowly, giving thanks to God that they had decided to fire the end of the village furthest from him.

The door to the barn faced off to the main path through the village so there was no way he could use that entrance without being seen. On this side, however, there was a small window, just over half a man's height up the wall. It would be tight but he was sure he could squeeze through without too much difficulty.

Once on the inside, he ran to where he had left his weapon, up in the rafters wrapped in his torn and blood-stained cloak, the pungent smell of it bringing back painful memories of the battle. He grabbed hold of the shaft, feeling a new sense of strength and courage coursing through his veins, dispelling the torpor that had threatened to swamp him. He hefted the weapon, taking pleasure in its familiar weight and balance. He had not had a chance to sharpen it since the battle so it had lost some of its edge and still bore more than a few nicks and notches from where it had bitten iron, wood and bone. Nevertheless, he was confident it would still serve its deadly purpose.

Next to it lay his battered shield, emblazoned with the tattered remnants of the Wessex wyvern and still with one or two arrow heads protruding from the battered boards. In truth, it was well beyond its useful life and would never see service in the shieldwall again, but needs must. It might yet block a blow or two. Twinges of pain shot up his forearm as he lifted the shield into position, but they soon faded. He flexed his grip on the leather strap, testing the strength and resilience of his arm. It had not been called upon since the battle for anything other than the most basic of tasks. To his delight, the newly knitted flesh held firm. Nor was his movement hindered in any way. The muscles seemed ready to go to work and the memory of long hours spent training with the heavy shield had not been forgotten. Though not at his best, he was stronger than he had dared hope.

A series of shouts from without reminded him of the job ahead of him. By the sounds of it, the two other soldiers had taken once again to beating poor Eahlmund. Thurkill didn't understand the language but the tone was enough to go by. Most likely they were demanding to know the whereabouts of other fugitives in the area. It did not really matter, though; they would pay dearly whatever the case.

Standing by the door, Thurkill used the narrow gaps between the warped wall planks to peer outside. The wounded man had now slumped over to one side, unconscious at least, but quite probably dead. *That's one fewer to worry about,* he smiled. Nevertheless, there were still four of them and he would have to work quickly if he were to survive. He had to act while they were still separated. Dispatch the two men by the church while the others were out of reach. To take on all four together, would surely see them all killed.

There was no time for sophistication in his planning; surprise, speed and aggression would have to see him through. He just hoped Hild and Brithnoth were ready. He took one final look through the slats to fix the location of the two nearest soldiers precisely in his mind, and then took and held a deep breath.

Then Thurkill raised his right foot and smashed it through the rickety barn door, splintering the wood with a noise that seemed to echo off the surrounding buildings. In the same instant he was out into the open and running towards the nearest Norman, screaming in rage. As he thundered over the packed earth, he saw two things happening; Brithnoth, the brave as he would henceforth be known, had leapt from cover and was charging towards the other man with his spear held out firmly in front of him. At the same time, Hild had taken up position to one side and was now nocking an arrow in place ready to draw. Confused by the sudden commotion, the two other soldiers, still busy firing the thatched rooves at the far end of the village, turned to stare in astonishment. Moments later, they started to run back, dropping their torches and dragging swords from scabbards as they came.

The two nearest soldiers, however, were frozen to the spot, torn between the twin threats of the archer and spearman on one side and the death-bringing warrior charging out of the barn. Their indecision proved to be their undoing. With a huge lunge, Thurkill ploughed into his man, shoving his shield boss into his chest, and knocking aside his sword which he had managed to raise at the last minute to meet the threat. The force of the impact sent him sprawling backwards a full six feet. Before he could recover, Thurkill was on him, smashing the axe blade against his skull.

Without a moment's hesitation, he spun round to face the second man. To his credit, Brithnoth's had scored a hit on his upper thigh opening a wound which, if not immediately life threatening, was enough to hamper his movement. The two of them were now circling each other, the Norman trying to keep his damaged leg to the rear while using his sword to fend off Brithnoth's jabs. Fifty or so paces away, he could see Hild, her bow drawn back to her chin, waiting for an opportunity to loose an arrow, but the Norman was no fool, deliberately keeping Brithnoth between him and her as much as possible.

None of his skill and guile, however, could prevent an attack in the rear from Thurkill. There was no honour in it, but he had no choice. The man had to be put down before his two remaining comrades could reach them. Relying on brute force more than the axe's blunted edge, he swung it as hard as he could in a horizontal arc, connecting with the side of the Norman's helmetless head. It was like a tree being felled; his eyes rolled up into the back of his head as he collapsed on the spot, unconscious, his legs unable to support his weight.

"Look out!" Hild's urgent shout from behind alerted him to the imminent danger. Twisting round, he raised his shield more in hope than expectation, but his instincts were good. The onrushing Norman's sword crashed heavily into its battered edge, severing a large segment of the wood in the process. It had done its job, though, saving his life one final time. In fury, he hurled what remained of it at his assailant's face. It took him by surprise, forcing him to take a step back and to one side. Seizing the opportunity, Thurkill unleashed a wild flurry of vicious two-handed blows, driving his opponent back step by step as he hurriedly parried each strike.

To his right, Brithnoth was now sorely pressed by the fourth soldier. The poor lad was not a warrior by any stretch and was fighting desperately for his life. He had done well to injure the first man, but had been helped by the initial surprise of the attack. It was surely only a matter of time before he fell victim to the more experienced and deadlier fighter. With his own fight on his hands, though, Thurkill was powerless to help him. He could only pray that he could hold out a while longer.

Meanwhile, he wasn't having it all his own way either. His opponent was blessed with an abundance of skill with the sword and – having withstood his frenzied attack with aplomb – he was now starting to assert himself. Thurkill took a moment to weigh up his options, deciding subterfuge would be the best, albeit riskiest, option. He took a step or two back, as if trying to disengage from the fight. At the same time, he puffed out his cheeks blowing heavily through his mouth, taking great gulps of air as if struggling for breath. As he hoped, the Norman came on at him. Backing off still further, he offered no more than cursory blocks until he once again leaned over, resting his hands on his thighs for a moment.

The ruse worked like a charm; grinning in triumph, the Norman closed in to finish Thurkill. But before his killing blow could land, the Saxon stepped neatly to the left and smashed the haft of his axe into the Norman's face with every bit of strength he had. The thick wood shattered the man's nose and mouth.

Teeth flew in all directions while blood sprayed from his ruined nostrils. Amazingly, he did not fall; he was so dazed, however, that he swayed where he stood, tears of pain streaming uncontrollably from his eyes. Without mercy, Thurkill kneed him in the balls and then punched his seax hard into his gut as he was doubled over in agony. This time he went down and did not move.

That left just one to deal with; he hoped he was not too late. Turning, he saw his worst fears were true. The Norman had Brithnoth at his mercy. The farmhand had lost his footing and had fallen back to land in a heap on his arse. But now Hild finally had the chance she had been waiting for and she let fly with her arrow. True to her word, her aim from fifty paces was good; the missile struck the soldier squarely in the chest as he raised his sword above his head ready to bear down on Brithnoth. Although it failed to penetrate his mail shirt, the punch it delivered was enough to make him stagger back. With surprising speed, Brithnoth was on his feet in an instant, running at the soldier, howling with emotion, fear and anger. He hit the soldier so hard that the blade punched its way through the mail shirt and out through his back. Pumping his legs hard, Brithnoth's momentum carried the two men several more paces until they slammed into the wall of the church close by to where Hild's father was still bound. The Norman clawed futilely at the spear, trying to free himself, but the damage was done. The blade had eviscerated his vital organs and it was just a matter of time until he bled out.

In shock, Brithnoth let go of the spear, staring dumbly at the dying man, as if unable to comprehend what he had done. "I've never killed anyone before," he mumbled, before turning his head to one side and puking profusely.

Thurkill strode over to him and placed a protective arm round his still heaving shoulders. "I'm proud of you, Brithnoth. I didn't think you had it in you but you have shown great courage and strength to defend your friend."

Hild, meanwhile, had rushed over to her father and removed the bindings from his wrists and the rope from around his neck. Now Nothelm stood there, rubbing his forearms to get the blood flowing again, while shaking his head at the carnage around him. By now, half the village was in flames but with the wind blowing as it was, the rest of the houses should escape the conflagration.

Before Thurkill could speak, however, a low groan sounded just behind him. Eahlmund! Spinning round, he saw his friend lying on his side, vainly trying to pull himself over to where his father's body lay. His face was a mask of blood and dirt through which tears had worn a streaky path.

He rushed over to help him. "Rest easy, my friend. There's nothing you can do for him now."

The poor lad was in a sorry state. Both eyes were swollen, half closed and rapidly blackening. The angle of his nose was crooked, clearly broken, and there was blood caked around his mouth. Thurkill wasn't sure how many teeth had been missing before, but there certainly seemed to be more gaps there now than he remembered.

"They have made a bit of a mess of your face, I'm afraid, but perhaps that's no bad thing. It could not be any worse than it was before."

Despite his anguish, the young man managed a brief smile, before wincing in pain. "I know you mean well, Thurkill, but please don't try to make me laugh, it hurts too much. I think I most of my ribs are broken as well."

Hild emerged from her father's house carrying a bowl of water with a rag in it. As gently as she could, she knelt beside Eahlmund to begin wiping the worst of the dirt and blood from his ravaged features, working her way deftly round the worst of the bruises. Once she had finished, she leaned forward to plant a delicate kiss on Eahlmund's forehead, carefully selecting one of the few spots on his face that had not been damaged.

Thurkill then helped his friend to his feet and, supported between him and Hild, they made their way over slowly to where Nothelm knelt next to the body of Ealdric. He had his arm round Estrith, who had now emerged from her hiding place, comforting her as best he could. The intensity of her sobs made it hard for them to hear the headman as he spoke.

"You should be proud of him, Eahlmund, and you too Estrith.

168

He was a brave man who did more than most to stand up for his people. He shall not be forgotten in this village, I promise you that. He will be buried with honour by the altar, in pride of place."

His mother was still too distraught to speak, so Eahlmund took it upon himself to speak. Thurkill noted how quickly his friend appeared to have dealt with the horror of seeing his father killed before his own eyes. In the heat of the moment there simply wasn't the time to dwell on it. Eahlmund shrugged but otherwise showed no emotion. "I am proud to call him 'father', Nothelm. He died trying to protect me and his home. If I am ever half as good a man as he, I will have done enough to earn his respect. But not before then."

Thurkill coughed to break the awkward silence that followed. "What now, Nothelm?"

"We rebuild, that's what. This village has stood here as long as anyone can remember; perhaps back even to the time of the first of our people to come to this land. We will not let a few Norman thugs stop us."

Thurkill frowned. "I applaud your spirit, but what if others come looking for these fellows?"

"We'll bury them deep in the woods where they won't be found and claim that they passed through once they had burned the place. What's more important is that the people come back to the village to help us begin again. Will you help us? A man of your strength and leadership would be a great asset to us in our time of need, not to mention that some people," here he glanced sideways at his daughter, "would not want to see you go."

Thurkill blushed and stared at his feet, unable to meet the eyes of either Hild or her father. "I would like that more than anything but I fear I must leave. Almost ten days have passed since the battle and I have tarried here longer than I would have liked, as grateful as I am for your hospitality. I have kin who need me to the east among the people of Kent and, having seen what has happened here today, I fear for their safety."

As soon as he had finished speaking, Hild turned on her heel and ran into her home, but not before an involuntary gasp had escaped her lips. Thurkill made to follow her but Nothelm placed his hand gently on his shoulder to hold him back.

"If I know my daughter, she will want to be on her own for a while. She'll come around soon enough. It was the same when her mother died. Give her space or you'll risk a punch to the face. Trust me, I still have the bruises for my pains. For my part", he continued, "I respect your decision, as disappointing as it may be. I would do the same in your position."

***

She came to him in the dead of night. He had moved his bed to the barn so as not to intrude on Estrith and Eahlmund's grief after they had buried Ealdric that evening in a solemn service at the church. Unable to sleep, he lay there staring at the roof beams, listening to the gentle cooing and occasional fluttering of the doves that made their home there. Hild was never far from his thoughts. He didn't want to leave her but he had no choice. He had sworn an oath to protect his sister and he had left it too long already. What if she were already dead? Ravaged and defiled. Foul images flooded his mind, pushing his thoughts of Hild to the far recesses of his brain. If Edith had been hurt in any way, he would never be able to forgive himself. Nor, he thought grimly, would he ever forgive those that committed such foul deeds. They would regret the day they ever crossed his path.

His mind was in such turmoil that he almost didn't hear the door of the barn being gently pushed open, its base scraping almost imperceptibly across the earthen floor. He tracked the gentle padding of her footsteps as she crossed to where he lay and shivered as she lifted the edge of his cloak that he was using as a blanket, to slide in beside him. His heart began to race as he realised she was naked. Ignoring the blocks of ice that were her arms and legs he wrapped himself around her, driving his warmth into her. Deep waves of pleasure flowed through him, everything about her was perfect; her scent, her soft hair against his face, the smooth skin of her body…everything.

"Hild, I …."

Before he could say another word, however, Hild lifted herself on one elbow and pressed her index finger against his lips. Then she buried her head into his shoulder and held him tight. He lay there once more, staring at the roof, his mind awash with a thousand different emotions. Hild's breathing was smooth and even, showing that she had already fallen asleep, though his shoulder was still damp where her tears had flowed unchecked.

TWENTY-THREE

24 October, Brightling

The villagers paused in their work to watch him leave. He wore his mailshirt, burnished to a fine hue by Estrith, and hiked up at the waist by a new leather belt - gifted by Nothelm – into which he'd slotted his axe. Over the top, helping to keep his armour and weapon hidden from the casual observer, he wore a new woollen cloak, a deep green in colour and wonderfully warm. It had been Hild's leaving present to him, left for him by the hay bales where they had lain together the previous night.

For now, though, she was nowhere to be seen. She had left before the dawn's first light, saying that she would not watch him go. She understood why he had to leave, but that did not mean she could be happy about it. For his part, Thurkill had held her tight one last time, pressing her against his chest. He had promised to come back for her as soon as he could. It was a promise he had meant and one that he hoped he could keep. Leaving her now was more painful than any physical wound he had ever received, but he had no choice. His first duty was to his kin. With his father gone, there was no one else to care for them. In his mind, he foresaw a time when he might bring his family back to Brightling, or else have Hild join him at his hall. First, however, he had to make sure that the village still stood and that Aga and Edith were alive. He could not silence the nagging fear that all might not be well.

Feeling lonelier than he had for a while, he cast around for one last time, seeing only blank expressions on those who had gathered in the village square. Even Eahlmund was not there. He had seen him earlier that morning as he had paid his final respects by the side of Ealdric's grave. His friend had said little as he'd stood, head bowed, deep in thought. He feared more than anything that Eahlmund in some way might hold him responsible for his father's death. *Perhaps if I hadn't been messing about with Hild in the woods, he might not have died?*

He pushed the thought from his mind. If he had been there, there was a good chance he would have been captured or killed by the Normans as well.

Other than the few buildings that still smoked from where they had been fired, there was little sign of the previous day's fight. The bodies had been removed and buried in the darkest recesses of the forest. Blood-stained earth had been turned over to remove all traces. Even the ruined buildings would soon be replaced; men had already started to bring back newly felled trunks from which they would fashion new planks. In a few days there would be little or no sign of anything untoward having happened. Thurkill just hoped they managed to finish the work before any more Normans came snooping.

He took one last look around the village, hoping more than expecting to see Hild appear. Then he turned and headed along the east road. He had only gone a few paces, however, when a voice called out.

"Wait."

He turned, his heart quickening, hoping Hild had changed her mind after all, but it was not to be. Instead he saw his friend, Eahlmund, lumbering up the path towards him, weighed down with spear in one hand, a shield slung on his back and a bulging sack on his right shoulder. He kept running until he had pulled level with Thurkill whereupon he stopped, hands on knees, panting as if his lungs would burst.

"What are you doing, friend?"

He was still trying to catch his breath, the words flung out in between gasps for air. "I... couldn't... let you go... on your own. You might... get yourself killed."

Thurkill laughed but not unkindly. "Well, I am grateful for your protection, Eahlmund, but what about your mother? Surely her need is greater than mine now that your father is gone?"

"Don't you believe it; she is quite happy to have me out from under her feet. She has moved in with her sister so that Brithnoth and his family can have our home as theirs has been burned down. With her in there too, there's not a lot of room and especially not if you add me into the mix too."

"Nevertheless, is this what you really want? Who knows what lies ahead? We will doubtless find ourselves in more fights before too long."

"It will be as God wills it. You saved my life yesterday so there is a debt to be paid, that's how I see it."

"But not one that I expect you to pay, friend. You are not bound to me in any way."

"Look, the fact of the matter is that you are stuck with me and that's that. Now, which way are we going?" With that, Eahlmund strode off purposefully in the direction Thurkill had been walking, leaving him smiling and shaking his head in his wake.

"And anyway," Eahlmund called back over his shoulder. "I'm hoping you'll put in a good word for me with your sister. Though if she's as ugly as you I may not hold you to that."

"Why, you cheeky bastard! She's way too good for you and..." Thurkill caught himself as he realised it was a joke. Eahlmund had doubled over again, this time made insensible by uncontrollable peals of laughter.

TWENTY-FOUR

26 October, Haslow

It was late afternoon on the third day after leaving Brightling when Thurkill and Eahlmund arrived at the outskirts of Haslow. It had been an uneventful journey, deliberately so on Thurkill's part as he had stayed away from the major roads and paths to avoid any chance meeting with marauding soldiers. If truth be told, though, he had no idea where the Normans were. Surely they would have advanced on Lundenburh or Wintanceastre by now? Nonetheless, it could do no harm to be cautious.

They approached from the south, careful to remain out of sight until they knew what awaited them. The land on this side of the village was thickly wooded and given over to foraging for upwards of fifty pigs. If Thurkill's memory served him right, they were cared for by a father and son who went by the names of Osfric and Osfrith. Their family had been swineherds for as long as anyone cared to remember and it was often said that old Osfric loved his pigs more than he did other people. Thurkill smiled at the memory, hoping that the old man was still thrived.

"Is it far now?" Eahlmund asked for the umpteenth time that day, his cheeky grin showing he was deliberately trying to irk Thurkill.

The young warrior decided not to rise to the bait. "Just on the other side of these woods, then across the meadow and we'll be there."

"Good, because I'm starving. One of these pigs," he pointed to large sow that was snuffling its way from tree to tree searching for mushrooms and truffles amongst the mast, "would be nice. Can we take one with us?"

"You'll have me to answer to if you do, you young scamp."

"Osfric!" Thurkill was genuinely pleased to see him.

The old man came over to them, leaning heavily on his staff, keeping the weight off his left leg as much as possible. "It's good to see you, young master Thurkill. There's many here who thought you were lost along with your father in battle, but I knew differently."

"You've had news about Scalpi?"

"I'm sorry to say we have. One of the lads who went with you to the battle made it back here a few days ago. Just the one mind; I don't suppose the other three will ever come back. Anyway, he – Aethelnoth it was, the smith's son – he told us that he had seen your father killed, dying with honour while defending the king. He also said he saw you lying nearby but had lost sight of you when he was swept up in the rout."

"I was as good as dead, knocked unconscious and separated from one my ears." He pushed his straggly hair back to reveal the ugly, red scar where his ear had once been.

Osfric eased himself down onto a fallen log, grunting as he stretched his left leg out in front of him. "Hmmm, better an ear than the whole head, I suppose. You must have left before Aga arrived then."

The news shocked Thurkill, causing his legs to almost give way beneath him. "My aunt was at the battlefield? When? Why?"

"She made Aethelnoth take her back to the battlefield. He didn't want to go, I can tell you, but she made him all the same. She wanted to find her brother's body and bring it back. Yours too, I shouldn't wonder. In hindsight, though, it proved to be a bad idea."

Thurkill felt his heartbeat racing faster with each moment. "Why do you say that? Is she alright?"

"Yes, yes, she's fine," Osfric said impatiently, irritated at the interruption. "She found Scalpi alright, but she also found some Normans."

"Tell me what happened, for God's sake." He realised he had raised his voice in his eagerness to find out. "Quickly," he hissed, more quietly.

Osfric grinned knowingly. "You always were the impatient one, young Thurkill. I see this has not changed."

The old man hawked and spat into the pile of leaves to his side, clearing his throat to begin his tale. "Well, as I had it from Aethelnoth, the Normans were still camped by the battlefield when they arrived and it was not long before their presence attracted the wrong sort of attention. She was taken before their

Duke William so he could ask her what her business was there.

"Well, she's a proud woman as you know, so she held her head high and calmly stated that she had come to claim the body of Scalpi, loyal thegn of King Harold so he could be buried with honour back at his hall. This amused the Duke but, apparently, he was impressed with her courage and fortitude so he allowed her to proceed and even provided an escort. A dozen of his knights were assigned to help her find the body and to bring it back here."

"She was treated with honour and respect?" Despite himself, his hand strayed to his seax as if he would be able to strike down anyone who had harmed Aga right there and then.

"No one says any different, Lord."

It was the first time that Osfric, or anyone for that matter, had used that title when addressing him and it shocked him. Of course, with his father dead, he was – in name at least – the Lord of Haslow; though it would not be true in law until confirmed by a king. Either way, he felt a sense of responsibility that had not occurred to him before. The people of Haslow were now under his protection. They looked to him for security and justice.

"They returned here not three days since; Aga and Aethelnoth riding on a wagon pulled by two oxen on which lay Scalpi's body, dressed in his armour and wrapped in a fresh cloak. The escort came with them, riding six in front and six behind. Now I don't mind telling you that they were the finest but also the foulest looking fellows I ever saw. Covered head to foot in armour and with faces as grim and as hard as any you might hope to encounter. The leader in particular was an especially ugly brute. All glowering looks, scowling and an ugly red scar running across his face. It wouldn't pay to cross that one, I daresay."

Thurkill caught his breath. It couldn't be, could it? Surely many men bore the scars of battle on their faces, especially after the events of recent days. He put the thought from his mind; it was coincidence, nothing more or less. Nonetheless, it might pay to tread carefully just in case. "Where are they now, these knights?"

"Still here, Lord, and showing no signs of leaving just yet, if I'm any judge."

Thurkill raged inside. This was his village by rights; to have it infested with these foul scum was beyond the pale. "What makes you say that, Osfric?"

"Well, they've made themselves at home, that's for sure. Kicked your aunt and sister out of their hall and installed themselves in there instead. Doing their best to eat their way through all your stores as well. In fact, I've been sent out here to bring in yet another of my herd for tonight's feast, if you please. And I doubt they'll pay me for it either."

"Has no one tried to stop them?" Thurkill could feel his ire rising once again. This was his land and he was not going to stand by and allow it to be pillaged by these Norman whoresons.

Osfric looked hurt, as if the challenge had been directed at him personally. "If you could suggest how a bunch of farmhands and shepherds are supposed to stand up to a dozen heavily armed warriors, I'd be all ears." He paused... "No offence intended, Lord, but we can do no more; to do so would be to invite death and we all have families that depend on us. A few of us already have bumps and bruises to show for our pains." He pointed at his leg which he proceeded to rub tenderly for good measure.

"My apologies, Osfric. I did not mean to suggest a lack of honour or courage on your part. It is the situation that angers me, not you. If my father were here, I'm sure he would have a plan all figured out by now." Thurkill sat down heavily on the log, next to Osfric, resting his chin on his palm as he did so.

Eventually, Thurkill lifted his head. "Wait. You said that my kin had been kicked out of the hall?" Osfric nodded. "Where are they now?"

"They have taken up lodging with old Swifhilda in her hut on the edge of these woods. She lives on her own and had room to spare for them."

"I will go there now. It's getting dark and we need a place to bed down for the night. My thanks, Osfric." Thurkill stood, clapping the swineherd on the shoulder as he rose.

***

It was a short walk to Swifhilda's hut. The door had seen better days and was in need of replacement. Through the gaps where it no longer fitted snugly within its frame, he could see a shimmering light. He shivered in anticipation; both of the warmth of the fire that burned within and with the thought of seeing his kin again for the first time since he had left to go north with Harold to face the Vikings. It seemed like an age ago now; so much had happened in between.

The sound of a dog barking inside the hut brought him back to the moment. It was whining and scrabbling at the door, as if desperate to be released.

"Who's there?" His aunt's voice, although tremulous still retained a shadow of its familiar strength. Nevertheless, Thurkill was shocked to hear the change in her; she had once been so confident and commanding, sure of her position. All that had changed.

Without waiting to be invited, Thurkill pushed open the door and strode in, followed closely by Eahlmund. In unison, the three women within shrieked in response to his war-like appearance. At the same time, the dog bounded over and launched himself head first into his midriff, before proceeding to jump up at him repeatedly.

"Eric", he beamed, pleased to be reunited with his hound. "Down!" he roared more in jest than anger, trying fruitlessly to push the daft mutt away from him. But it was no good, Eric was not to be put off. Accepting the inevitable, Thurkill sank to his knees, allowing the dog to place his front paws on his shoulders and slobber his face with great sloppy licks of his huge, rough tongue.

In the meantime, Aga and Edith stared dumbly at him, open-mouthed in shock. "What?" he laughed, pushing the dog away as he rose to his feet. "Is your favourite nephew and brother not worthy of a hug to welcome him home?" Then with pretend peevishness, he added, "At least Eric is pleased to see me."

The spell was broken. As one, the two women threw themselves forward, wrapping Thurkill in their arms, crying and laughing in equal measure. It was Aga who recovered first.

"Thank the good Lord that you live, nephew. When you

179

didn't return from Senlac we feared the worst, especially...what with your father," she hesitated over this last, suddenly fearful that he might not yet know.

Thurkill nodded solemnly. "I was there with him at the end. Rest assured he died bravely, sword in hand, giving his life to defend his king."

Aga sniffed, her eyes welling with tears of pride and sorrow. "It pleases me to know that he did his duty until death." She gathered herself with a visible effort. "Anyway, look at the state of you. When was the last time your face saw water, it's filthy! And – good God – what's happened to your ear? I let you out of my sight for a few days and this is what happens?" She had to stand on tip toe to push his hair away to get a better look.

"Ach, don't fuss, woman," he grumbled good-naturedly. "'Tis no more than a scratch. This, on the other hand, was much worse." With an evil grin, he pulled back the sleeve of his tunic to reveal the long, jagged scar which ran half the length of his forearm from his wrist. "That almost did for me, I don't mind telling you" he said with boyish pride, with one eye on Edith to see her reaction. "But for the work of an old healer at Eahlmund's village, I would have died, I'm sure."

"Eahlmund? Is that the poor boy stood behind you whom you have, 'til now, failed to introduce?" she scolded.

Thurkill bowed respectfully, though his words dripped with playful sarcasm. "My sincerest apologies, dearest aunt and honoured sister. This," he waved his arm theatrically in the direction of his friend, "is Eahlmund, son of Ealdric, from the village of Brightling which stands three days' march to the south and west of here and but a mere stone's throw from the site of the battle. Eahlmund," he turned to face him, "This is my aunt, Aga, sister of my noble father, Scalpi and this is my sister, Edith, daughter of Scalpi."

With the introductions made, Thurkill went on to explain all that had happened at Senlac and beyond, while Swifhilda and Edith busied themselves preparing a simple meal of bread, cheese and apples. As they ate, Thurkill turned the conversation round to Aga and what had happened in the village.

"Why do I find you here, Aunt, lodging with Swifhilda, for

which," he nodded to her, "you have my everlasting gratitude, instead of in my father's hall where you belong?"

Aga looked down at the table, shame-faced. "There was nothing I could do, Killi. We were powerless to stop them. There may only be a dozen of them but they are warriors all and not afraid of a few farm-hands, women and old men. Though we are many, we are no match for them. They've already killed poor Aethelnoth."

Thurkill had not known this and he fought to control his emotions with difficulty. As a boy, he had trained with him with spear and shield on many occasions and had considered him a friend, a brother almost. "In God's name, why? What sort of threat was he to them?"

"He took exception to our eviction from the hall. Perhaps they were in a bad mood, or perhaps they wanted to make an example of him to the rest of us, but either way their leader simply drew his sword and cleaved him almost in two after he dared to stand up for us." Tears came once again to Aga's eyes as she called to mind what she had witnessed.

Thurkill hugged her reassuringly then released her. "Tell me more about their leader. What sort of man is he?"

Aga shuddered involuntarily at the thought. "As cruel a man in looks and deeds I never did see. He introduced himself as Richard, eldest son of the Count of Gilbert, though whoever or wherever that is I couldn't tell you.

"He is a dark-haired man, not as tall as you by any means, but thick-set. There's something about the way he looks at you that sends shivers down your spine. He doesn't have to raise his voice; it is the look in his eyes that pierces you and stops you cold; it's enough to make you do his bidding without question. The worst thing, however, is that scar. Long it is, all the way from the corner of his mouth to his ear, almost. When he speaks, it's like it's alive, dancing up and down across his face in time with his words."

Aga stopped, seeing the look on her nephew's face. "Do you know him, Killi?"

"I know of him, if it is the same man. He came to Lundenburh carrying a banner from the Pope, with a monk who demanded that Harold give up his throne. He was also the one who mutilated Harold's body without care or mercy. An evil bastard without any redeeming features."

Aga tutted absent-mindedly at the language, more out of habit than anything, causing Thurkill to laugh. "Aunt, I am not a boy to be molly-coddled any longer. Those days have passed. What's more I am now lord of this village with a duty to defend and protect those that live here. If I am to do that, I will have to do far worse than utter a few choice words."

Aga gave him a look of pride mixed with fear and determination in equal measure. "Your father would be proud if he could see and hear you now, of that I am certain. But what are we to do? Haslow is in the hands of these thugs who have set up home in your father's hall. We are forced to wait on them, to prepare feasts for them which they eat at your father's table. What's more," Aga continued, lowering her voice so that Edith would not hear, "I have seen the way this Richard looks at your sister. The longer this goes on, the more I fear for her."

Blinded by rage, Thurkill strode over to the door and punched his hand into the frame, oblivious to the pain. "That foul foreign filth will pay with his life if he so much as looks at her the wrong way."

Aga waited until the outburst had blown itself out before responding. "Have a care, nephew. Using violence against such numbers would not be wise. But perhaps, now the rightful lord of Haslow is back, things may be different. We should try at least to reason with them. After all, the reason they came here at all was because they said we needed their protection with you and your father both believed to have been slain on the battlefield."

Slumping down in his chair once more, Thurkill grunted, though it wasn't clear whether he was in agreement with Aga or not.

TWENTY-FIVE

27 October, Haslow

Thurkill woke just as the first rays of watery autumn sunshine began to stream through the gaps in the walls of Swifhelda's hut. The wind moved the tree branches back and forth making the light dance continually across his face, blinding his eyes every few moments, until he was unable to ignore it any longer.

Sitting up he panicked a little when he noticed that neither Aga or Edith were there, until he remembered his aunt saying they would be gone before dawn to oversee the preparation of breakfast for FitzGilbert and his men in the lord's hall. The knowledge that his kin were little more than slaves for the foreign invader in his own home did nothing to assuage his foul mood.

Perhaps sensing the strained atmosphere, Eahlmund's tone was overtly respectful. "God's blessings this fine morning, Lord. I would know your pleasure for the day."

Despite himself, Thurkill could not help but chuckle at his friend's awkward attempt at formal conversation; he was clearly unused to it. "There is no need for such ceremony between us, Eahlmund. Particularly when it is so clumsily done."

Eahlmund shrugged but smirked nonetheless, relieved at being excused such strictures. "Your pardon, Lord. I'm not used to talking to lords and all. Right then, so are we going to teach these Norman bastards some manners or what?"

"I fear it may not be as simple as that, my friend. Our guests control the playing board; they have many more pieces than us and arranged against ours in the strongest positions. We will need no small amount of luck and subterfuge if we are to come through this with all our pieces intact. First of all, however, we wait; and while we do that, I see no reason not to set about this fine meal that has been left for us."

***

Not long after they had finished, Aga came into the hut and placed a large bundle on the ground. Straightening up, she pushed her hands into the small of her back, trying to ease the muscles that ached with the effort of having carried the heavy burden all the way from the hall.

"I think that's everything you wanted. Well, at least I hope it is as I don't have time to fetch anything else. I need to get back before I am missed."

"My thanks, aunt. I will follow on shortly."

"You see that you tread carefully, Thurkill. I won't lose a brother and a nephew all within the same moon."

"Fear not. I have no intention of being reunited with my father just yet. Besides, I have Eahlmund here to keep me out of trouble."

Eahlmund laughed. "Some chance I'd have of stopping you from being a fool."

With Aga gone, Thurkill squatted down to open the bundle. Inside he was pleased to find all that he had requested. His father's best mail shirt which had been lovingly repaired and polished since it had been recovered, along with its owner's body, from the battlefield. There were also two sets of clean clothes, the finest they possessed, including a new cloak with golden brooch and other of the finest accoutrements the family possessed. He intended to make an impression and he hoped that what he had available to him now would do just that.

"Right, Eahlmund. You're to play the part of my trusted captain. It will be a stretch, of course, but I need you to get out of your farmer's rags and put on these nice clothes. On top of that you can wear my mailshirt and this new cloak here. I'll take my father's shirt."

Eahlmund looked dubious, but began to remove his clothes all the same. "You know that if you put a pig in a dress, it's still a pig?"

Thurkill laughed. "Yes, I know few would ever believe you are of noble birth, but if you keep your mouth shut and let me do the talking then we should be alright. Just concentrate on looking as menacing as you can."

Although he was considerably larger in build than his father had been, Thurkill found that the mail shirt was a decent fit; a little snug under the armpits but not so much as to affect his agility too much. He wondered whether Aga had adjusted it in some way. With it on, he marvelled at how shiny it seemed in the light of the sun that streamed through the windows. The smell and touch of it brought a lump to his throat as it brought back memories of the day he and his father had set off to Lundenburh to join up with Harold's army.

Shaking his head to clear his mind, he got back to the task in hand. He buckled the leather belt around his middle, pulling it tight so that it helped take up some of the weight of the heavy mail. From the belt he hung his seax and axe, one on either side of his body. Then, reaching down, he picked up the cloak Hild had given him, throwing it round his shoulders before using the ornate golden clasp to fasten it at his left shoulder. To finish, he grabbed the bone comb that Swifhilda had left on the table and proceeded to force it through his unkempt mop of hair. Multiple curses and painful winces later, he gave up. It would have to do. Shrugging to himself, he turned to check on Eahlmund's progress.

He could not prevent a sharp intake of breath. "By God's hairy scrotum, but you gave me a shock. I almost didn't recognise you for a minute." The transformation was nothing short of remarkable. Gone was the grubby farm worker and in his place stood, for all intents and purposes, a full-blown huscarl. Not as tall as Thurkill but no less imposing for that. Years spent working the land had left him with a frame that was as muscled as any warrior. The mailshirt fitted him like a second skin, and he was clearly relishing the feel of the fine clothes, never having worn anything so luxurious in all his life.

The only thing that ruined the look was the fact that he stood there grinning like an idiot; like a new-born foal filled with wonder at its first steps into the world. Removing the sword from its sheath at his side – a weapon no one of his station could ever hope to afford, let alone use – he proceeded to swing it wildly around his head, making cuts and thrusts at an imaginary enemy, accompanied by challenges and insults shouted at the top of his voice.

Thurkill laughed and clapped his hands appreciatively. "Well, there's no faulting your enthusiasm, but your sword-skills could do with a bit of work."

"I think I could get used to this, my friend. Prancing around like a pretty peacock seems preferable to slaving away in a muddy field on a rainy day. Is this all that you noble boys do all day?"

"That and stuff ourselves silly and drink ourselves insensible every night; it's a great life, for sure. Right, it's time we were going. Remember, leave the talking to me but keep your wits about you. I've no idea how this may turn out and we may need to be fleet of mind and foot if things go awry."

***

They were met at the door of the hall by two Norman soldiers. If the full impact of his situation hadn't been apparent to Thurkill before, then this simple barrier brought it home beyond all doubt. He had not imagined to find the way into his own hall barred by the outstretched, mailed arm of a grim-faced soldier. The soldier barked some harsh words in his own tongue in a voice that exuded authority. Having no idea what had been said, Thurkill simply made as if to push past. "Out of my way, man. Would you dare stop me from entering my own hall?"

The soldier took a step to his left, now fully blocking Thurkill's path. Simultaneously, he placed his gloved hand squarely in his chest and gave a firm shove while repeating the same words, but even more aggressively than before. Taken by surprise, Thurkill was forced to take a couple of steps back to avoid losing his balance.

He was momentarily confused, unsure how to react. He felt his cheeks colouring; anger mixed with the embarrassment of being treated in this way on his own land. To make matters worse, a number of villagers had stopped to watch the exchange, doubtless having recognised Scalpi's son. He could not afford to lose face this early in proceedings, but he was equally aware that he must tread carefully. He was supposed to be the Lord of Haslow and he could not afford to act like a rampaging bull. Not just yet, at least.

He took a step forward and drew himself up to his full height, squaring his shoulders as he did so in order to maximise the effect. He stood a good head taller than the soldier, resplendent in his Saxon lord's finery. With an exaggerated flourish, he swept the cloak back to reveal the hilt of his axe, a gesture that he hoped could not be mistaken. At the same time he put his hands on his hips and barked. "My name is Thurkill, son of Scalpi, and I am lord of this village. I demand entrance to my own hall so that I may speak with your lord." He knew that the soldier could not understand a word he said but hoped at least that his tone, as authoritative as he could muster, would leave no doubt as to his importance.

The solider, however, remained steadfastly unimpressed. He repeated the same words but also added a few more while pointing meaningfully at Thurkill's axe.

From behind him, Eahlmund leaned forward. "I think he wants us to leave our weapons here with him before he'll let us in." It was an age-old tradition amongst their people too, dating back to more volatile times. Only the lord and his bodyguard were allowed to carry blades of any kind within the hall. Quite apart from the fear of assassination, there was always the chance that a drunken argument could get out of hand, so the absence of weapons helped keep the carnage to a minimum. It was a further kick in the balls to have to comply but he had no option unless he wanted to start a fight right there and then.

Irritably he snapped at Eahlmund. "That much is clear, even to me. It doesn't mean I have to like it though."

Nevertheless, he removed his axe, handing it and his seax to the soldier and indicating that Eahlmund should do likewise. The door warden then nodded his satisfaction and stepped to one side to allow them entry.

Once inside, the memories came flooding back. Though it had been not much more than a month since he was last here, it still felt like a lifetime. Familiar smells assailed his nostrils: the wood fire in the central hearth; meat roasting on a spit being turned by a young churl. He almost expected to see his father seated in the lord's chair at the far end of the hall.

When he did look, however, it was not his father he saw but the same, scar-faced Norman who had come to Harold's feast in his palace in Lundenburh before the battle. The same man who had so cruelly and so foully butchered the king as he lay wounded on the field of battle. He was slouched in his father's chair with one leg draped over the arm, In one hand he held a goblet of wine and had what looked like a pork rib in the other, the juices of which were dripping down his chin and onto his tunic. Thurkill had to fight hard to stifle the feelings of revulsion and anger that washed over him.

He walked forward slowly, giving himself time to slow his breathing and to take in the rest of the occupants of the hall so he might see what they were up against. Sat behind the same bench as scar-face were two more Normans, presumably captains whose rank entitled them to eat with their lord. Elsewhere, a further half-dozen soldiers lounged at benches along the side walls. Most of them were too engrossed in the food and drink set before them to bother with him, but one or two looked up, looks of undisguised disdain on their faces.

Aga and Edith were also present. Both had immediately taken notice of his arrival, worry etched on their faces.

FitzGilbert had appeared not to notice the newcomers, however. He was more concerned that his cup was empty. "Hey, woman! More wine." His grasp of the Saxon tongue was basic to say the least but effective, his barked order sending Edith scurrying away to fetch another skin.

By now, Thurkill – with Eahlmund no more than a pace behind his left shoulder – had reached the dais on which the top table stood. He stood there, shoulders back, head held high, waiting to be invited to speak. After several moments, during which his impatience grew immeasurably, FitzGilbert finally looked up from the conversation he had been having with the soldier to his right.

"Who are you?" His words were terse and to the point.

With a great effort of will, Thurkill managed to remain respectful as the old Saxon traditions of hospitality demanded. "Lord, my name is Thurkill, son of Scalpi, lord of this village and the land surrounding it."

There was no sign of recognition or emotion on the part of the Norman; rather, he looked bored by the whole affair. "And what do you want with me, Saxon?" He spat the last word to make clear that he felt it to be an insult.

"I have come to offer my thanks to you for taking care of my lands in my absence and to relieve you of that burden. I have returned to claim this estate as my own in keeping with the laws of our fathers and their fathers, as the eldest surviving son of the previous lord."

"Returned from where?"

Thurkill hesitated momentarily, unsure whether he should reveal his presence in the recent battle. In the end he decided that he would gain nothing by trying to hide it. "From the battle at Senlac, where I stood with my father who died with honour defending his king."

The Norman yawned. "So, your father paid the price for standing against Duke William, the rightful king of this god-forsaken land. Do you not know that he was promised the throne by your King Edward? A claim which Harold himself swore on holy relics to support. Your Harold was no king in the eyes of God; he was a usurper and all those who fought for him were no better than traitors. And – also according to your laws – the lands of a traitor are forfeit. Haslow, and all the land which surrounds it, is mine now." As he finished he waved his hand dismissively as if indicating there was nothing more to discuss.

For a few moments, Thurkill was too stunned to reply. Eventually, though, rising indignation got the better of him, anger causing his voice to crack. "By what right do you dare deprive me of my birth right?"

"By right of conquest, boy; no more, no less. You fought and you lost. I cannot explain it any more simply than that." Turning away from Thurkill as if there were no more to say on the subject, FitzGilbert then yelled, "By God's bones, woman, where is my wine? If I have to come and get it myself, you'll feel my belt across your back."

Thurkill bridled but held his peace with a huge effort of will, despite the double provocation of being called a boy and hearing his sister, the daughter of a lord no less, treated as if she were a common slave. Before he could reply, however, Edith returned with a fresh wineskin.

"Finally, by God! A man could die of thirst. Hurry up and fill my cup, Saxon whore."

Thurkill was about to speak when, out of the corner of his eye, he caught sight of Aga who – almost imperceptibly – shook her head as if to tell him to let it pass. The gesture reminded him of his father's advice; a man should be judged on knowing which battles to fight and which to avoid. Winning the war is more important that a single battle that gains you nothing.

By now, Edith was leaning over FitzGilbert, pouring a stream of the dark red liquid into his cup. As she did so, the Norman took the opportunity to grab a handful of her backside. As he did so, he grinned lasciviously and made a comment in his own tongue to his companions. In her shock at being groped, Edith stumbled, spilling wine all over FitzGilbert's tunic and crotch.

He jumped to his feet. "Merde! You stupid whore!" Without a moment's hesitation he swung an arm catching Edith squarely on the cheek with the back of his hand. The force of the blow was enough to send her sprawling to the ground where she lay sobbing with pain. Aga rushed to her side to comfort her as best she could.

Scalpi's words of wisdom flew out of his mind. This was more than he was prepared to stomach. Nonetheless, he retained an icy calm as he glared at FitzGilbert. "Touch her again and you die, Norman."

A hush descended across the hall. Every single one of the Norman soldiers now turned to stare at the Saxon. Though they might be ignorant of the meaning of the words, the cold fury behind them was unmistakeable. Even FitzGilbert paused in the act of wiping down his wine-soaked clothes. Eventually he resumed his seat and smiled. "I am sorry, Thurkill son of Scalpi, but it sounded to me like you just threatened me in my own hall."

Though the smile could not hide the murderous intent in FitzGilbert's eyes, Thurkill was not to be cowed so easily. "Your ears do not fail you, Norman. And it is a threat I will make good on if you harm her again."

"Perhaps I was not clear before. My mastery of your tongue is not good, after all. This hall, everything in it, the whole village and all the people that live here belong to me now. And as their lord, I will do what I will with them, all of them."

To emphasise the point, he moved over to where Edith now sat, wrapped in her aunt's arms. Without a word he bent down, grabbed her by the hair and hauled her to her feet. Once upright, he then seized her by the throat and pulled her towards him. Forcing his mouth over hers, he held her in place for what seemed an age, before roughly pushing her away. For her part, Edith endured the ordeal, allowing herself to go limp until she was released.

Before Eahlmund could stop him, Thurkill charged forward, bounding on to the dais and lunging forward to try to reach the smirking Norman. Blinded by rage, with no weapon to hand, he had no idea what he would do if he reached him, but that was not the point. It was an act born of desperation and was doomed to failure, but his honour could not allow the insult to his own sister to stand.

But, anticipating just such a move, the two captains were quick to intervene. One grabbed him by the arm and throat, forcing his face down hard against the table's solid oak surface while the other held a deadly looking dagger to his neck, pricking the skin so hard that he felt a trickle of blood. At the same time, two more soldiers rushed in from either side, pinning Eahlmund's arms to his sides and rendering him immobile.

Unfazed, FitzGilbert grinned. "A foolish reaction, but one that was not unexpected from a brainless Saxon oaf such as you. It is no wonder you were defeated."

Thurkill struggled against his captors but it was useless; their grip on him was too strong. At any moment he expected the knife to be rammed home, ending his life and condemning his sister to her fate. Inwardly, he cursed his impetuosity; he was no use to anyone dead. Would he ever learn to curb his temper?

FitzGilbert, meanwhile, was pacing up and down behind his chair, apparently deep in thought. "I don't understand you, Saxon. Why forfeit your life for this serving girl, pretty though she may be? It makes no sense."

Thurkill kept silent, suddenly aware of the danger he had created for Edith by his foolhardy outburst. His heart beat furiously against his chest as he felt the panic rise in him.

"I understand something of your culture, so I know that a lord has a duty to take care of all those who rely on him for protection, but that alone does not explain your actions. There must be more to it. What more is she worth to you?"

Suddenly, he stopped pacing, coming to a halt right beside Thurkill. Bending over he pushed the shaggy mane of hair away from the Saxon's face, chuckling as he caught sight of the missing ear. Having stared straight at Thurkill's face for several moments, he then looked over to where Edith stood. After two or three more looks, he began to nod, realisation dawning in his mind.

"All becomes clear. Same nose, same cheek bones, same eyes. I would say that makes you part of the same family." He paused, as if running the calculations through his mind. "Not that different in age from what I can see; she's your little sister, isn't she? Now that would explain your behaviour."

Thurkill said nothing. The truth was out and there was no point denying it. Both their lives now hung by a thread; a thread that could snap at any moment.

"Luckily for you, you find me in a good mood today. I have killed men for much less, but I am inclined to be magnanimous. We have only just been introduced and no doubt you would have hoped for this encounter to have played somewhat differently. I can understand your anger; I, too, would not be pleased to lose my ancestral home, but then I didn't lose the battle, so what would I know?" He could not stop himself from laughing at his own joke, before becoming serious once more.

"But you should know that this is the first and the only warning that I shall give you. If I see you on these lands again, I will hand your pretty little sister over to my men so that they may take turns with her. After that experience, I think it's safe to say that she will no longer be quite so sweet and pretty. That said, she might even enjoy it – make a woman of her. Most girls her age are married with children where I come from. In fact, I have a good mind to do her the honour of making her my whore. She has a certain comeliness that I find not unattractive. I trust I have made myself sufficiently clear?"

FitzGilbert then waved to his two soldiers, indicating that they should let Thurkill rise.

Despite his predicament, Thurkill was determined not to show weakness in the face of this callous dog. "Your time will come, Norman. Perhaps not today, perhaps not tomorrow but I will have my lands back. And if I hear that any harm has come to my sister it shall be visited upon you ten-fold. I will take pleasure from slitting your throat and watching you die."

Richard threw his head back and laughed. "A delightful image to be sure. I'm almost tempted to see you try." Almost immediately though, his face changed to a murderous stare, his cold, blue eyes piercing to the back of Thurkill's skull. "Do not try my patience, Saxon. I have agreed to let you live, now be gone before I change my mind."

TWENTY-SIX

28 October, Haslow

Thurkill threw his drinking horn against the wall of Osfric's hut, splintering it into several pieces. It was late into the night and he showed no signs of slowing down, driven on as he was by a burning anger and shame at the day's events. The room's three other occupants – Osfric, his son, Osfrith, and Eahlmund – looked up momentarily from where they sat, talking in hushed tones, but said nothing. No one wanted to provoke his ire any further, preferring to let it run its course. Surely soon he would either collapse in a drunken stupor or fall asleep.

He'd already downed several horns of ale, from a barrel that Osfric said he had been saving for the forthcoming Yuletide festivities. The old man had muttered grumpily at having been made to open it, but Eahlmund had convinced him that his lord's need was greater. Osfric had relented but not before he made it clear that he would expect coin to be paid in due course.

"Bastard!" Another crash as Thurkill kicked the stool he had been sitting on, sending it flying against the door.

Osfric looked imploringly at Eahlmund. "Can't you do something? Before he drinks all my ale and destroys my home in the process."

Eahlmund looked from father to son, as if to ask why it had to be him. When no help was forthcoming, he shrugged his shoulders, sighed and pushed himself to his feet. Trying to look bolder than he felt, he walked over to where Thurkill stood staring out of the window, righting the stool and placing it where he might coax the young man to sit back down.

"So, today did not go as we hoped, but it was never going to be easy, my friend. But all is not lost."

Thurkill swore viciously. "It's not your sister at the mercy of these Norman scum."

"I know that, Thurkill, but smashing up this place piece by piece isn't going to help, is it? You're still alive; you still have your strength. You can still protect her."

Despite everything, his friend's reassuring words managed to have a calming effect. Thurkill's shoulders slumped and he allowed himself to be guided over to the stool, where he sat down putting his head in his hands.

"What can I do, though? There's at least ten of them and there's but one of me."

"Well, you have me as well, so that makes two. Though how much use I'll be is a matter of conjecture."

Thurkill lifted his head to look at Eahlmund and smiled through the fog of drink and rage that clouded his brain. "Your loyalty and friendship do you credit, Eahlmund. Your father would be proud. But two is not much better than one when there are so many of them."

"Four."

"What?"

Osfric stood, puffing his meagre chest out. "I said that we number four. My son and I will fight for our lord. It is our duty."

He didn't know whether it was the ale, tiredness or a combination of both but Thurkill felt his eyes misting. He blinked several times and shook his head in an attempt to clear it but when he looked at the father and son, now stood proudly side by side, his vision was still somewhat blurred. "A lord could not want for more loyal followers than you, but I cannot ask you to do that. These are trained warriors we're up against. They would kill you both as soon as look at you."

"We have both stood in the shieldwall before, both trained with shield and spear. We still have them here in this house, hidden in the rafters above. We will gladly raise them again in your cause, Lord."

Thurkill shook his head with bemusement. The room was swimming before him as the effects of the drink caught up with him, but he was also starting to feel burgeoning shoots of hope take hold in his heart. "I would be honoured to have you stand with me, Osfric, and you, Osfrith. You have served my family well for many years and it will not be forgotten. However, we must be realistic; even four will not be enough, I fear."

Osfric shrugged. "Let us worry about that in the morning. I will send Osfrith out at dawn to rustle up a couple more lads. There are others here who have done time in the fyrd. Till then,

Lord, might I suggest that you get some sleep before you empty my ale barrel?"

***

Thurkill awoke the next morning with a mouth as dry as a barn floor at the height of summer and a head that felt like every blacksmith within two days' walk was hammering inside his skull. He groaned as he pushed himself upright, but this only made things worse. He slumped forward, pressing his fingers to the sides of his head, as if he could somehow massage the pain away. After a few moments he could stand it no more. He lurched over to the corner of the room where there stood a pail of fresh water into which he dunked his head, taking great gulps to try and rid his mouth of the taste of the ale.

"Urgh. Why does it taste so good the night before and then hurt so much the next day?"

At that moment, Osfric came in with his son and two other men. "Ha! You young 'uns never learn to hold your drink. That kind of skill takes maturity and wisdom far beyond your years."

Thurkill grinned ruefully. "I'll be alright once I've broken my fast. But tell me, who's this with you?"

The taller of the two men stepped forward stiffly. "Lord, I am Leofric, and this is my brother, Leofgar, sons of Aelfgar, your father's loyal tenant who has tilled these lands these past many years. We are sorry for your loss; Scalpi was a fair and wise lord. To honour his memory, we have come to fight for his son so that he may take back what is rightfully his."

Thurkill nodded solemnly. "You are welcome at my side, Leofric, as are you, Leofgar. I remember your father well, though I am surprised not to see him here with you. I trust he is in good health?"

Leofric sniffed. "He is well indeed, Lord, and remains loyal to you. He wanted to come but our mother forbade it, saying he would be more of a hindrance than a help."

Thurkill clapped him on the shoulder good-naturedly and laughed. "I meant no slight on his honour. I was just fearful that he must have passed on as I remember him to be a stout fellow who would not willingly shy away from a fight."

"'Twas ever thus, Lord. The only fight he has ever been

known to avoid is one with our mother. He knows that is a battle he can never win no matter how hard he were to fight."

Behind them, the door opened again. Standing there was a grinning Eahlmund, holding his arms wide with a freshly caught rabbit in each outstretched hand. "Breakfast."

As they ate, Thurkill turned his mind to the matter in hand. "So, what to do now with our little army? I cannot pretend it will be easy and we must not throw our lives away unnecessarily. There are still twice as many of them as there are of us; it would be foolhardy to try and take them on man to man."

"It would be best if we could even the odds in some way. We can't take them all on at the same time."

Thurkill grabbed another rabbit leg from the wooden platter in the centre of table, ripping the meat from the bone and allowing the juices to flow unhindered down his chin. "A fine point, Eahlmund, but how do we achieve that? We cannot simply ask them nicely if they would oblige us."

"We won't have to, Lord. Not if we use the brains that God saw fit to give us."

"How so, Osfric?"

"Most days, a few of the soldiers head off into the woods to hunt boar and deer. I suppose it stops them getting bored, puts meat on the table and they get to practise their horse-work at the same time."

"A few? I need more details, man. How many?"

"I would say it varies. Never seen more than six, but never fewer than four either."

Thurkill took a moment to ponder the information, tearing the last remnant of meat off of the bone before tossing it carelessly into a corner where it was immediately devoured by Osfric's huge lurcher dog. "That sounds promising. Four should be alright, but six would be a challenge. But with surprise on our side, we might just be able to carry the day. It will not be easy, though, and we may pay dearly for our efforts. Speak now if you would not be part of this; I will not think badly of you were you to do so."

He held their gaze one by one, trying to delve into their

minds to divine their true feelings. Not one of them moved or spoke, though. Not one eye failed to hold his gaze. After a few moments he smiled broadly; they were steadfast fellows. What they lacked in skill, they more than made up for with courage.

***

They spent the next few hours preparing their weapons and discussing the plan. Osfric found a local boy and sent him out with instructions to keep watch on the hall and to report back as soon as he saw any Normans leaving to go hunting. Thurkill didn't know how long they would have to wait or even if any of them would venture out that day, at all. It was cold but dry so there was no reason not to go, as far as the weather was concerned. A mist was starting to form, clinging to the low ground in places, but not enough to hamper a hunting party. *This might even work in our favour*, Thurkill thought, *if it helps to obscure our true intent for that little bit longer*.

They did not have long to wait. No more than two hours after he had been dispatched, the boy breathlessly burst into the house gabbling that six soldiers had ridden off westwards into the woods, accompanied by three men from the village and a pair of hunting dogs.

"They'll be out for the rest of the day now," Osfric asserted confidently. "That should give us plenty of time to prepare."

Thurkill nodded. "We need to use the time and the land to our advantage. We're evenly matched for numbers but they'll be on horseback and are all trained soldiers. Anything we can do to push the odds in our favour will help."

"I think I know a place, Lord."

"Speak, Osfrith. Let's hear your idea."

"If they have gone west, then I know that area well. I used to hunt rabbits and squirrels there as a boy. On the way back to the village there is a sunken path that is bordered on both sides by ancient hedgerows. It's narrow and I doubt there's room for any more than two men on horseback to walk abreast. And you can't go around it as the woods are dense on either side."

Thurkill nodded. "I like the sound of that. In fact, I think I recall the place you mean. If it is the lane I'm thinking of then it will serve our purpose well. Take us there now."

As soon as he saw it, Thurkill knew it was perfect for an ambush. The path between the impenetrable hawthorns was a good two hundred paces long. So dense was the thicket that Thurkill doubted anything bigger than a rabbit or fox could get through. Once the trap was sprung there could be no escape that way.

He smiled approvingly at the young swineherd. "You have done well, my friend. I could not have chosen better. Now, to spring the trap I propose that four of us," he nodded at Eahlmund and the two brothers, "hold the line here at the front. We'll form a shieldwall here across the path. If we stand strong, they'll not be able to pass."

Leofric and Leofgar looked doubtful but nodded all the same, perhaps anxious at the prospect of facing mounted warriors for the first time.

Eahlmund saw the look on the faces and tried to bolster their courage. "Don't worry, lads. I was in the shieldwall at Senlac. The Norman bastards could not break us, not until we were undone by their trickery. Horse or no horse they shall not pass."

Thurkill smiled, grateful for the support of his friend. "That's right. We stay close together and they won't get through. Keep the shields overlapped and use your spears to stab at the horses, if you can't reach the men. If we bring down but one of their mounts, it will cause confusion and fear and give us the edge for sure."

Osfric was almost beside himself with anticipation, literally hopping from foot to foot, belying his age. "What of us, Lord? What would you have us do?"

"Don't worry, you'll not miss out. I want you and your son to hide at the far end of the lane. With them focussed on us, they won't be expecting an attack from behind. Use your spears to deal whoever's at the back and that will sow panic amongst the rest. But be careful if they have some of our villagers with them. Be sure to let them get away safely."

With arrangements made, the two groups split up to position themselves to wait for the return of the soldiers. Thurkill took the time to wander off away from the others to gather his thoughts. He sat down by the edge of the lane, his back leaning against a gnarled beech trunk. He wondered, idly, if FitzGilbert would be with them. The boy hadn't known for certain one way or the other and, if he were honest, Thurkill was not sure whether he hoped he was or not. It might make things easier to kill him today and have done with it, but what would that mean for Edith, Aga and Haslow as a whole? At the very least, though, they could even the odds now so that he was better placed to bargain with the Norman. Perhaps with his strength halved, FitzGilbert would be more inclined to leave?

His thoughts turned to the struggle ahead. He knew Eahlmund could fight but his faith in the rest of them was less sure. True, Leofric and Leofgar had been trained to fight in a shieldwall, but had they ever been tested against men who were trying to kill them? Who knew how a man might react until the moment was thrust upon him? At least he and Eahlmund would be there to keep them steady. Osfric and Osfrith were hunters, well used to the art of killing, although neither had ever had cause to kill another man. From their position at the back they would be less exposed to danger, though, and that was probably the best and safest place for them to be.

Thurkill realised he was starting to become anxious. He could not help but feel protective towards these men. One or more of them might well be killed today – fighting for him – and he would have to carry that on his conscience for ever. The weight of responsibility hung heavy over him as he sat there waiting. He supposed it must have been the same for his father but that did not make it any easier to bear. He knew when his time came he would have to answer to God for the lives of men that had been lost because of him; to be able to justify their death in pursuit of a worthy cause. He offered up a silent prayer that the tally did not begin today, no matter how just the conflict.

Thurkill had no idea how long they had been waiting before he heard the hoot of an owl, once and then repeated twice more. It was the signal Osfric had said he would use as soon as the swineherd sighted the returning hunting party. It was now late afternoon and the light was already fading as the sun began to slip towards the tree line. The temperature had fallen with it and the mist began to form once more, clinging to the low ground and making the lane look more eerie than ever.

Turning to the others he sought to encourage any hearts that might yet be faint. "Here they come, lads; ready yourselves. Remember; they are not expecting trouble so we have surprise on our side. Stand firm, show no fear and victory will be ours. You have my word." He looked to either side; to his left stood Eahlmund his jaw set and his knuckles showing white against the dark wood of his spear where his grip tightened. To his right Leofwine and Leofgar looked as calm as if this were the most natural thing in the world. One of them was even humming some kind of tune. Thurkill shook his head, non plussed. His fears for their courage were seemingly misplaced.

"Forward, lads; steady now." He directed them to take a few steps further down the lane to a point where a tree trunk encroached on the path. It served to narrow the lane yet further and would also secure their right flank, as if it were a fifth, immovable warrior. Once there, he craned his neck, trying to make out the advancing Normans. He could now hear the thud of their horses' hooves interspersed with bursts of coarse laughter as the men made their way home, content with the day's activity, unaware of what lay just ahead of them.

As the boy had said, there were six of them, all on horseback, riding two abreast; the width of the lane would allow no more. A short distance behind them he could also make out three men on foot, men from the village who were burdened with the day's haul, a couple of lurchers trotting dutifully at their heels. And then the Normans saw them; they reined in their mounts, apparently uncertain of what to make of the men who blocked their way. As far as Thurkill could tell, they wore no mailshirts. He had suspected that this would be the case but had not dared to hope. Without armour to protect them, the balance had swung that little bit further in their favour. Both he and Eahlmund wore mail and helmets while the two brothers were well protected with boiled leather jerkins and head gear.

From where he waited, he could hear the Normans arguing. Voices were raised and one or two of them were gesticulating wildly in their direction. Thurkill supposed that at least one must be advocating retreat. The lack of shields and armour must have caused a certain amount of concern amongst them when faced with determined, armed men. Whereas others favoured a more aggressive response, perhaps confident in their superiority and their horses. It did not take long for a conclusion to be reached. Suddenly, the two horsemen in front heeled their mounts to urge them forward, readying their spears as they rode.

"Steady, boys. Remember… Hold fast and they won't break us. Get those shields up."

The four Saxons hoisted their shields into place and levelled their spears, pointing them slightly upwards to aim at the horses' chests. At the same time, they turned slightly to the side and planted their right legs square behind them, ready to absorb the impact of the charge. Their shields, each one touching its neighbour, were thrust forward to form an impenetrable barrier. At the right-hand side of the line, Leofric's shield butted directly against the protruding tree trunk, while on the left, Eahlmund was as close as he could be to the hedgerow without actually being in it.

And then the Normans were upon them, riding their mounts as hard as they could against the shields. Although trained for battle, the horses still hesitated to confront a hedge of sharpened spear points. Their eyes were wide with fear, their nostrils flared as they whinnied with terror as they were compelled forward remorselessly.

The wall buckled under the impact but did not break. Both Thurkill and Leofgar in the centre had to take a step back, ducking beneath the rim of their shields, but the others moved with them, preventing the wall from breaking. At the same time, Eahlmund and Leofric thrust their spears straight at the exposed chests of the horses. With a heart-breaking screams, both beasts stumbled to their knees, blood gushing from the gaping wounds left by the blades. The two riders were pitched forward, unable to keep their seat as the horses collapsed. Dropping his spear, Thurkill darted forward and stabbed down at the nearest man with his seax, plunging the long knife into his exposed chest. To his right, Leofgar followed his example, impervious to the supplications of his stricken foe. Within moments it was over; the first two soldiers were dead, and the two Saxons had recovered their spears and their place in the shieldwall.

Just four of the hated enemy remained. Angered by the fate of their comrades they strove to press home their attack, but found their way blocked by the fallen horses whose limbs still thrashed wildly in agony. The sounds and smells of the dying horses were enough to stop the next two beasts from stepping forward into the morass, despite the savage beating being meted out to them by their riders.

Osfric and his son chose that moment to make their presence known. They charged forward from where they had been hiding, making as much noise as they could, striking fear and confusion into the hearts of the remaining Normans who, unable to turn their horses easily, had to twist in their saddles to see what new threat now assailed them. It was too late, though, as the two swineherds were already upon them. Together, they drove their spears into the unprotected backs of the two rearmost soldiers. Death was almost instantaneous as they fell to the ground.

Glancing at each other, the two surviving horsemen made up their minds. With a roar they threw themselves forward, callously raking their heels as hard as they could down the flanks of their panicked mounts. They aimed directly for the gaps between the four waiting warriors, hoping to make good their escape.

Amazingly, one managed to vault over the wall, between the two brothers, jumping higher than Thurkill had thought possible. The other was not so fortunate, however. His mount stumbled at the point of take-off, its front legs entangled in the slippery mess caused by the spilt blood and guts of the wounded beasts to its front. With a shout of triumph, Thurkill thrust his spear as hard as he could at the rider, grunting with satisfaction as he felt the point pierce the man's unprotected torso. The strength of the impact lifted the Norman bodily from his saddle and threw him backwards, wrenching the spear shaft from Thurkill's hands.

Forgetting him, Thurkill turned to see what had happened to the last man. Miraculously, his horse had kept its footing after the jump and was even now hurtling up what remained of the lane as its rider continued to dig his heels into its sides, eager to put as much distance between him and the scene of carnage behind him as possible.

"Spear!" Thurkill grabbed Eahlmund's proffered weapon and hurled it after the fast-disappearing Norman. His aim was true but at the last moment, the Norman ducked down alongside his horse's neck. Whether or not he had heard and understood Thurkill's shout or simply expected some kind of missile to be thrown, the move saved his life. The spear sailed harmlessly over his head, missing him by no more than a hand's breadth.

"Shit!" Thurkill yelled in frustration.

Eahlmund clapped him on the shoulder, grinning from ear to ear as the adrenaline of the fight still coursed through his veins. "Worry not, my friend. Five of his friends lie dead or dying behind us. Victory is ours."

Thurkill rounded on him angrily. "You fool! Don't you realise he will warn the others? We needed to kill them all if we were to have any chance at all. Now they will be ready for us; our task just became ten-fold harder." In his anger, he kicked out at one of the fallen men.

Eahlmund said nothing but hung his head, abashed. Behind him the swineherd and his son went on with the gruesome business of slitting the throats of the two mortally wounded horses. "Brave animals, both, to charge a shieldwall like that; but at least there will be meat aplenty for many folk this winter."

A groan brought Thurkill out of his mood. He spun round, cursing himself for forgetting to check on the health of his men. He had a lot to learn yet about being a lord. Sprawled on the ground before him was Leofric, an ugly-looking gash to the side of his head. His brother knelt beside him, cradling his head in his lap and dabbing at the wound with a piece of cloth ripped from a dead man's tunic.

"How is he? What happened?" The worry in his voice was, however, real enough.

"Hard to say, Lord, but I think he'll survive. Stupid sod forgot to duck when that horse leapt at us. Caught him on the side of the head with one of its hooves. Hopefully it's knocked some sense into him, though. God alone knows he didn't have much to start with."

Despite his concern for Leofric, Thurkill laughed. The injury did not appear to be life-threatening, after all, though it remained to be seen whether he would be fit enough to continue the fight. Time was pressing; he needed to attack now before FitzGilbert had time to prepare his defences. With every hour that passed, his position grew weaker while that of his enemy grew stronger.

"Do what you can for him, Leofgar. If you can patch him up so that he can fight again, then so much the better."

The young man nodded and turned back to his brother, who was now attempting to sit up. Although groggy and dazed from the blow, he conscious enough to call for a slug of ale. Leofgar hushed him while binding his head with another strip of cloth which served, for the time being at least, to staunch the flow of blood.

"Lord." Eahlmund stood alongside him, his hand on his shoulder. "These men have asked that they be allowed to fight with you." He pointed in the direction of the three men standing to one side, by the hedgerow. They had discarded the slaughtered game and stood alert and ready, eager to impress.

Thurkill beckoned them forward. "Well met, lads. You are most welcome here." As they stepped up, he recognised them from the village. "Eopric, Copsig, Eardwulf. I know you all; good men every one of you. I would be glad to have you in my little war-band but this is not your fight; I cannot force you to put your lives at risk."

Copsig took a step forward and bowed his head before his lord. "We have served your father and now we serve his son. It is the way of things. Your fight is our fight and if we are to die in its pursuit then so be it. We may not be warriors but rest assured we will give a good account of ourselves. Besides, you are not the only one to have a score to settle with those Norman whoresons."

Thurkill nodded solemnly. "Then, let us all go to my father's hall and finish this."

TWENTY-SEVEN

28 October, Haslow

Dusk was falling when they arrived back at the village. They left Leofric in his home; still too groggy to stand unaided, let alone fight. It was a loss, Thurkill knew, as he was a good man, but the arrival of Copsig, Eopric and Eardwulf more than made up for it, even if they had neither swords, shields or armour. He now had eight in his war-band, stout fellows all, whatever their experience. That they were farmers and swineherds up against trained warriors did not matter. What was to come would be less about spears and shieldwalls and much more about cunning and stealth. If they could get in close, the seaxes they all carried – and learned to use from childhood -would come into their own.

At the outskirts of the village, Thurkill skidded to a halt, signalling to the others to do likewise. Even at this distance, Thurkill could tell something was wrong. Watch fires had been set all around the hall, casting their glare against the growing darkness; no one would be able to sneak up undetected with their light. From where he stood, no more than fifty paces from the hall, he could see a number of shadowy figures moving between the fires. As he had feared, the remaining Normans were ready for them. The escaping hunter had done his job well.

With five men now dead, there would be seven Normans up there, including scar-faced FitzGilbert. They would have had little time to prepare, but enough to don their mailshirts, to ready their weapons and to light these fires. This would be no easy fight, that much was clear. There was little they could do about it though; the die had been cast. There was no backing down now; for all he knew, his sister and aunt were at the hall and every hour that went by the more their lives were at risk.

No sooner had the thought entered his mind than his worst fears were confirmed. FitzGilbert, together with one of his captains, emerged from the hall, each leading a woman by a halter fastened around their neck. They dragged them to the space where the fires were brightest and stopped. The light of the flames lit up their faces, revealing their terrified expressions.

"Can you hear me, Saxon dog?" FitzGilbert shouted out into the gloom in his heavily accented English.

Thurkill kept his silence, unsure of what to do. By his side, he bunched his hands into fists, clenching and unclenching as he stood aghast at the scene before him. He had been afraid of something like this happening but had refused to accept it, hoping it might not come to pass. Now it was real, his mind raced to find a solution, but nothing was forthcoming.

"Answer me, Saxon. You are in no position to bargain. Do I need to spell out what I will do to your beloved sister and your dear aunt should you fail to surrender to me?"

With no apparent option, Thurkill's shoulders slumped in defeat. He took a step forward, only for Eahlmund – by his side – to grab his arm, stopping him from going any further. "Don't go, Lord. He'll kill you as soon as look at you."

He turned to face his friend. "But what choice do I have? If I don't, he will kill them. You know what a bastard he is; he won't even hesitate. I am sworn to protect them; I cannot allow them to die whilst I still have some power to prevent it."

"I'm waiting, Saxon. You have killed five of my men. That is a crime in any land and you must answer for it before my Lord, William of Normandy. Did you expect to be able to get away with it?"

Eahlmund still held him back, hissing in his ear. "We could take them. There's enough of us. Look around you."

Thurkill glanced back to see the faces of those who stood with him, every one of them set in grim determination. Each of them gripped whatever weapon they had to hand, ready to play their part. He knew he just had to give the order and they would willingly go forward to their deaths. It was too much to bear.

He shook his head. "I can't risk it, my friend. Quite apart from the number of men we might lose, as soon as we broke cover he would slit their throats, just to have them out of the way. I know his type, killing two innocent women wouldn't give him a moment's pause. If I thought we could reach them in time to stop it, I would gladly give the order."

"You have had long enough. I can't wait all day." FitzGilbert pulled Edith towards him, drawing his knife from his belt as he did so. Holding the wicked blade against her throat, he turned back towards where he knew the Saxons to be. To her credit, Edith stood silent, resigned to her fate, but Aga could not prevent a shrill scream of terror bursting from her lips.

"Well? This is growing tiresome."

Thurkill shook himself free of his friend's grasp as he stepped into the light. "Wait."

The Norman nodded in apparent satisfaction. "I am glad that you have seen sense, boy. You had no other option if you wanted to spare their lives." Turning to one of his soldiers he issued orders for Thurkill to be bound by the wrists, and for his weapons to be removed.

Thurkill winced as the soldier lashed two lengths of cord around his forearms, the fibres digging in painfully as he pulled the ends tight together. As the knots were tied off, Thurkill bowed his head, unable to meet the petrified gaze of his kin. He had done what he must to protect them; it was not cowardice, he told himself. At least this way, they would live and he could find a way to save them another day.

"You have me now, Norman dog. Let my family go as promised."

FitzGilbert looked at him, a quizzical look in his eyes. "I recall no such promise. Far from it. There is a price to be paid for killing five of my men in cold blood. An eye for an eye and a tooth for a tooth, as I think our God teaches us."

A terrible realisation dawned on Thurkill. FitzGilbert's face took on a look that was nothing short of diabolical, his scar seeming even more red and angry looking in the light of the flames. He turned and spoke to the soldier holding Aga. Thurkill had no idea what he said but the accompanying gesture of drawing his thumb across his throat was unmistakeable.

Stepping behind Aga, the Norman yanked her forehead back, baring her throat and slowly drew the blade of his knife across the exposed flesh. Aga bore her fate with stoic defiance; fixing her nephew with a gaze that bore into his soul; pleading with him, not for herself as her time was over, but for his sister. He knew that the vision of her face as she slipped lifelessly to the ground would never leave him for as long as he lived. The look in her eyes would be forever burned into his mind's eye. He knew he could not allow Edith to suffer the same fate.

Stung into action, Thurkill rammed his shoulder into the guard to his left sending him sprawling to the ground. In an instant he was rushing towards Edith, desperate to reach her before she could be murdered as well. He had no idea what he could do as his wrists were still bound, but he did not care. He had to do something; he had to stop them somehow. As he drew closer, he put his head down ready to butt, like he'd so often seen the stags do in the hills around Haslow as they fought for supremacy in rutting season. With his arms unavailable to him, his forehead was all he had left. His aunt had often said it was as hard as stone, impervious to even the most basic thought, and he prayed she was right. He was now but a pace or two from the soldier holding Edith.

But before he could reach her, there was a blinding flash of light in his head, accompanied by a searing burst of pain. He felt his legs begin to buckle, powerless to prevent himself from crumpling in a heap. As he lay on the ground, he could feel himself drifting into a black void of unconsciousness, but not before he saw Edith's screams cruelly cut short as the knife sliced her throat open almost from ear to ear. Unable to speak, unable to move, Thurkill lost his battle to stay conscious. The last image he saw was his precious sister slumped on the ground before him, her sightless eyes staring glassily at him as blood still pumped from the gaping wound in her neck.

TWENTY-EIGHT

29 October, Haslow

When Thurkill opened his eyes, it took him a few moments to work out where he was. At first he feared the blow to his head had made him blind as he could see nothing. To make matters worse, he couldn't move either. *What in God's name…?* Almost immediately though, his memory returned with sudden and blinding intensity. Aga! Edith! Murdered in front of him by that sick, grinning bastard of a Norman.

He had never felt more alone in his life. In the space of a few short weeks he had lost his father and now his aunt and beloved sister. His youthful oath to protect her to his dying day had been torn to pieces. Tears stung his eyes as he lay bereft in the solitude and darkness of his surroundings. He swore a new oath; for what remained of his life, he would dedicate himself to avenging his family. He would kill any and every Norman, beginning with – and most especially – the devil's spawn who had slaughtered his kin.

Fuelled by new-found rage, he tried once again to move. He was lying on his side, that much was obvious, but his wrists and ankles had been bound so tightly together that he could hardly shift at all. His head was the only part of him that was free, but even that was restricted as he found when he banged his forehead painfully against some unseen object. As his senses slowly recovered, he realised he must be in the woodshed; the smell of freshly chopped logs was unmistakeable. He knew it to be a small building at the back of the hall, so small that it surprised him that there was room for him.

He began to wonder why he had not been killed. Why keep him alive? For what purpose? Whatever the reason, he fervently prayed that it would be a mistake that FitzGilbert would come to regret, and soon. He was not afraid of death: the priests promised an eternal life after death and he knew that he would be reunited with his family there. He had no intention to rush blindly to their embrace but, when the time came, he would welcome the release from this world.

To add to his misery, it was freezing lying there on the damp earth. He had been stripped of his mail and cloak so that he wore no more than his tunic and trews. He had no idea how long he had been lying there but it was long enough for the cold to have penetrated deep into his bones. He shivered uncontrollably as his muscles vainly attempted to generate some much-needed warmth.

Sometime later he became aware of a faint scratching sound. At first he thought it was merely his teeth chattering, but when he clamped his jaws together he could still hear it. *Rats! That's all I need,* Thurkill thought. *They could at least wait until I'm dead before they come to feast on me.*

"Thurkill? Thurkill? Can you hear me?" Eahlmund's whispered voice was unmistakeable. "Are you still alive in there?"

Despite his situation, Thurkill could not stop himself from smiling. Perhaps all was not lost. "Aye, you great pudding. Trussed up like a chicken ready to be roasted on a spit, but otherwise alright, I think. Nothing seems to be broken, at least. Though my head hurts like a bastard."

"Thanks be to God. We feared the worst when we saw what they did to your family."

His ire rising at the memory once again, Thurkill hissed. "God willing, FitzGilbert will pay dearly for that. I will not allow it to go unpunished. An eye for an eye, Eahlmund. An eye for an eye."

For a moment, silence fell between them; Eahlmund having no words of comfort to offer. Eventually, Thurkill spoke, more wearily this time. "Are you still there, my friend?"

"Yes, Lord."

"Tell me, is it day or night? What is happening out there?"

"It is some time before dawn, already the sky begins to brighten in the east. They have set a guard on you but he prefers to stay closer to the hall, by the fire where he can keep warm. I think he is also fearful of an attack and does not want to be too far away from his comrades. Either way, I was able to sneak up here without being seen or overheard. Whilst we can talk, I can't get you out of there; the walls are too sturdy and any attempt to

211

free you would not go unnoticed."

Thurkill grunted. The men of Haslow took pride in their work. Their buildings were strongly built so that they would not fall down in the first gales of winter. He never thought he would ever have cause to curse them for it.

"What's more, FitzGilbert has sent a man off south."

"For what purpose would he reduce his strength yet further?"

"I know not, though rumour has it that William the Bastard has yet to move far from Senlac. Word is that he has sent emissaries to Lundenburh, calling on the lords there to pay him homage as King of England and he awaits their response."

"So, FitzGilbert's man goes to William. What is his plan and how does it involve me, I wonder?"

Before Eahlmund could reply, there was a rattling of chains and the door of the hut was thrown open, casting him into the light of the braziers by the hall. Two soldiers stood in the doorway looking down at him with mocking eyes. The sudden rush of cold air caused Thurkill to shiver even more as leaves skittered across the uneven floor. He hoped they had not seen his body shaking or, if they had, that they did not take it for fear. With his family all dead, he had nothing left to fear. He did not care for his own life anymore. What pain they might inflict on him would be fleeting when compared to an eternity in heaven with his family. He gritted his teeth stared back with what he hoped was an expression of fierce contempt.

"Up!"

It might have been the only word of English that they knew but it made little difference. Thurkill could not move, let alone stand. In frustration the nearest of the two men strode into the enclosed space and dragged him out by the scruff of his tunic. Out in the open, he drew his dagger and bent over his captive. Thurkill steeled himself, half expecting the knife to be shoved into his ribs or throat, but he did no more than slice the bonds that held his ankles. With his legs now unencumbered, they could manhandle him to his feet, albeit unsteadily as it took a moment for the circulation to return to normal.

The two soldiers then bundled him across the short distance to the hall where they pushed him through the open doorway so forcefully that he was sent sprawling amongst the straw and detritus of the previous night's meal, a dog yelping in protest as the bone on which it had been gnawing was sent skittling across the floor.

"Get up." The order was barked from the lord's table. Thurkill looked up but his view was obscured by the smoke rising from the hearth in the middle of the hall, where a churl was busy rekindling the embers of the previous night's fire. Too slow to comply, he was hauled to his feet by two guards and roughly manhandled forward until he came once more face to face with FitzGilbert.

"Welcome, Saxon. I trust you slept well? Your accommodation was to your liking?" The evil leer on his face merely reinforced the malice with which the words were delivered.

Thurkill said nothing but, ignoring the pain, lifted his head so that he could stare directly at his oppressor, his piercing blue eyes burning with an intense hatred that caused the Norman to look away briefly, momentarily disconcerted.

FitzGilbert then cleared his throat, attempting to regain his composure. "Perhaps it was too comfortable. Maybe the pigs will make better bed fellows tonight? Anyway, you are no doubt wondering why I have brought you before me, perhaps even why I have allowed you to live?" He did not wait for a reply. "Well, as you know, by the ancient right of conquest, William is now the rightful ruler of this accursed, rain-soaked country. Nevertheless, this fact seems to have escaped many of your countrymen. Envoys have been sent demanding the capitulation of those lords that still live after the battle, cowards that did not fight with you at Senlac in the main, but no response has yet been received.

"The Duke grows impatient; he will not wait forever. Sooner or later he will march to take the country by force if need be. Every day he grows stronger as more and more men and supplies cross from Normandy, making good the losses sustained in battle."

Thurkill yawned, ignoring the pain in his bruised jaw. "All very interesting, Norman, but what does any of this have to do with me?"

"I would have hoped that was obvious, but it matters not. William has a desire to be seen to be performing his duties of a king, such as dispensing justice. You, my friend, will have the honour of being the first defendant to be brought before William, King of England, the first of that name. You will be tried for your crimes and, doubtless, sentenced to hang as a rebel against his royal authority. I hope you are suitably humbled by this great privilege that has been bestowed upon you?" He threw his head back and laughed uproariously at the prospect.

Thurkill stood, expressionless and unmoved. "It matters not to me, Norman. Your William is no king of mine. Whether you murder me or he does makes no difference. Murder is murder. But if I were you, I would kill me now before it's too late."

FitzGilbert snorted derisorily. "Too late for what, dog?" Disdain dripped from his words.

"For what you did to my aunt and sister, you deserve to die. I will have vengeance for their deaths and I will be the instrument of your doom. I have sworn it before God; I will send you to hell myself. The longer you keep me alive the more chance I have to fulfil my oath. Are you willing to take the risk?"

If FitzGilbert was in any way concerned by the threat, he betrayed no sign of it. "I have to admire your courage, boy. You people simply don't know when you're beaten, do you? It matters not, though. William's soldiers will be here in a day or two and that will be the last I see of you. Before you go, however, your insolence is worthy of a parting gift."

He barked orders to the two guards and before Thurkill had a chance to defend himself, the blows began to rain down on his unprotected head and body. With his arms tied, there was little he could do to defend himself. He fell to the ground, pulled his knees up to his chest and his arms up to his face as best he could and simply waited for it to end.

***

He had no idea for how long the beating went on; he was unconsciousness long before it was over. He awoke sometime later, back in the log shed, his legs tied once more. There was a bitter taste in his mouth which he soon realised was blood. Moving his tongue around, he also found that one of his teeth was loose to the point of having becoming dislodged. Filling his mouth with saliva he hawked and spat the whole sorry mess, tooth, blood and saliva, as far away from him as he could.

"Ah, you're awake then?"

"Eahl..." he coughed to clear his croaking voice. "Is that you, Eahlmund?"

"Aye, and Osfric too. We have been lying here for ages waiting for you to regain your senses. That must have been some kicking they gave you; you have been out for hours."

Thurkill flexed his jaw, trying to ease the pain he felt when talking. He didn't think it was broken but it hurt like hell all the same. "I've had worse punches from my sister." It was as well they couldn't see him, though, else they would all too easily see through his feigned bravado. It was probably only the fact that the Normans were supposed to send him to Duke William that had kept them from being truly brutal. It would not have done to send a corpse before their lord, after all.

Eahlmund paused before replying, as if not believing him. "What now, Lord? We need to get you out of there and away from this place."

"And how will you do that? Soldiers are coming to take me before William where I am to stand trial before him, all so he can be seen to be dispensing justice as if he were king of this land."

"But he's not the king." Osfric was indignant. "A new one has been proclaimed in Lundenburh."

The news shocked Thurkill, causing him to forget his pains. "What? Who? Tell me all that you know, Osfric."

The old man hesitated. "Well, I don't know for certain, but Osfrith met some men on the road earlier today; foreign merchants making their way to the coast to get back to Flanders. They came from Lundenburh with news of the goings on there."

Eahlmund interjected. "Mostly turmoil and chaos by the sounds of it."

"Yes, but they also spoke of a meeting that took place in old King Edward's abbey at Westminster. All the great lords of the

215

land were there. Those that didn't die in the battle, that is."

"That would include Earls Eadwine and Morcar, I don't doubt, amongst others. What we might have done if we had them and their men with us on the field."

"You are right, Lord, those names were mentioned, but I forget any others."

"No matter. Continue with the story. What of this king?"

Thurkill's excitement grew. Perhaps with a new leader, the country might rally round and throw the bastard Normans back across the channel. He racked his brains to think who it might be. The old King Edward had had no sons to inherit, that's how they had ended up with Harold. Harold had sons but they were surely too young to rule? What about Eadwine or Morcar? The crown did not have to pass from father to son after all; just to someone to whom all the great nobles would agree to pledge allegiance. Beyond Eadwine and Morcar he could think of no one else; and their reputation had suffered badly with the defeat at Eoforwic which made them unlikely candidates. But in a time of crisis such as this, who knew what strange events might come to pass?

"They said that the lords acclaimed a new king of the English, a man who goes by the name, Edgar, a prince of the house of Wessex."

Edgar! Of course. The last surviving heir of the house of Wessex.

"Who the hell is Edgar?"

"Edgar, my poor ignorant Eahlmund, is of the same family as the old King Edward. If I am not mistaken he is Edward's great-nephew, being the grandson of Edmund who was known as Ironside who ruled briefly some fifty years ago, before the Dane, Knut, conquered the land."

Eahlmund spoke slowly, as if concentrating hard. "So... Edmund will have been Edward's... brother?"

"Half-brother, but yes. After Knut took the throne, Edgar's father – who also went by the name of Edward – went into exile to a land far to the east called Hungary, I think. He only came back to these shores about ten years ago, if I recall what my father said."

"So why not have this other Edward as king then, instead of Edgar?"

"I suppose we would have done had he been alive – ahead of Harold even – but he died shortly after his return, leaving his son, Edgar, who could have been no more than a boy of five summers at the time."

"But surely he's still only a boy now? How can he be expected to rule let alone defeat William?"

"He can't be much older than fourteen, maybe fifteen at best, Eahlmund. Probably hasn't even started to grow his moustache yet."

Eahlmund chuckled. "Whereas you, Lord, have a full beard."

Even though it was meant in jest, Thurkill bristled at the implied criticism. "The difference, my friend, is that I am not responsible for the lives of hundreds of thousands of people and nor do I have to muster and lead an army big enough to defeat the Normans."

"Well, if we don't get you out of here, you won't be doing anything at all either way."

"And we don't have long to work that out," Osfric chimed in, "before they come to drag him off to see William."

TWENTY-NINE

1 November, Haslow

The door to the woodshed was flung open so fiercely that Thurkill was jerked out of the uneven sleep into which he had finally fallen. With the way his bonds had been tied, it was almost impossible to find a position that allowed any comfort, meaning he had been awake for most of the night. Intense fatigue made his eyes feel as if they were lined with grit and dust; he had to blink several times before he could bring his vision into focus.

"Out!" As ever the soldier was brief and to the point.

Slowly, painfully, he pushed himself to his knees but could manage no more. Two soldiers, men that he had not seen before, barged into the confined space and, with a hand under each armpit, lifted him – not ungently – to his feet. Then they stood by his side, supporting his weight, helping him to move, with tiny shuffling steps, under his own volition. Blinking into the early morning daylight he tried to make sense of his surroundings. In front of him stood an open-topped wooden cart, hooked up to a pair of huge oxen. Around it, before and aft, stood a dozen soldiers, cloaked, helmeted and armed with spear, sword and shield. In front of them, FitzGilbert waited, hands on hips. His smile exuded a sense of power and superiority, betraying his determination to enjoy every moment.

"Good morning, Saxon. I trust you are refreshed and ready to meet your new king? You might have cleaned yourself up a bit for the occasion, though, don't you think?"

Thurkill offered no reply other than to spit a gobbet of blood and phlegm disdainfully on the ground mid-way between him and the Norman.

"No matter. I can't say that I am sorry to see you go, though it would have been nice to have had the pleasure of killing you myself. I could have added you to the collection along with your aunt and sister." A malicious grin accompanied his words, as if doing all he could to try to goad Thurkill into a reaction; any excuse to beat him to a pulp once more. When Thurkill made no move or sound, however, he sniffed, disappointed, before continuing.

"But when one's king commands so must one obey. These men," he waved his hand at the twelve new soldiers, "have come to take you to William's camp so you may face royal justice for your actions."

"Don't be so sure that you have seen the last of me, Norman. I have not forgotten my oath to kill you."

FitzGilbert laughed heartily. "Your optimism is truly admirable, boy. I hope that when they hang you, your dance of death is both long and painful." With that the Norman turned on his heel and strode back into the hall, dismissing the young Saxon for good.

Strong hands grabbed him by the shoulders, propelling him forcefully up and into the wagon. Unable to use his arms, he was powerless to stop his head from bashing into the wooden planks along the edge. Dazed, it took a few moments for his head to clear but when it did it dawned on him just how desperate his situation was. Six soldiers had formed up behind the cart and six more were in front, not to mention the two who rode on the cart itself. He had no idea what had happened to Eahlmund, Osfric and the others but they had left it too late now for sure. His fate was sealed; he would be delivered to William where he would be executed. The trial would be short - for show purposes only really. There was no way he would be allowed to live, not after what he had done.

I'm sorry, father. I have let you down. Not only will the family name die with me but I failed to protect your sister and daughter. Nor will I be able to avenge their death as honour demands. Feeling more miserable than he could ever remember, he buried his face in the dust of the wagon's bed. Shielded as he was from the view of the following soldiers, he allowed the tears to flow unchecked.

***

He awoke, shivering. The Normans had not seen fit to give him a cloak to protect him from the late autumn chill and so he was dressed still only in tunic and trews. *On the bright side*, he mused, *at least it's not raining*. It was dark all around him except for the deep orange glow of a dwindling fire about ten or so paces away. At that moment, he wished for nothing more than to be lying within reach of its warmth.

He could make out numerous shapes wrapped in cloaks and blankets huddled around it; many of whom appeared to be snoring heavily. Closer to him, two soldiers stood guard, stamping their feet and flapping their arms heavily against their bodies in an effort to keep warm. They were deep in conversation with each other. Though the foreign words were unintelligible to Thurkill, the intonation made clear their obvious disgruntlement. He allowed himself a small smile; all the world over, it seemed, soldiers belly-ached about having to stand watch at night, in the cold, while their comrades slept.

Just then he froze. What was that noise? It sounded like an owl hooting but, having grown up in these parts, it was like no owl he had ever heard. In fact, he would have sworn it sounded almost human, as if someone was trying to imitate an owl. There it was again. Yes, it was unmistakeable now. Thurkill tensed; something was afoot. Surely the guards must realise, as he had, that the sound was a signal of some kind? He turned his head slowly towards the two men, keeping his breathing as even as possible to give the impression that he was still asleep. With relief he saw they showed no signs of alarm; they were blissfully unaware of any imminent danger.

Next he sensed rather than saw two shadows passing him, creeping silently along either side of the wagon. Even at such close proximity, he could not hear them at all. Thurkill's heart thumped heavily against his chest. To his ears it sounded deafening; he was amazed that his guards could not hear it. The adrenalin pumping through his veins made him itch to be part of whatever was going on; the frustration of being unable to move was overwhelming. He knew, however, that he must lie still. He could not give the soldiers any reason to turn around, lest the would-be assassins be discovered. He wondered who the men were; it was impossible to tell in the dark. Their features were masked by hoods which were pulled up over their heads. One seemed to be somewhat taller than the other; he wondered if that, perhaps, could be Eahlmund?

Time seemed to stand still as step by critical step, the two indistinct shapes edged closer to their quarry, keeping in step so that they were at all times equidistant from the Normans. Then, as if by pre-arranged signal, they took the final step that brought them within killing range. Simultaneously, each man clamped their left hand over their victim's mouth from behind, yanking their head back to expose their neck. Then, in one seamless movement, they brought their right arms round, the dwindling firelight glinting off the metal seax blade that each man held. With swift, practised hands the assailants viciously scored the knives across the pale white flesh, opening each throat with a wickedly deep incision that severed the windpipe, ensuring the dying men would utter no sound.

Blood gushed from severed blood vessels, soaking the front of their mail shirts. The two attackers held their prey upright for what seemed an age, waiting until all life had fled from their bodies, before lowering them gently to the ground, careful to avoid any excessive clanking of metal. All the while both they and Thurkill stared at the sleeping forms around the fire, willing them not to awaken. Mercifully, not one of them moved or even so much as stirred; none of them was even remotely aware of the mortal danger that now threatened them.

Almost immediately, several more shadowy figures surged forward like wraiths past the wagon. With great stealth they advanced on the camp fire, where they fanned out in a circle until there was one man behind each soldier. Then, at a signal from the tall leader, they struck down as one, over and over again, stabbing and slashing at each man's head and neck.

It was all over in moments. Not one man had managed to cry out and – even if he had – it would have been to no avail as there was no one there to help them. Every single one of them was either dead or dying. The leader who had given the signal to attack was now stalking around the outside of the circle, checking each man. Here and there he stopped and listened before kneeling to finish any that still lived. Only then did the attackers return to the wagon where two of them clambered up and began to cut away at Thurkill's bonds.

It took a few moments for the circulation to return to his arms and legs; he had been bound hand and foot for more than two days now and every time he had struggled, the knots had seemed to get tighter. His wrists had been rubbed almost raw where the cords had chafed continually against the skin. Eventually, though, he was able to stand unaided and climb down from the cart.

Immediately, he was mobbed as the wraiths – now revealed to be his comrades from Haslow – gathered in a circle around him, throwing questions at him, slapping him on the back and trying to find out if he were unharmed. Eahlmund, who had indeed been the tall leader, said nothing but just grinned with affection, like a dog greets its absent master. Even in the dark, Thurkill could see his face was splattered with blood, giving him a devilish appearance. In truth, they were all giddy with excitement, revelling in their night's work. Thurkill was happy to let them have their moment. No doubt they would tell the story for years to come, of the time they massacred a band of deadly Norman knights.

There might have been little honour in killing defenceless men in such a way – like gutting pigs ahead of a feast day – but needs must. Without their efforts, Thurkill knew he would have soon been dancing on the end of a rope in front of a crowd of baying Normans. They would have his eternal gratitude; any feelings of distaste would soon be forgotten. Once the noise had died down sufficiently, Thurkill raised his hands to speak.

"That was well done, my friends. I am forever indebted to you."

His words were met with a loud and raucous cheer accompanied by further back slapping. It was some time before he could continue.

"But a line has been crossed now. You could have left me to my fate and gone on with your lives and no one would have thought any the less of you. It was I who decided to attack their hunting party, it was my aunt and sister who were murdered and it was me that was to be punished. It was not your fight. But now your actions have made it your fight too; they will hunt you and they will kill you for it if they can. This is not some wild, youthful adventure that ends up with a cuff round the ear when you get caught by your father. This ends in death; it's just a matter of deciding whether it's ours or theirs."

The group was quiet now, like men who come home drunk from the tavern only to be scolded by the wives. For some time, no one moved or spoke, each alone with their own thoughts, Finally, Eahlmund stepped forward into the centre of the group.

"I think we all knew that in our hearts before tonight, Lord. But that did not stop us from taking this path, for I swear this was the right thing to do. We are at peace with our souls on this matter. The Normans may have won a battle and killed our king but they have not taken the country from us just yet. We have a choice either to bend the knee like our grandfathers did before Knut or to fight back and protect our land and our families. And if we are to do that, we will need strong leaders like you."

Thurkill nodded his understanding. "Then I salute your courage, one and all."

"What now, Lord?"

Thurkill was unsure who had called out, it was too dark to be certain, but it sounded like the swineherd's son, Osfrith. "It is time to make a choice, friends. I know where my path lies and you must decide whether you wish to follow that same path or pick another."

"I'm with you, Lord." Several others muttered in agreement.

He smiled. "And I would welcome your company, Eahlmund, even though you have not yet heard my plan. I urge you to choose wisely, and be assured that I will respect your decision, whatever it may be.

"I go north to Lundenburh where a new king has been acclaimed. I go there to pledge my sword to him and I will gladly take as many of you who would join me.

"If you decide this path is not for you, then my counsel would be to leave here. It will not take the Normans long to work out what has happened and you can be assured their vengeance will be merciless. Rather, you should gather your belongings and your families and go. If you have family in villages nearby, go there; otherwise start afresh somewhere else. Either will be better than remaining here waiting to be killed."

One or two of the men looked uneasy, as if unsure of

themselves and what to do for the best. Others shuffled their feet and looked anywhere other than at Thurkill. *Those men will most likely not come with me*, he thought. *But that is understandable; they have a duty to keep their family safe which is just as powerful to them as what I must do.*

"Nope, I'm still coming with you." As ever, Thurkill was grateful to Eahlmund for setting an example to the others.

"I lost my father to these bastards and my mother has been taken in by her sister's family, so I am free to do as I please. And I choose to stand with you and fight."

"Will I never be rid of you, you ugly devil's spawn?" Thurkill slapped him on the shoulder, grinning broadly. Several others also agreed to follow, whilst the remainder held their tongues, one or two of them looking distinctly awkward. Thurkill was happy not to press, though, as there was still much work to be done that night.

"Anyway," he clapped his hands and laughed to lighten the mood. "You don't all need to decide now; it can keep for a while longer. But there is the small matter of my oath to avenge Edith and Aga. I have a pressing need to pay my respects to FitzGilbert before this night is out. Who's with me?"

THIRTY

2 November, Haslow

By Thurkill's reckoning there was about an hour left before dawn when they arrived back at Haslow. As well as the men who had faced up to the hunting party a few days ago, two or three more of the villagers had now joined their ranks. Happily, he was also able to welcome back Leofric who had recovered from the blow to his head. He was still groggy and suffering from continual headaches but not enough, so he said, to stop him from standing side by side with his brother and his lord.

As soon as they reached the outskirts of the village, Thurkill gathered them all together to discuss his plan. From where they stood, Thurkill could see that the watch fires still burned in their iron braziers in front of the hall. But in contrast to before, now only a single soldier stood guard. *No doubt with me out of the way, FitzGilbert sees little need for more,* he smiled to himself.

He turned back to face his followers, leaning in close to keep his voice low. "Looks like there is just one guard. Eahlmund and I will deal with him, the rest of you position yourselves in groups of two or three facing each door. Go now and wait for the signal. Two hoots of a barn owl and then you go. Understood?"

Everyone nodded assent before scurrying off to their appointed places. Left alone with Eahlmund, Thurkill paused for a moment's reflection. This was his home after all, where he had spent the last years of his childhood in happiness with his family. All that was gone now and all at the hands of the Normans. There was nothing left for him here anymore, certainly not once the slaughter of the escort party was discovered. They would not allow Haslow to survive; an example would have to be set. There had already been tales of settlements on the coast being pillaged and burnt to the ground and that was just to take supplies to feed their army. Who knew what they would do to a village involved in the murder of their soldiers? He was brought out of his reverie when Eahlmund placed a hand on his shoulder. "The others are in position, Lord.

It's time."

Thurkill grunted. "God be with us, Eahlmund. And may He forgive us for what we are about to do." Having crossed himself hurriedly, he scurried off towards the side of the hall, careful to stay low and out of sight of the guard. As soon as he was in position, in the lea of the main wall, he stopped and turned to look back in the direction whence he had come. In the pre-dawn gloom, he could just about see his friend, crouching down, his back pressed against the wall of a house. He waved his arm to indicate he was ready and, as he watched, Eahlmund got to his feet and stepped out into the open. He began to walk with a slow, measured pace towards the hall. As he walked, he stretched his arms out wide to show that he carried no weapon and meant no harm.

When he had covered half the distance to the hall, the guard became aware of his presence and called for him to halt. As if pretending not to understand the command, Eahlmund continued his slow walk. As he grew closer and came more into the light from the brazier, Thurkill could see he was even smiling; he nodded appreciatively to himself, the lad was playing his part to perfection.

The soldier repeated his warning and took a few steps towards Eahlmund, drawing his sword as he did so. This time, Eahlmund stopped, tilting his head quizzically to one side and shrugging to show he did not understand. Thurkill heard the soldier mutter what sounded like a curse under his breath and smiled to himself. *He's unsure what to do. He does not know whether he's dealing with a real threat or a complete simpleton?*

After a few more moments of hesitation, the soldier made up his mind and began to walk towards the Saxon, confident that he could manage the situation on his own and perhaps eager not to wake up the hall's occupants without good reason. He did not make it within five paces of Eahlmund, however, as he fell in an unconscious heap as his legs buckled beneath him. Stood behind him, Thurkill hefted from one hand to the other the piece of wood he had taken from the forest, as if testing its weight and density. "There's nothing like a decent bit of oak."

Eahlmund grinned, his eyes now filled with evil intent. "That's one out of the way. Now for the rest."

"You know what to do."

With a nod, Eahlmund strode off to the nearest brazier to put the agreed plan into action. Once there he cupped his hands around his mouth and gave the signal for which the others had been waiting. Together, they all rushed forward, dragging carts and heavy barrels which they used to block the entrances, to prevent anyone from leaving. They worked quickly and efficiently with a minimum of noise. It was almost inevitable, however, that one or two of the occupants might stir and venture outside to see what the fuss was, so they had to move fast to make sure all was ready.

When they were done, just the main entrance, by which Eahlmund and Thurkill now stood, was left unblocked. Reaching forward, they each grabbed a brace of burning logs from the brazier and hurled them high on to the thatched roof. Although the air was cold, it had not rained for several days now and so the straw was dry. There was a momentary quiet, long enough for Thurkill to worry that the plan might fail before it had even begun. But then the straw suddenly ignited with a fearful whooshing sound. Almost immediately the flames began to spread rapidly across the entire roof. The night sky was lit up with an angry orange glow and the air was filled with plumes of thick, billowing smoke.

Thurkill stood back, aghast at the sudden intensity of the conflagration; his emotions conflicted between shame at destroying his father's hall and the overwhelming desire for revenge against the Norman scum who had murdered his family. He prayed to God that there were no Saxons within; when concocting the plan he had assumed that the Normans would not wish to share the living space with anyone but their own, and that assumption was being put to the test now.

By his side, Eahlmund stood with a look of steadfast determination on his face. "Now they will come, for sure."

No sooner had he spoken than the first shouts of alarm were heard from within, just about audible over the noise of the burning roof. Already the flames were starting to lick at the thick wooden posts that supported the walls, and here and there they were even alight. Confident that the other doors were barred sufficiently to prevent escape, four of the villagers had now made their way to the main door, leaving only a couple of men to watch over the other exits. Now they stood grouped around the entrance, scythes, clubs and spears in hand, to await developments.

It did not take long for the first man to emerge, coughing and rubbing his eyes from the effects of the smoke as he stumbled out into the cold, night air. He never stood a chance. Leofric rushed forward and thrust his spear deep into the man's unprotected gut, before wrenching it out again in one smooth movement that ripped a deep gash across his abdomen. No sooner had he fallen than Leofgar was there to drag the body away, out of sight of the next man to emerge.

"FitzGilbert is mine. We take him alive!" Thurkill roared to make himself heard above the flames, desperate to make sure he was not going to be robbed of his moment.

Two more Normans came bursting out of the hall. These men were better prepared, however, having seen what had befallen their comrade. Although they were not wearing mail shirts, they had managed to grab sword and shield from within. Shoulder to shoulder, they came barrelling out of the hall having determined this was their best hope of survival. At first their plan worked as the speed and ferocity of their charge took the Saxons by surprise. Leofric, standing to the left of the doorway, was barged over as he was struck by the kite-shaped shield with the full force of a dipped shoulder behind it. The man to his right was less fortunate, though. Too slow to heed the warning that Thurkill yelled at him, he was struck down by a savage sword blow that took him between the neck and shoulder, cleaving him almost in two.

Thurkill had not even had time to learn the man's name; he had not seen him before that evening; but nonetheless he felt the loss just as keenly as if he had been a close companion. He had hoped that none would be lost in the night's escapade and it pained him that he was unable to hold good to that promise. In truth it was the man's lack of experience that had cost him his life, he was no warrior for sure; but even knowing that did not make the loss any easier to bear.

The two Normans made it no further, however. In the time it took for them to kill the young lad, the remaining Saxons closed in for the kill. On the far side, Osfrith shoved his spear between the running legs of the furthest soldier, causing him to go down in a tangle of limbs. Quick as a flash, his father, displaying surprising agility for a man of his advanced years, darted in to finish him by burying his seax in his neck before he could regain his feet. Seeing that his time was up, the surviving soldier hurled his shield at the nearest opponent and then ran headlong at Thurkill, his sword held aloft in both hands, ready to deliver a killer blow. The blade gleamed in the light of the flames, blood from the dead farmhand dripping down his hands and arms, making him appear all the more fearsome. He came on with reckless abandon, having no regard to his own safety. It was one last, wild charge to try to escape his fate; kill or be killed.

Thurkill did not panic; the situation called for calm. He stood, feet shoulder-width apart, balancing lightly on the balls of his feet as he had been taught by his father. He held his axe loosely in his hands, taking comfort from its well-balanced weight and the neat fit of the grip in his palms. With just moments to spare before the onrushing Norman crushed his skull, Thurkill took a deft step to the left, his attacker's sword sailing harmlessly past his head. In the same movement he brought the shaft up sharply, smashing the wooden end into the Norman's unprotected face. There was a sickening crunch as the nose was smashed and teeth dislodged from his gums. He was unconscious before he even hit the ground.

By now the hall had been almost entirely engulfed in flames and was in danger of collapse. Nevertheless, there had still been no sign of FitzGilbert. By his reckoning, Thurkill thought there must be at least one other soldier in there along with his nemesis. Surely, they could not stay there much longer? He could not believe they would willingly choose a fiery death over the chance to fight. It did not take long for him to be proved right. The next soldier came out, warily, hunched low behind his shield. Thurkill stared hard at him, trying to determine his identity. No one dared approach in case it was the leader. Then, Thurkill caught a glimpse of a shock of blonde hair; it was only fleeting but it was enough to confirm that the man was not his hoped for target. Turning his head, he shouted out to the half dozen men gathered around him.

"Take him! It's not FitzGilbert."

The words were hardly out of his mouth when the most horrendous animalistic noise he had ever heard came from inside the hall. It sounded more like a wounded bear than a man. Turning back to face the hall, he was just in time to see his nemesis sprinting towards him, sword flailing around his head as he came, smoke rising from his clothing where the incredible heat within the hall must have been on the verge of setting it on fire. He was naked but for his braes; his skin blackened in places where it had been seared by the intense heat inside the burning hall. The pain he felt must have been unbearable.

Taken by surprise, Thurkill had just moments to react. There was time only to raise his axe, an almost futile attempt to parry his opponent's blade. It was late and it was desperate, but it proved to be just enough to save his life. FitzGilbert's sword made contact halfway along his before slipping down all the way to the blade where it grated with the most terrifying screech of metal on metal. He doubted he had ever been hit harder; the force of it caused a jarring sensation all the way along his arm from wrist to shoulder, threatening to numb the muscles completely.

The Norman's momentum brought him face to face with Thurkill and it was an horrific sight. His features, already disfigured by the age-old scar, were contorted in pain, his cheeks and forehead blackened from soot and blistering in places where he had been exposed to the intense heat of the flames. Furthermore, much of his hair had been singed away, the effect of which combined to give him the most gruesome appearance. None of it seemed to have affected his strength or dexterity, though. It was all Thurkill could do to hold FitzGilbert at bay. The Norman's teeth were bared, seared lips stretched back over the gums in some devilish grimace. He could feel his hot breath on his cheek as he screamed obscenities at him in his own tongue, apparently driven mad by a combination of pain and anger. Thurkill felt as close to death at that moment as he had ever been.

Suddenly, he felt an intense pain in his groin. The Norman had retained enough lucidity to lift his knee and drive it hard into his unprotected balls. The impact caused him to double over, the air forced from his lungs. Despite the blinding pain, he had the presence of mind to drop to his knees and roll away out of arm's length. It was a good job that he did as FitzGilbert followed up his success with a powerful downward hack of this sword which, instead of splitting open his back, sailed uselessly through the air before hitting the muddied ground.

The Norman roared in frustration, spinning round to face Thurkill who was struggling to regain his feet, using his axe as a crutch. Through tears of pain, Thurkill could see his opponent's eyes light up in triumph, believing victory was within his grasp. He must have known that he was going to die, there was no escaping that fate, but at the moment he was consumed by an animalistic urge to kill Thurkill.

Swallowing down the bile that had risen to his throat, Thurkill was happy to let FitzGilbert think he was beaten. Despite the agony he felt in his crotch, he knew he could keep him at bay until he had recovered enough to turn the tide. Until then, the more the bastard thought he was winning, the more likely it was that complacency might lead to a mistake.

For now, though, he had to keep his wits about him as the Norman was keen to press home his advantage. He rushed forward once more, hacking at Thurkill's head and body with incredible speed. Pretence or otherwise, it was as much as he could do to fend him off. He was still moving awkwardly; the pain had eased a little but his bruised balls were still restricting his movement. He needed to bide his time until an opportunity presented itself. The rest of his warband had gathered around them, anxiety etched on their faces, but not daring to intervene. They could see that FitzGilbert had the upper hand and feared for their lord's life.

The next attack was accompanied by the sound of the hall collapsing as the fire finally wrought its full destructive power.

He had no time to mourn the loss of his home and the memories it held, though. Again and again he had to block the wild lunges aimed at his head and body. FitzGilbert's sword seemed to be a blur in front of his face so fast was it moving. *How much longer can this devil keep up this pace? More to the point,* he thought, *how much longer can I hold him off?*

The sound of metal clashing against wood and metal was ear-splitting, echoing off the walls of the dwellings around him. His arm jarred with every strike; his muscles screaming with the effort required to parry the Norman's sword, to prevent it from cleaving his skull in two. Slowly but surely, he was being forced backwards, step by step, as the onslaught showed no signs of abating.

Suddenly, without warning, Thurkill felt himself toppling backwards, his left foot snagging on the outstretched leg of one of the dead Norman soldiers. He could not stop himself; it was as much as he could do to keep hold of his axe as he landed heavily on his backside, his spine jolting painfully with the impact.

FitzGilbert roared in triumph, a blood-curdling howl filled with hate and pain. He rushed forward, eager to end the fight before the Saxon could regain his footing. In the little time available to him, Thurkill could do no more than twist his body despairingly to one side. He prayed it was enough but at the same time, he prepared to meet his end. The blow – when it came – missed his head by a whisker. He felt the waft of the air as it swept passed his skull, glancing instead off his mailed shoulder. The pain made him cry out and he feared at first that the bone might have broken.

He knew he was just a heartbeat from death. But at the same time, the opportunity for which he had been waiting was now staring him in the face. In launching what he had expected to be the killing blow, FitzGilbert had over extended himself. In an instant, Thurkill let go of the axe and twisted his hand back to his leather belt where he found the comforting grip of his seax. Grabbing hold of it in a reverse grip, he released it from its sheath and, using every ounce of strength he could muster from his prone position, he slammed the point down as hard as he could into Richard's bare foot. The force he used was so great that the blade went straight through the flesh and bone and buried itself a full hand's breadth into the soft earth beneath.

FitzGilbert screamed in agony, dropping his sword and flopping to the ground to grasp his injured foot. Meanwhile, Thurkill used the time to push himself back to his feet, picking up his axe as he did so. He stood over the wounded form of his enemy, blade poised squarely over his exposed neck. His family's faces flashed before his eyes, flooding his brain with emotion as he stood victorious over the hunched form of his mortal enemy. His eyes brimmed with tears, a mixture of relief and hurt that threatened to engulf him.

"Finish him!" He was unsure who it was who called out but it brought him back to the moment. Looking up, he smiled wanly at those around him, suddenly exhausted by the events of the night. In truth, he had had enough killing for one day but FitzGilbert deserved death, of that there was no doubt. Shaking his head as if to clear his mind, he took a step back before launching the hardest kick he could muster directly at the side of his head. The Norman collapsed, unconscious.

***

"Wake up, you whoreson." Thurkill flung the contents of the wooden pail directly in FitzGilbert's face. It was a foul-smelling mixture of water and pig manure that Osfric had gathered from his farm. It had the desired effect though as the Norman came back to life, coughing and spluttering as some of the foul effluent filled his mouth, nose and eyes.

The indignant look on his face was replaced almost immediately with one of fear as he realised the full horror of his situation. He was standing with his back to a tree on the outskirts of the village, his arms pulled back and bound firmly behind the trunk. The cords had been pulled so tight that he was unable to move. Another bond had been placed around his forehead keeping his head up and his face pointing forwards. As he tried to move, the gash in his left foot opened once more, oozing a fetid mixture of blood and pus, covering the thick red crust that had begun to form.

FitzGilbert's voice was thick, his lips cracked. "What do you want with me, Saxon? Kill me and be done with it."

Despite his fear, there was still a cold, hard courage in his eyes which Thurkill could not help but admire. He must have known his doom was both inevitable and imminent, yet he would not beg for his life. His pride would not allow it.

"Don't worry," Thurkill smiled without humour. "I have every intention of killing you. But it was important to me that you did not die in combat. You are not worthy of that honour. Instead you will die here, by my hand, like the animal scum you are, bound to this tree with no weapon in hand. It won't be a quick death; I won't allow you that mercy. You will have time to watch the life slowly seep out of you as you contemplate your sins and how you will answer for them before God. Then I will leave your body here to be devoured by wolves and your bones picked clean by the crows. You deserve nothing more for what you did to my kin."

"I care not, Saxon. Your time is over anyway so you will not enjoy your pathetic little victory for long. Harold is dead and your army defeated. Soon your whole country will submit to William and your kind will be wiped out for good."

"That may be, but when my time comes, be it soon or when I am old and grey, I know that I will meet my family once more with my head held high, having avenged them. Your soul, however, will wander the land forever, finding no peace without a Christian burial."

Whether the thought scared him or not did not show. Instead, FitzGilbert stared implacably at Thurkill, a sneer slowly spreading across his face that showed his contempt.

"Enough!" Thurkill drew his seax and strode forward. The Norman let out an involuntary gasp as he prepared himself for death, but quickly regained his composure sufficiently to mount one last act of defiance, hawking a great gobbet of phlegm directly into Thurkill's face. Without pausing to wipe himself clean, Thurkill drove the blade deep into his exposed gut. FitzGilbert grunted but did not cry out, as if determined to deny the young Saxon any satisfaction at all from the kill. Staring intently into the Norman's eyes, Thurkill twisted the blade until it was horizontal and then dragged it slowly across the base of his belly, opening a huge gaping wound out through which spilled blood and intestine.

"Rot in hell, you bastard."

EPILOGUE

5 November, Lundenburh

Thurkill pulled back on the reins as he crested the rise. Placing his hands at his sides he arched his back, trying to ease some of the ache brought on by long miles on the road. Ahead of and below him, the ground sloped away down to the wide expanse of the great river which snaked its way across the land, as far as the eye could see in both directions. To his right, where the sun was now slowly rising, weak and watery in the late autumn dawn, he could just about make out the coast where the river spewed out into the cold, grey sea that divided their little island from the land of the Normans and Franks to the south and the Danes and other Norse peoples to the north and east.

Directly ahead of him the long, wooden bridge stretched across the river from the settlement of Suthweca on this southern side to the walled city of Lundenburh itself to the north. Not far west of the bridge, the river took a sharp turn to the south and there, on the far side of the river, he could make out the new abbey that the old King Edward had built and where he had been buried.

"There she lies, lads. The greatest city in the country. And by all accounts it's where we will find Edgar, the new King of England."

There were six others with him. First among them, as ever, was Eahlmund, who now hardly ever left Thurkill's side, having assigned himself as his lord's personal bodyguard. Then there were the two brothers, Leofric and Leofgar, both of whom had decided that their fortune lay with their young lord rather than by staying on in Haslow. The party was completed by Copsig, Eopric and Eardwulf, the three young men who had joined them after the ambush in the forest. The rest of the warband had decided to stay with their families to make a new life out of the ashes of the old, including Osfric, who had claimed he was too old to be fighting at his age, and his son, Osfrith, who felt his duty was to stay with his father to help look after him and his mother. Thurkill had been sorry to see them go; especially the young lad as he had proven himself a staunch fighter in the short time they had been together; but he understood the decision and could not, in truth, hold it against either of them.

"Sod Edgar! I don't know about the rest of you but I just want a good beer, a good bed and a good woman; and not necessarily in that order. In fact, the more I think about it, all three at the same time would be ideal."

There'd been precious little joy since they'd left Haslow so it was good to hear the men laughing at Eahlmund's joke, offering their own ribald comments about how they intended to enjoy the delights of the city. Dutifully, Thurkill laughed along with the rest but said nothing; he wasn't sure how long it would be before he felt the need for happiness once again or was even capable of allowing it into his life.

"Come on then, lads. If you shift your arses we can be there in time for breakfast."

A short while later they reached Suthweca; a moderate-sized collection of houses, inns, shops and a church or two that had grown up simply because it stood at the southern end of the bridge into the city. Many had been the time that travellers had arrived after dark when the gates had been closed for the night, needing somewhere to stay until morning. Enterprising traders had not been slow to see the opportunity and now the community had a thriving life all of its own, separate to the city to its north. This morning, however, it was deserted. It was still early, admittedly, but surely by now there would be people about? Shopkeepers setting out their wares, travellers starting out on their journeys?

They saw no one until they reached the small fort that guarded the entrance to the bridge. There they were met with a line of warriors, each one dressed as if ready for war, and all carrying spear and shield. They formed a solid shieldwall, an interlocking line of men, blocking the gateway to the fort which, in turn, prevented access to the bridge. It was a narrow lane that passed through the walls of the fort, underneath a wooden palisade which was also lined with men, though these warriors were armed with bows; each one notched with an arrow and pulled back ready to loose at Thurkill and his little warband. As they came within range, a bare-headed warrior in the middle of the line of bowmen raised his arm, palm outstretched towards them, and shouted. "Halt! State your business and whence you come to Suthweca."

Thurkill looked from side to side, but there was no other way to reach the bridge other than through that gate. Staying calm, and careful to make no sudden movements lest he incite an overly nervous bowman, he took a couple of steps forward, his arms held out to the side, palms facing forward to show that he meant no harm.

"I am Thurkill, son of Scalpi, loyal thegn to King Harold. I am come from my father's village at Haslow, two days' march to the south and, before that, from the battlefield at Senlac ridge where I fought alongside the king and my father and saw them both perish. My business is to seek refuge for my warband within the walls of the city to the north and to pledge our swords to the new king, Edgar, should he accept our troth."

The warrior lowered his arm and nodded, a new-found respect showing on his grizzled face. "I welcome one who fought at Senlac; I was there in the shieldwall until the end also. If you bring men and loyalty, then I dare say you will be welcome here as both are in short supply in these troubled days. Wait there, I will escort you over the bridge."

The speaker introduced himself as Wulfnoth. He had fought as a hearth warrior for Harold's brother, Gyrth, and had only just escaped with his life after the ill-fated charge. After the battle, when he saw there was nothing more he could do, he had used the night to cover his escape and then had made his way north to Lundenburh as quickly as he could, fearful that the Normans would be marching with all haste behind him.

Thurkill clapped his hand on the man's shoulder as they walked. "I knew your lord well. He was a good man, like his brother, and I mourn their passing daily."

By the time they had reached the end of the bridge, Thurkill had told Wulfnoth what had happened to him since the battle and the look of sympathy on the other man's face was genuine and heartfelt.

"I am sorry for your loss, truly. But I fear there are many

more such days ahead for many of us before we can be rid of this whoreson, William, and his men who maraud across our lands. With Harold dead and no other proven war-leader to hand, we have to look to Edgar as our one remaining hope."

"Where will I find the king? I would pledge my sword to him and those of my men."

"I'll take you to him. He's holding court in the palace at Westminster, making plans for war. I am sure he will be pleased to see you and will welcome you to his army."

Eventually, they arrived at the island of thorns where old King Edward had built his beloved abbey next to the existing royal palace from where he had been able to keep a close watch over its construction. The palace itself, however, was not much more than a great hall surrounded by a collection of smaller buildings that had made up the king's private dwellings.

As Wulfnoth pushed open the main door, Thurkill was immediately struck by the incredible noise and bustle within. All around, men stood in groups amongst the richly carved, wooden pillars that ran all the way along the sides of the hall. Many of them appeared to be arguing furiously with each other, gesticulating wildly or jabbing fingers in each other's chests. In the middle of the hall, the hearth was filled with a roaring fire which made the atmosphere stuffy despite most of the smoke being drawn up through the central vent hole in the roof. Beyond the hearth, a number of scribes stood at their writing lecterns, frantically scribbling away at their parchments. Messengers stood next to them, waiting for the orders to be finished so they could gallop off to deliver them.

At the far end of the hall, on the raised dais, a smaller party was gathered. In the centre, sat on the ornate wooden throne, was a young, beardless man, little more than a boy in fact. By his side were three others: two men and a woman. Thurkill immediately recognised the former, for he had met them on the march to Eoforwic several weeks before. Eadwine and Morcar had not changed since that time; their mood appeared as dark and as foreboding as it had been after Harold had lambasted them for their defeat at Fulford Gate. The woman stood between them, dressed in a long black woollen dress, must be their sister,

Ealdgyth, Thurkill reasoned, who was still in mourning for her husband, Harold.

What struck Thurkill most, however, was the young lad on the throne. The contrast with Harold could not have been greater. In place of the imposing, experienced war-leader now sat a boy who, whilst not that much younger than himself, seemed completely out of place. He looked ill at ease in the large wooden chair so recently occupied by his predecessor. Even the royal robes in which he was clothed seemed too big for him, as if they had been made with someone else in mind. He was a slight lad, yet to develop much in the way of muscle or bulk. On top of which his short dark hair, pale complexion and sallow features did little to give any impression of authority. Thurkill wondered to what extent the power of the throne now rested with this young man or with the earls beside him. Either way, his heart sank, his confidence for the fight ahead waning.

He did not have time to dwell on his thoughts any further, however, as their arrival had not gone unnoticed. Earl Morcar leaned down and spoke in Edgar's ear, causing the young king to look over in their direction. Smiling, he beckoned for them to approach the throne.

Wulfnoth placed a hand on his shoulder to urge him forward. "Follow me, Thurkill, and speak only when spoken to."

As they came close, Edgar rose to speak. Immediately, Thurkill saw that he had misjudged the boy, as he spoke with a calm assurance and a regal bearing that belied his years. Perhaps there was more to being a king than just being an inspiring presence on the battlefield, he mused.

"Well met, Wulfnoth. Tell me, who is this fine and noble warrior by your side?"

Wulfnoth bowed his head before replying, nudging Thurkill as he did so to follow his example. "Lord King, I present to you Thurkill, son of Scalpi, loyal thegn and huscarl for the late King Harold. He hails from Senlac where he stood in the front rank of the shieldwall, alongside Harold, against William the Bastard of Normandy."

Edgar threw his arms wide in a gesture of welcome. "I am honoured to have you at my court, Thurkill, you and your warband. There are many here who, like you, have come from that field; some who will never fight again, so grievous are their wounds earned in defence of this land. But there are many more who stand willing to fight again, and again, for as long as it takes us to be rid of this Norman usurper. The throne of England is mine by birth right as the great grand-son of King Aethelraed, who was himself the father of King Edward who was buried at the abbey here less than a year ago.

"Though we have lost the first battle, we are by no means defeated. William holds but a small part of the realm to the south and with every day that passes he must grow weaker while we grow ever stronger."

Thurkill had no idea how much truth lay behind these words but he didn't care. His initial misgivings had been replaced by a feeling that this was a man he could follow; a man he could fight for and – if need be – die for. He had killed the scar-faced whoreson, FitzGilbert, and he knew he would have to kill many more Normans before he was done. A surge of pride and furious anger grew within him and he found himself shouting Edgar's name and thrusting his fist into the air along everyone else.

As the noise died down, he became aware of shouts coming from outside the hall. At first he thought the cheering had carried beyond the walls of the palace to those without, but it soon became apparent that he was wrong. The door burst open to reveal a huscarl who ran straight to the dais. He was sweating with the exertion despite the cold, his blonde hair matted and stuck to his face beneath his helmet. Without waiting to be invited to speak, the warrior blurted his message.

"Lord King. The Normans attack."

"Impossible!" Edgar sounded more indignant than frightened. "My scouts told me they were in Dover not four days ago, and showing no signs of moving."

"'I swear 'tis true, Lord. I have seen them. They approach the fort at Suthweca even as I speak. They were about two miles distant when I came hither and must be close to half that distance away by now. The men at the fort are preparing the defences but the captain begs you to send reinforcements with all haste."

"So be it." Edgar turned to face Eadwine and Morcar. "Gather your men and march to the defence of Suthweca. The Normans must not be allowed to cross the bridge; else all is lost. The defence of my kingdom starts here."

END NOTE

Thurkill's Revenge is set within the tapestry of the calamitous events of 1066; one of the most fateful years in British history. Whilst many of the events – such as the battles of Fulford Gate, Stamford Bridge and, of course, Hastings – took place largely as described, much of the rest is a work of fiction woven around that skeleton.

Scalpi is one of the few Saxon warriors that we know was present at Senlac Ridge on the fourteenth of October and it was a small leap of faith to create a son for him, one that would have been old enough to fight alongside him. Thurkill would have been a typical, albeit young, huscarl – essentially a professional soldier in the paid service of a noble – trained from a young age to fight for his lord and die for him if honour demanded.

If this book has piqued your interest in this

fascinating period of our history, you could do worse than invest in *The Norman Conquest* by Marc Morris. I've read few better, more approachable works in all my years studying history. My description of King Harold's demise was inspired by his research and references to primary sources such as the *Carmen de Hastingae Proelio (Song of the Battle of Hastings)*. It deviates somewhat – and very realistically in my opinion – from the version of events we all learned in school. Arrow in the eye? I think not.

Should you have enjoyed reading *Thurkill's Revenge*, then please do leave a review. I would also welcome feedback direct to me on Twitter via @Paul_Bernardi or by email to pvbernardi@gmail.com.

Thurkill will return for more adventures in *Thurkill's Battle*.

Paul Bernardi.

DEDICATION

This book is dedicated to my wife, Julie, whose long-standing support and encouragement have given me the strength to follow my dreams of being an author of historical fiction. Her position as editor-in-chief is less secure, however, as she tends to become too caught up in the story to remember to spot all the typos and other errors, of which there are, no doubt, many.

Printed in Great Britain
by Amazon